Office Ladies and Salaried Men

Office Ladies and Salaried Men

Power, Gender, and Work
in Japanese Companies

Yuko Ogasawara

UNIVERSITY OF CALIFORNIA PRESS

Berkeley / Los Angeles / London

The costs of publishing this book have been supported in part by an award from the Hiromi Arisawa Memorial Fund (named in honor of the renowned economist and the first chairman of the board of the University of Tokyo Press) and financed by the generosity of Japanese citizens and Japanese corporations to recognize excellence in scholarship in Japan.

University of California Press
Berkeley and Los Angeles, California

University of California Press, Ltd.
London, England

Library of Congress Cataloging-in-Publication Data

Ogasawara, Yuko, 1960–
    Office ladies and salaried men: power, gender, and work in
Japanese companies / Yuko Ogasawara.
        p.   cm.
    Includes bibliographical references and index.
    ISBN 0–520–21043–3 (alk. paper). —
ISBN 0–520–21044–1 (alk. paper)
    1. Women white collar workers—Japan—Interviews.   2. Busi-
nessmen—Japan—Interviews.   3. Women—Japan—Psychology.
4. Sex role in the work environment—Japan.   5. Office politics—
Japan.   6. Control (Psychology)   I. Title.
HD6073.M392J36   1998
331.4′816513′0952—dc21   98–5332
                                                                CIP

Printed in the United States of America
9   8   7   6   5   4   3   2   1

For my parents,
Furuyama Kazutaka and Furuyama Masako

Contents

Illustrations

Table

Figures

Acknowledgments

My first and biggest "thank you" goes to the men and women who shared with me their experiences in the Japanese workplace and to the many people who introduced me to these wonderful sources of information and inspiration. I was often surprised, and indeed touched, by the generosity and openness of my contacts. My only hope is that this book does them justice.

I would also like to thank Matsuo Kazuyuki of Sophia University in Tokyo for making it possible for me to enroll in a U.S. graduate program. As an undergraduate at Sophia, I was a typical Japanese college student, sitting silently at the back of Professor Matsuo's classroom, never imagining that I would pursue a graduate degree. Four years after graduation, when I decided to apply to the University of Chicago for graduate work in sociology, I asked Professor Matsuo for a letter of recommendation. Although he could barely remember me, he listened carefully to my plea and agreed to write the required letter. When I later thanked him, he chuckled and said, "I believe in the spirit of 'Why not?' rather than 'Why?'" Denny Petite at Sophia, who also kindly supplied a letter of recommendation, further prepared me for my graduate study by lending me numerous sociology volumes from his bookshelf.

My graduate training at the University of Chicago was unusual in that I was physically present on the campus for only three years. After becoming an "ABD" (All But Dissertation), I packed up my research notes and followed my husband as he was transferred from post to post in Minneapolis, Tokyo, Amsterdam, Hereford (England), and finally Tokyo again. Throughout my travels, I was fortunate enough to receive much-needed guidance from three Chicago faculty members. It was Wendy Griswold, now at Northwestern University, who taught me what qualitative analysis could be. She was my mentor in every sense of the word, always urging me to push forward in my work. I am also deeply grateful to Bill Hanks for his intellectual and moral support. I remember the warm welcome he gave me when I first stepped into his office in the anthropology department—I was happily surprised to find that he would listen intently to the ramblings of a strange Japanese sociology student. Mary Brinton in the sociology department was a source of great comfort for me, not only because she is so familiar with Japan but also because she is a sympathetic and understanding soul. She encouraged me to turn my dissertation into a book and generously dispensed advice. Among my University of Chicago friends, I would like to thank Julle Cho, Juliette Ferrari, Chan-ung Park, and Vipan Prachuabmoh for sharing with me the difficulties and joys of graduate student life.

When I returned to Japan, numerous people helped me adjust to Japanese academic society. Watanabe Hideki at Keio University was one of many to offer me assistance when I most needed it. He invited me to present my work at his seminar and later introduced me to various groups of scholars. Tanaka Kazuko at International Christian University (ICU) provided me with my first institutional affiliation in Japan. Other people who gave me valuable advice include Hioki Koichiro, Kanemitsu Hideo, Kariya Takehiko, Kawashima Yoko, Osawa Machiko, Takai Yoko, Takazawa Norie, Tsuya Noriko, Ueno Chizuko, Watanabe Fumio, Yoshino Kosaku, and Yoshida Kensaku. My colleagues at Edogawa University, including Hasegawa Tomoko, Hirayama Maki, Murata Sadao, Oyane Jun, and Takayama Machiko, provided a supportive and stimulating environment for writing this book.

I would like to extend my special thanks to Martha Debs and Kanno Takashi, my former colleagues at a management consulting firm. Takashi spent hours on the telephone, patiently serving as a sounding board for my ideas. Martha's help, based on her expert knowledge of editing and rich understanding of Japanese culture, is visible on every page of the book.

I would also like to express my pleasure in working with the expert staff at the University of California Press, notably Laura Driussi, Sue Heinemann, Carolyn Hill, and Sheila Levine.

My final word of thanks goes to my family. I feel an immeasurable debt to my parents, Furuyama Kazutaka and Masako, for nurturing whatever good there is in me. They have patiently watched me grow into my own in a society where such growing and such watching are not always easy. My sister Furuyama Yoko read the manuscript and gave me valuable comments based on her experience working in a Japanese firm and her training as a lawyer. My father-in-law, Ogasawara Susumu, who retired prematurely from an academic career because of fragile health, sent me numerous clippings from newspapers and journals. Anyone who knows the status of *yome* (bride and daughter-in-law) in a typical Japanese family would agree that I am fortunate to have such a supportive father-in-law. Finally, I thank my husband, Ogasawara Yasushi, for his love, patience, encouragement, insight, and delicious dinners. I could not ask for a better partner with whom to share the long journey from its early days in Tokyo. Not only this project but my career would not have been possible without him.

Introduction

As a Japanese woman studying in the United States, I was often asked about the status of women in Japan: Is women's role still primarily at home? What opportunities are there for working women in Japan? How do women office workers who serve tea and do simple assignments view their work? Have things changed in the last ten years?

I was delighted to have the chance to talk about my native country, yet I wanted to give as accurate an account as possible. Initially I spoke of the intense sex discrimination in Japan. I described the severe obstacles women faced in establishing a professional career in a male-dominated society and how many women who had graduated from top universities ended up typing documents and serving tea in the office.

Most Americans I talked to in university circles had heard of the male-biased career structure in Japan, and they did not seem surprised by my story. They might, however, ask: "Is it really *still* like that?" When I replied with an emphatic yes, my American friends responded with sympathy for Japanese women and wondered how these women can stand it. One person even wondered why more Japanese women did not emigrate to the United States. Many people I talked to had a preconception of Japanese women as gentle, shy, and obedient. My account seemed to tally with this image and confirm that Japanese women, submissive and deferential, were the victims of society.

I began to feel uneasy and to state my argument less vigorously. Are Japanese women miserable? I wondered. Do they feel that they are victims of society? Are they really submissive and deferential to men? I was not sure. I was not even convinced that these women feel oppressed or are unhappy with their lot. I realized that I had given my American friends an impression of Japanese women that I myself did not believe to be entirely true.

I changed the emphasis of my account. I mentioned that, despite being discriminated against, Japanese women have considerable say both at home and in the office. In addition to pointing out that among Japanese couples it is the wife who usually controls the family budget, I gave as an example the case of a married acquaintance of one of my Japanese friends. The husband rented a lovely condominium in a popular Hawaiian resort for his wife and eight-year-old son during their summer vacation, although he knew that he himself could not join them there. He had a promising career in one of the leading trading companies and was too busy to take time off. Summer in Tokyo happened to be especially hot and humid that year, and the husband had to sweat in the urban concrete jungle, while his wife relaxed by the sea.

Most of my American friends seemed surprised by this example. They sympathized with the man and said they were glad they were not in his position. They wondered who was really oppressed, whether Japanese men didn't suffer from the burden of earning a living in Japanese society. My friends' reaction made me uneasy. Apparently, my description had wiped out the image of Japanese women as victims of oppression. Instead, women now loomed large as tyrants enjoying the easy life while men exhausted themselves mentally and physically in the strenuous business world.

The more I tried to be accurate, the more I failed to communicate. I was frustrated: I had failed to impart the "truth" about relations between men and women in Japan. When I emphasized how much women as a group are discriminated against, I made individual women seem more vulnerable to oppression than they really are. When I described how influential individual women often are both at home and in the office, I downplayed the glaring discrimination they face. I was confused. Are Japanese women oppressed, or not? Are they powerless, or powerful? The questions guiding my research thus emerged.

In gender studies, Japan is an important case. Many observers and scholars, both Japanese and non-Japanese, agree that sex roles are strictly delineated in Japan. In terms of wages, employment status, occupational roles, and any other ways in which we choose to measure gender stratification, Japanese women are more disadvantaged than their counterparts in other industrial countries. The unequal and low status of women in Japan has been exposed and severely criticized in the international community.

In spite of the sharply delineated sex roles, the Japanese public often claims that once you look beyond the immediately observable, you see that women have the real power over men. In popular opinion, the Japanese woman manages and controls the home as her own space, enjoys unlimited autonomy there, and frequently prevails over her husband in decision making about the home and family life in general. Derogatory terms such as *sodaigomi* (a large piece of garbage that is difficult to dispose of) and *nure-ochiba* (wet, fallen leaves that cling irritatingly to the ground even if you try to sweep them away) refer to men who have no authority in their homes and are fearful of their wives. Recently, there has been a reversal in the preferred sex of a newborn in Japan: more mothers nowadays want girls than boys. Girls, the argument goes, will provide emotional support to their parents in the future, whereas boys will only comply with their wives' wishes. Observing the strength of the mother-daughter bond, some scholars even predict that Japan will become a matrilineal society in the near future (Sakai 1995).

How are we to interpret the seemingly contradictory depiction of women's status in Japanese society? How can the two conflicting views be reconciled? What makes it possible for women to enjoy autonomy despite their limited roles in the economy? What is the nature of their influence on men? Is it only at home that women exercise control? What about women's voice in the public sphere? These questions are central to this book.

Study of Japanese Women

The Japanese economy has attracted the attention of many Western social scientists, who have attempted to explain how and why it works. Concentrating on male employees in large corporations, their studies focus on the "lifetime" employment system and other distinctive features of Japanese companies (Abegglen 1958; Clark 1979; Cole 1971, 1979; Dore 1973; E. Vogel 1975). Only recently have women's roles in Japanese society begun to be investigated in depth.

The rapidly expanding literature on women in Japan reflects the two opposing views of women. Many studies describe how women face intense sex discrimination and, as a result, are relegated to low-paying and dead-end jobs. Other studies, many of which examine the woman's role at home, emphasize that women have considerable leverage in society. What accounts for these opposing views? In order to answer this question, let us first examine the two perspectives.

Women's disadvantaged position in the economy is well documented, mainly by labor economists and sociologists working with statistical data. Sociologist Mary Brinton and labor economists Ōsawa Machiko and Ōsawa Mari each analyze why women's economic roles are limited in Japan.[1] Together with quantitatively sophisticated work that examines women's workforce participation (Hill 1984; Shimada and Higuchi 1985; Shinotsuka 1982; Tanaka 1987; Yashiro 1983), these writings draw an overall picture of gender stratification in Japan. However, because they deal primarily with macro-level phenomena and statistical data, these studies do not reveal how women exert influence in face-to-face interactions and negotiate power in forms other than wages, occupation, or status.

Rich ethnographic material on Japanese women's lives has been offered by anthropologists such as Takie Lebra (1984), who collected life histories from women in a small city in central Japan. Many other authors have focused on women in selected occupations.[2] There are some English-language writings on women and Japanese law (Cook and Hayashi 1980; Lam 1992; Parkinson 1989; Upham 1987), and a broader picture of women's status in Japan can be found in the works of Iwao Sumiko (1993), Mary Saso (1990), and Robert Smith (1987).

Many of these studies examining micro-level phenomena refute the stereotypical view that the Japanese woman is dependent, deferential, and powerless. Takie Lebra (1984), for example, confirms that in most Japanese homes, it is the wife who controls household finances. In addition, she finds that many husbands are totally dependent on their wives for housework, which includes not only cooking, cleaning, and ironing but also "around-the-body care" (*mi no mawari no sewa*): the wife helps the husband change his clothes, serves him at dinner, and fetches him cigarettes, an ashtray, a cup of green tea, and the like, while he relaxes before television. According to Lebra, the husband's childlike dependence gives the wife leverage to exercise power by making her services absolutely necessary. She observes: "If one looks at the wife's complete control of the domestic realm apart from its structural context, one might be led to the conclusion that women are more powerful than men in Japan, or that Japanese women enjoy more power than

American women, for whom the division of labor is no
(1984, 302).

A similar view of women's role specialization appears in
Roberts's work (1994), which presents a speech delivered by the p
dent of a lingerie company. According to the president, women as pro
fessional wives manage men much as a puppeteer manipulates a puppet:
although men are always at center stage, it is women who make the
male puppets dance.

Perhaps one of the most optimistic views is presented by Iwao Sumiko (1993), who argues that men's formal superiority is matched by
women's informal dominance. It is true, Iwao argues, that women are
excluded from formal arenas such as policymaking and business. But
because of this, they have more freedom than their male counterparts,
who must spend long hours on the job to support their families. Not
only do women have the chance to engage in a broad range of culturally enriching activities, but they can also decide to work on their own
terms, part-time, without the worry of making a living.[3] Iwao concludes,
"Today it is, in a sense, the husbands who are being controlled and the
ones to be pitied. The typical Japanese man depends heavily on his wife
to look after his daily needs and nurture his psychological well-being.
The Confucian ethic of the three obediences formerly binding women
could be rewritten today as the three obediences for men: obedience to
mothers when young, companies when adult, and wives when retired"
(1993, 7). The fearful fate of retired men is also noted by Anne Allison
(1994).[4]

Although most works refer to female autonomy in the household,
Dorinne Kondo (1990) examines women's position in a workplace. At
the factory where she conducted her research, middle-aged female part-
time workers play the role of surrogate mother for younger male full-
time artisans. The women invite artisans home for a hot meal, lend them
money, and run bank errands for men who cannot leave work during
the lunch break. According to Kondo, superordinates, such as parents
or bosses, assume the position of caregiver in Japan, and subordinates
seek indulgence. Therefore, by casting themselves as mothers, these
women workers gain power over the younger men and claim a central
space for themselves within the informal structures of the workplace.
Because female part-timers are vital to the informal relations of the
workplace, they can scarcely be called marginal.

These ethnographies reveal an aspect of women's status in Japan

analyses provided by labor economists and
r, they do not offer a convincing analysis
. Why is it that women can exert influence
's monopoly of formal power? What is the
is? Lebra (1984) and Kondo (1990) provide
ir perceptively written texts. However, it is
become so totally dependent on their wives,
ir female coworkers' kindness. Are Japanese
and spoiled, or is something more structural
involved? In other words, is men's dependence on women a result of
their individual, voluntary action, in which case they can presumably
become more independent if they choose to do so, or it is more sys-
temically determined? These questions are left largely unanswered because the existing literature fails to integrate ethnographic observations
with large-scale quantitative data.

Literature on Women's Measures of Influence

If the contradiction in Japan between women's collective
economic status and individual women's day-to-day experiences is not
well explained, neither is the discrepancy between collective status and
individual experience in society in general. Although men as a group
on many occasions exercise a disproportionate amount of power, individual men often do not *feel* powerful in their everyday relations with
others (Gerson 1993). Similarly, individual women sometimes find that
they can get what they want in concrete day-to-day situations despite
their limited power as a group (Collier 1974; Rogers 1975; Wolf 1972).
Why? In order to answer this question, we need to analyze the links between collective status and individual lives. It is necessary to understand not only how men's collective power puts them in a position of
advantage, but also how it constrains individual men's choice. Likewise, we need to examine ways in which women's disadvantaged position as a group provides opportunities for individual women. Investi-
gating these less visible power issues has important implications. For if
men feel they are getting a bad deal, and if women feel their lot is better than it seems, then there may be less impetus than we would expect
for change toward a statistically egalitarian arrangement.

A number of excellent studies investigate how women prevail in domestic decision making in spite of their husbands' opposition. Many

of these ethnographies come from researchers in southern European (mainly rural) societies (Dubisch 1986; Friedl 1967; Gilmore 1990; Reigelhaupt 1967; Rogers 1975; Uhl 1985), but there are also studies of women's primary roles in family life, including reproductive and distributive activities, elsewhere in the world (Boddy 1989; Chinas 1973; Collier 1974; Gullestad 1984; Swartz 1982; Weiner 1976; Wolf 1972).[5] In this literature, women's power in marital relations is typically described as being unofficial and informal but nonetheless real and is contrasted to men's official, formal, and sometimes cosmetic power. In her watershed article on a peasant village in France (1975), Susan Rogers maintains that because of social science's traditional preoccupation with authority structures, men appeared to be dominant. In reality, however, women's power in the household, although informal and covert, is more effective than the overt, formal power of men. Women grant their husbands authority, prestige, and respect in exchange for power, thus perpetuating the "myth" of male dominance.[6] A parallel argument is put forward by Pierre Bourdieu (1977) in his study of Kabyle villagers, a Berber-speaking community in Algeria. He maintains that women often wield the real power in matrimonial matters, but that they can exercise it only on condition that they leave the appearance of power to men.[7]

One of the difficulties of studying women's domestic power is that autonomy and segregation are so intertwined for a wife that it is difficult to separate their effects. Idealized observations may sometimes overestimate female control. For example, the fact that many women hold the family purse strings has frequently been considered the symbol of women's domestic autonomy. However, instead of regarding budgeting as a source of power, some women feel this responsibility is a burden (Ōsawa Machiko 1994; Ueno 1987; Zelizer 1994).

Because the overwhelming majority of studies have examined women's control at home in a rural community, it is interesting to see how the shift of focus from rural households to urban workplaces affects the studies' arguments. Not only do the new studies have relevance for many of us living in cities, but they also allow us to test the prevailing assumption that women are most disadvantaged in modern bureaucratic organizations.[8] Susan Rogers (1975), for example, attributes wives' power to the domestic-centeredness of the community and the importance of informal face-to-face interactions. She therefore predicts that as the locus of identity moves outside of the family and community to the workplace, women's informal power will become much less effective. Is this prediction correct? Must women's capacity to influence necessarily be based on their homemaking skills? Is it only in the traditionally feminine sphere that women enjoy autonomy? In order to answer these questions, it is important to examine whether women can create opportunities outside the household. As Carol Mukhopadhyay writes, "Focusing on women solely as wives (especially brides) and (young) mothers overemphasizes the limitations on women's powers and sphere of action, even for the most male-dominated cultures" (1988, 465).

Compared to the accounts of women's activities in the household, discussions of women in the workplace tend to focus on their vulnerability (Kondo 1990 and Lamphere 1987 are exceptions to this). Women are depicted as victims of hierarchical work structures who must cope with limits, dilemmas, and uncertainties. In her classic study of the treatment of men and women in a large American corporation, Rosabeth Kanter (1977) describes the unequal and nonreciprocal relationship between a male boss and a female secretary. The boss evaluated the secretary, whereas she rarely evaluated him. Because the boss's opinion of his secretary determined her fate in the firm, but her opinion did not affect his fate, the secretary tried to please her boss by expressing her loyalty and devotion to him.

A remarkable piece of research on how the work environment affects human feelings has been conducted by Arlie Hochschild (1983). She, too, assumes that women's subordinate position requires them to control their own feelings more than men must. Therefore, she argues that women are expected to make themselves "nicer" than men and, for example, compliment others on their clothing. Women's niceness, according to Hochschild, is a necessary lubricant to civil exchange and keeps the social wheels turning. She writes: "High-status people tend to enjoy the privilege of having their feelings noticed and considered important. The lower one's status, the more one's feelings are not noticed or treated as inconsequential" (1983, 172).

There is a tendency to reaffirm the commonly held belief that the dominant can be assertive and the dominated must exercise discretion. Superiors, it is said, do not have to worry much about the opinion of others, especially the opinion of inferiors. Subordinates, in contrast, are supposed to be wary of what they say and do, lest they incur the displeasure of their superiors. Subordinates often attempt to appeal to the expectations of the powerful and curry favor (Scott 1985, 1990).

Contrary to such assertions, I show in this book that under certain circumstances, Japanese men in positions of authority care more about the feelings of subordinate women than subordinate women do about the feelings of men in authority. Fear, self-control, perseverance, and indirectness characterize the emotions of men rather than women. In some cases, it is men who try to maintain harmonious relations between the two sexes by cracking jokes or talking about last night's TV programs.

In the following chapters I describe how Japanese men take pains not to offend women, how they study women's moods, and how they even curry women's favor. The extent to which these men feel constrained in their relations with women and take care not to arouse their displeasure is extraordinary. I therefore argue that macro-level power relations are not necessarily reproduced in micro-level interactions, and may even be *reversed*.

Some theorists refuse to attach much importance to power exercised unofficially. James Scott (1990), for example, argues in his finely crafted book on resistance that the fact that women must pretend to be powerless is not only a symbolic concession but a political concession, which only reaffirms men's power in the public realm. He also points out that men, as the formal title holders, may take away this "unofficial" power from women, who only exercise it on behalf of men. Such criticism, however, fails to take into account the *structural* nature of women's access to various means of control. If men's dependence on women is not the sole result of an individual, voluntary action, but one based on the institutional structures of society, men cannot deprive women of their "weapons" as easily as Scott envisions.

In fact, the assumption that formal forms of power are more effective and enduring than informal means of control may be adequate only in a certain social context. Frank Upham (1987) describes how conflict resolution in Japan is characterized by informality, where potentially general issues are particularized and universal rules are substituted for ad hoc decision making. For example, although Japanese Ministry of International Trade and Industry (MITI) lacked specific formal powers, this fact did not stop MITI from gaining firms' compliance with its policies. By emphasizing consultation and consensus, MITI exercised strong leadership in forming and implementing many of its industrial policies (Johnson 1982; Upham 1987). Indeed, Upham contends that MITI wished to avoid legal formality so as to minimize the power of individual firms to challenge MITI in court. Informality need not mean ineffective and weak control.[9]

In this book I argue that Japanese women's access to informal means

of control is not necessarily a temporary arrangement that can be easily redressed if men choose to do so. Women's empowerment may be
neither coincidental nor transient. I show how, under certain circumstances, the men's power and the effectiveness of the women's resistance to it become so inseparable that one necessarily entails the other.
The men described in this book cannot deprive the women of their
weapons without inflicting serious damage on their own power base.
The men must therefore accede to the women's use of manipulative
strategies if they are to exercise their power.[10]

"Office Flowers"

Although increasing numbers of researchers are studying
Japanese women, very little scholarly work has focused on female office
workers.[11] Whereas their male colleagues, *sarariman* (salaried men), have
attracted much attention, we know surprisingly few things about smiling receptionists and clerical assistants.[12] In a sense, the focus on male
employees in large corporations is understandable: they are the bene-
ficiaries of the unique Japanese employment system and are often regarded as the backbone of the Japanese economy. The result, however,
is a biased view of Japanese labor and industrial relations. As Robert
Cole argues: "Insofar as the benefits of the privileged male worker aris-
tocrats come at the expense of female employees, temporary workers
and those working in small firms, the experience of the latter is very
much part of the Japanese employment system" (1979, 3).

There are two other reasons why a detailed examination of the life
and work of female office workers in large firms is important. First, it
has been repeatedly said that unlike men, Japanese women do not enjoy various benefits of internal labor markets available for full-time employees in large companies—benefits such as high wages, good working
conditions, employment stability, and prospects for promotion. There is
an imbalance in the distribution of male and female employees by firm
size, with women concentrated in smaller establishments (Lam 1992).
Women also account for the overwhelming majority of the increasing
number of part-time employees (Ōsawa Mari 1993).

However, it is not that *more* women than men start out their employment in small firms and as part-time employees. Brinton (1993) has
found that the overwhelming majority of both sexes obtain their first
jobs as full-time employees, and that approximately one-third of them,

both men and women, initially work for large companies employing at least one thousand people. Although young men and women begin their work lives in similar ways, an increasing number of women move out of large firms and out of full-time employment status as they age, whereas men are less mobile.

The commonly cited explanation for women's movement is that they quit working upon marriage and, when their children are grown, they reenter the labor market in positions available to them—in small firms or as part-time workers. Such explanation, however, adds little to the data obtained from women's employment patterns. What we need to know is how young women feel, think, and behave while working in the office.[13] What factors influence their decision to leave supposedly advantageous positions in large firms as full-time employees? How do they arrive at this critical decision?

The second reason for focusing on female office workers is the need to analyze the implications of the "lifetime" employment system. Numerous scholars have documented how the Japanese management system discriminates against women (Brinton 1993; Lam 1992; Ōsawa Machiko 1993; Ōsawa Mari 1993). It is also of great interest to see how this system provides opportunities for women.

In their analyses of large Japanese firms, some researchers have noted the ironic implications of the "lifetime" employment system for female employees. Because women do not receive the benefits of the internal labor market, they feel free to criticize authority. Thomas Rohlen explains the situation: "Women have no career at stake in the organization and can always turn back to their parents. Office morale problems are quickly apparent among the women, and a great deal of effort is expended these days trying to find ways to keep the Uedagin woman happy. She has come to have a special kind of leverage because she is more willing to show her dissatisfaction and even to quit" (1974, 104). Similarly, Rodney Clark observes that women can refuse to transfer to another location, although such transfers are part of the usual career path for men: "If she had been a male graduate (and supposing that a male graduate would ever have failed to respond to such an order) her superiors would have been able to offer better chances of promotion and to threaten some kind of managerial oblivion to induce her to go. But a woman? Women were scarcely eligible for promotion in any event, and they could hardly be made to do more tedious jobs than they were doing" (1979, 217–18). Clark also mentions that women are late for work when it suits them and disappear into the office kitchen when their sections are particularly busy. Because female workers are less wedded to the company, they regard authority lightly. They can be more independent than men (see also Iwao 1993 and Kelsky 1994).

In this study I examine what this independence buys for women. What exactly is the leverage women are said to have? How do they exercise it? Under what circumstances? What is the response of the company authority? Of their male colleagues? To what extent does it affect the way men interact with women? How are the relations between men and women in the office shaped by it? Are there any limits to women's independence? Finally, what implications does women's exercise of their leverage have on women's current and future status?

Women working in the office are called *ofisu redī* (office lady), or OL for short, in Japan. OLs are recruited immediately from universities and two-year colleges. In the past, many were also hired straight from high school, but this number has declined, especially in large corporations in urban areas, as more and more women attain higher education.

Major tasks assigned to OLs include operating copiers and facsimile machines, performing elementary accounting, and doing word processing. They are also usually responsible for such chores as serving tea to their male colleagues or company visitors, wiping the surfaces of desks with wet towels, and receiving telephone calls. Sometimes they are even asked to go out on errands, such as to buy prizes for the men's weekend golf competition. Perhaps because their work seems wholly superficial and nonproductive, some say that OLs' major contribution to the office lies in their presence. Indeed, OLs were once frequently called "office flowers," implying that they served a decorative function and thereby inspired men to work hard. Partly in response to the influence of Western feminist thinking, this expression is no longer popular. However, the role OLs play in the organization has not changed much since the days when they were called "office flowers."

My analysis concentrates on OLs working in large corporations. The discrepancy between the level of educational attainment and opportunities available for women is greatest in large firms that recruit employees, both male and female, from the nation's most prestigious universities and colleges. In addition, there are reasons to believe that OLs in large companies have more in common than those in smaller establishments. Japanese companies are infamous for their conformity. Preferring to be in step with other companies, they constantly compare their policies, including how to treat female employees, against those of similar companies. This tendency is stronger among large, established companies, whose every move is watched closely by the mass media and the government. Consequently, women in large companies often face strikingly similar uncertainties and dilemmas despite differences in the specific workplace. In contrast, situations in smaller and less well-established companies are more various. Being relatively new or small, these organizations rely less on bureaucratic rules and more on personal management style. As a result, women's working conditions in these companies tend to vary, depending more on the personal opinions of an individual manager than on fixed organizational policies.

Some Thoughts on Methodology

One of the first questions I asked myself was whether my research could be carried out solely by conducting interviews, which are less time-consuming than participant observation. Many researchers emphasize that the key to a successful interview is knowing enough to ask intelligent questions without knowing too much.[14] I seemed to have the desired combination of knowing enough and yet not knowing all. I had in the past worked with OLs of several client companies when I was employed by a management consulting firm in Tokyo. I also had many friends who were or had been OLs. However, because I had never actually been an OL myself, I could inquire with genuine curiosity what it was like to be an OL.

Yet I wondered if respondents would readily answer such queries as "Why don't OLs refuse to serve tea?" and "Why are men afraid of their female colleagues?" The more I considered the prospect, the less confident I became. Offering an explanation requires simultaneous detachment and close attention; the respondent must disengage from the immediate surroundings yet observe them steadily. He or she must assume the attitude of an onlooker. The world must be objectified, which necessitates a conscious distinction between subject and object. Moreover, in order to draw a clear picture of the situation for someone who is unfamiliar with it, the respondent must deal with issues of presentation, with the distinction between representation and "reality."

Yet dividing the world into two separate realms—representations and "external reality"—is a habit of thought. According to Timothy Mitchell (1988), when Europeans, who nurtured this habit of binary vision, visited Egypt in the late nineteenth century, they found it disappointing; it was *impossible* to represent. These Europeans were baffled by life in Cairo, which Egyptians "understood in terms of the *occurrence and reoccurrence of practices*, rather than in terms of an 'architecture'—material or institutional—that stands apart from life itself, containing and representing the meaning of what was done" (59, emphasis added).

OLs and *sararīman* of contemporary Japan may be more familiar with modern instruments of representation than Egyptians in the nineteenth century. However, as I see it, many still prefer to understand their lives not in abstract terms, but in concrete everyday situations. Their perceptions are not fixed but vary according to relations among the persons involved, the time, and the circumstances. They find questions such as "What do you value in life?" difficult to answer because these queries force them to extract "meaning" from an everyday situation and give it a determinate form.

This situationally negotiated understanding is evident in the Japanese use of personal pronouns, which vary according to context. The available options include but are not limited to *watakushi, watashi, washi, boku,* and *ore* for men, and *watakushi, watashi,* and *atashi* for women. The pronouns differ primarily in their degree of formality but also invoke complex resonances in terms of class, age, regionality, masculinity or femininity, sophistication, and intimacy (Hamabata 1990; Kondo 1990). A white-collar businessman who usually refers to himself as *boku* among his colleagues will raise the level of politeness and say *watashi* when speaking to his boss; he will become even more formal and use *watakushi* when addressing a large audience in a meeting. When speaking to his wife or among close friends from school, he may find the tough, macho expression of *ore* appropriate.

Furthermore, there is a plethora of expressions that can be used in place of personal pronouns, such as kin terms, occupational titles, and proper names. It is perfectly normal practice for a man to call himself *otōsan* (father) when speaking to his children. The unitary "I" presupposed in the West shifts with social positioning in Japan (Bachnik 1982; Wetzel 1994). It is made anew each time according to the particularities of a given situation. As Kondo argues, "You are not an 'I' untouched by context, rather you are defined by the context" (1990, 29).

To interview Japanese *sararīman* and OLs, I would have to formulate questions that would not look for "meaning" outside everyday occurrence. Although I had some idea of what a typical Japanese office was like, I did not know enough to ground my questions in the concrete situations of daily worklife. Therefore, I decided to carry out the first part of my research with participant observation in a large financial institution in Tokyo, which is called Tōzai Bank in this book.[15] I worked at Tōzai Bank four days a week from ten in the morning to four in the afternoon as a temporary employee for approximately half a year between the months of October 1991 and March 1992. My job was to give miscellaneous assistance to fifty-one *sararīman* and eleven OLs belonging to three departments. I served tea, made copies, and delivered documents to nearby departments. Instead of being tied to my desk, I was able to visit different parts of the company building, meet various people, and listen to many discussions. Further details on both the bank and the workplace are provided in the first chapter.

Although my experiences at Tōzai Bank were revelatory and enriching, it was important to assess the universality of what I observed; for this purpose, interviews were indispensable. After completing the participant observation, I spoke to thirty *sararīman* and thirty OLs and ex-OLs employed in large Japanese firms. In line with the definition most commonly used in government statistics and in studies of Japanese employment (Brinton 1989; Brinton, Ngo, and Shibuya 1991; Cole 1979; Hashimoto and Raisian 1983), firms employing at least one thousand people are considered large. However, in most cases, the informants I talked to were members of superlarge companies that are famous worldwide and employ nearly ten thousand employees. In the following chapters where interviews are quoted, I refrain from mentioning each time that the speaker belongs to a large or superlarge establishment and specify only the business of the company.

I contacted the sixty men and women by asking my acquaintances for the names of associates who worked in large companies. Although such a nonrandom sample has inherent shortcomings, I compensated as much as possible by variation. I talked to informants who differed, among other things, in age, tenure, position, education, line of business, and type of industry. Above all, I made sure that no two interviewees worked for the same firm. As a result, I talked to men and women working in sixty different large-scale organizations, something that was perhaps uniquely possible in a city like Tokyo, where there is an exceptional concentration of business. Readers are advised to refer to appendix A for a full discussion of the representativeness of the interview sample, as well as other methodological issues. Profiles of sixty *sararīman* and OLs are given in appendix B.

In addition, I interviewed ten *sararīman* and ten ex-OLs of large Japanese corporations specifically about Valentine's Day gift-giving in the office, and thirty wives of *sararīman* about the White Day gifts their husbands give to OLs. Detailed profiles of these informants are provided in chapters 4 and 6 respectively. Altogether, I talked to more than one hundred men and women, whose lives were strongly connected to large Japanese companies.

At this point, a road map of the rest of the book might be helpful. I begin with a general description of women and work in Japan, placing emphasis on OLs and their daily lives in the office. In chapter 2, I examine the forces that inhibit OLs from organizing open rebellion. The next three chapters discuss forms in which OLs negotiate power: how OLs embarrass and irritate men with their critical and persistent gaze; how they publicly humiliate men through symbolic gift-giving; and how they annoy men by refusing to cooperate, sometimes gently, but other times bluntly. In all three chapters, attention is paid to the structural factors that contribute to men's vulnerability and to women's accompanying empowerment. Chapter 6 discusses men's lavish gifts to OLs as one of the most effective means of influencing women who work in the office. I conclude by noting the manner in which women's resistance is voiced through accommodation and the way it reinforces traditional gender relations.[16]

1

The Japanese Labor Market and Office Ladies

Women and Work in Japan

WOMEN'S EMPLOYMENT PATTERNS

To understand the role of office ladies, one must first look at women's employment patterns in Japan.[1] The number of employed women in Japan has steadily increased since 1960, reaching twenty million in 1995. The growth rate has been higher for women than for men, and women now account for almost 40 percent of all employed persons (fig. 1). Interestingly, the rate of women's participation in the workforce by age takes the shape of the letter *M*. The percentage of women working increases dramatically when women leave school, reaching almost 75 percent among women in their early twenties. After that age, many women leave the labor market to marry and raise a family. The percentage of women working bottoms out at slightly less than 55 percent for women in their early thirties, after which there is a gradual increase. The second peak comes when women are in their late forties: about 70 percent work. The number of women working diminishes again as they grow older (fig. 2).

The rate of women's participation in the workforce contrasts sharply with that of men, which takes a curvilinear shape. The percentages of men and of women working increase in similar fashion until age twenty-four, but the percentage of men working continues to expand after age twenty-four. It remains at more than 95 percent among men in their thirties, forties, and early fifties and only drops among those in their

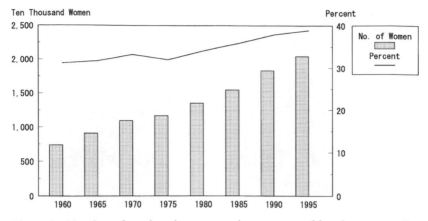

Figure 1: Number of employed women and percentage of females among all employees. *Source: Sōmuchō, Rōdōryoku chōsa* (Survey of the labor force), various years.

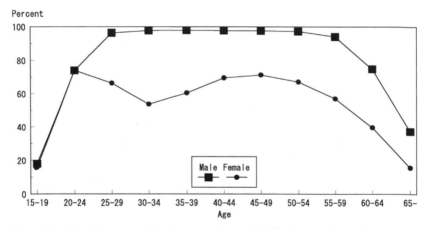

Figure 2: Workforce participation rate by sex, 1995. *Source: Sōmuchō, Rōdōryoku chōsa* (Survey of the labor force), 1996.

early sixties (fig. 2). Comparison of the percentages of working men and women indicates that the majority of Japanese women enter the labor market after leaving school, just as men do. However, a large number of women leave the labor market after marriage and childbirth. Many reenter the labor market later on. Because the overwhelming majority of large and prominent companies in Japan recruit female full-time employees only directly from school, reentrants seek employment either in smaller companies or as part-time workers and receive less pay

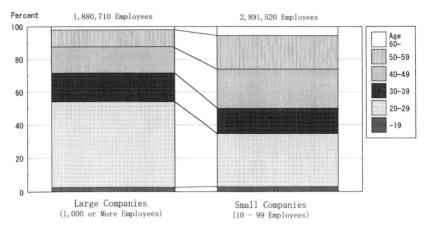

Figure 3: Female full-time employees by age, 1995. *Source: Rōdōshō, Chingin kōzō kihon tōkei chōsa* (Basic survey on wage structure), 1996.

and fewer benefits than full-time employees of large companies. These so-called part-time employees in Japan often work as long hours as regular employees, hence the name, *giji pāto* (quasi-part-time workers).

The difference in the ages of women working in large and small companies reflects this pattern of female employment. More than half the full-time female employees in large companies, with one thousand or more workers, are twenty-nine years old or younger. In contrast, in small companies with less than one hundred workers, there are nearly as many women in their forties and fifties as in their twenties (fig. 3). In either size company, there is a smaller percentage of women in their thirties, a fact consistent with the drop in the percentage of women of that age in the workforce.

Since 1960, the relative number of women in blue-collar jobs has decreased, and the percentage of women in clerical jobs has increased. As many as one-third of all women employed in 1995 held clerical positions, which testifies to the important place OLs occupy in the Japanese female labor market (fig. 4). In contrast, approximately one-third of all men employed in 1995 held blue-collar jobs; only 15 percent held clerical positions.

Only 1 percent of all women employed are managers or officials—a figure approximately one-seventh the equivalent percentage for men. In companies with one hundred or more employees, only 1 percent of *buchō* (general managers), 3 percent of *kachō* (section managers), and 7 percent of *kakarichō* (chiefs) are women. Overall, women account for

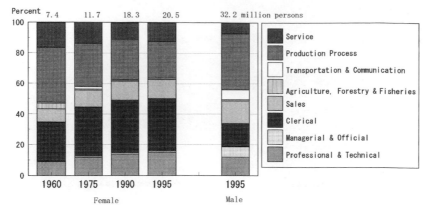

Figure 4: Employment structure by occupation. *Source: Sōmuchō, Rōdōryoku chōsa* (Survey of the labor force), various years.

only 4 percent of managers in these positions, whereas almost 40 percent of employees without such titles are women. The picture is even more bleak in large companies with one thousand or more employees. Women account for 1 percent, 2 percent, and 6 percent of *buchō, kachō,* and *kakarichō* respectively; overall, women account for only 3 percent of managers in these positions in large companies (table 1).

There are so few female *buchō* that labor statistics published by the government in *Chingin kōzō kihon tōkei chōsa hōkoku 1995* (Basic survey on wage structure 1995) contain numbers only for male managers; figures for female managers do not exist. What is extremely important to note, in this respect, is that not only are there few female *buchō*, but female *kakarichō* are almost equally rare. *Kakarichō* is typically the lowest rank of managers to have supervisory responsibility in a white-collar organization. Although the rank structure differs between companies, the rank of *kakarichō* usually carries nominal social distinction.[2] The fact that there are so few women even at this level of management speaks to the omnipresent pattern of "male managers and female subordinates" in Japan.

TŌZAI BANK

Financial institutions and real-estate companies employ the fourth largest number of women in Japan: 1.2 million in 1995. Only services, retail and wholesale, and manufacturing employ more. However, the percentage of female employees within the total workforce is

Table 1 *Percentage of Female Employees, 1995*

Company Size (number of employees)	Percentage of female managers			Percentage of female nonmanagerial workers
	Buchō	Kachō	Kakarichō	
100 or more	<1%	3%	7%	36%
100–499	2%	4%	9%	40%
500–999	1%	2%	8%	36%
1,000 or more	1%	2%	6%	33%

SOURCE: *Rōdōshō, Chingin kōzō kihon tōkei chōsa* (Basic survey on wage structure), 1996.

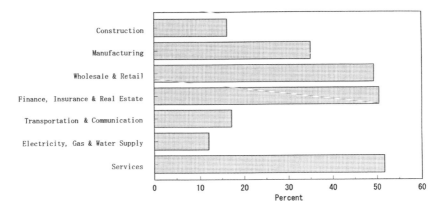

Figure 5: Percentage of female employees by industry, 1995. *Source:*
Sōmuchō, Rōdōryoku chōsa (Survey of the labor force), 1996.

among the highest in finance, insurance, and real estate: women account for half of the workforce in these industries (fig. 5).

Tōzai Bank is one of the largest and most prominent financial institutions in Japan. It was founded more than seventy years ago and belongs to a well-known *zaibatsu* (constellation of companies). The company has an extensive network of branches covering the entire nation
and extending overseas. At the time of my research, the bank employed
about four thousand men and three thousand women.

I worked as a temporary employee in the headquarters of the bank,
located in the central business district of Tokyo. The headquarters occupied a large building, with offices spread throughout its many floors.

The office in which I worked was on the first floor, in a large open space without any partitions or cubicles, which is the typical configuration in Japanese companies. In this office, there were three departments, which I refer to as Departments I, II, and III. Each department was headed by a *buchō* and a *jichō* (vice-general manager). Their desks were located in the back of the office. *Buchō*, two of them board members, also had private rooms on the second floor of the building, used primarily for meetings with important customers. Both *buchō* and *jichō* were often seen on the first floor, working in direct contact with their subordinates. Consequently, I was able to observe how OLs interacted with men in different hierarchical positions.

Each department was further divided into three sections. A section consisted of four or five men, including a *kachō*. These men's desks were grouped together facing inward, creating a circle. In addition to the three sections, there was also a planning group in Department I. It consisted of a man, his female assistant, and two OLs working as secretaries for the six *buchō* and *jichō*. My desk and a fellow temporary staff member's desk formed a ring with those of the four members of the planning group.

The front of the room functioned as a sales counter, and six OLs were seated there. The organizational positioning of these OLs was complex, for although two OLs worked in pairs for each of the three departments, they all officially belonged to an administrative group of Department III. This administrative group was located on the second floor of the building and consisted of four men, including a *kachō*, and twelve OLs. It was one of the constant complaints of the six OLs working for the three departments that their supervisor was the *kachō* on the second floor. They objected that his instruction often missed the mark because he did not have direct knowledge of work on the first floor. I later learned that this somewhat curious arrangement was the result of the managers' wish to make it easy to exchange OLs on the first and the second floor. Transfer within a department did not require the consent of the Personnel Department.

One OL had her seat not at the sales counter, but among men in a ring. This was explained to me as a temporary arrangement resulting from a recent merger of the section, which formerly belonged to a different department. True enough, when the OL left the bank for marriage, no one replaced her. There was also a group of four men, including a *kachō*, who had their desks in the room, although officially they were part of another department located nearby. Because their business

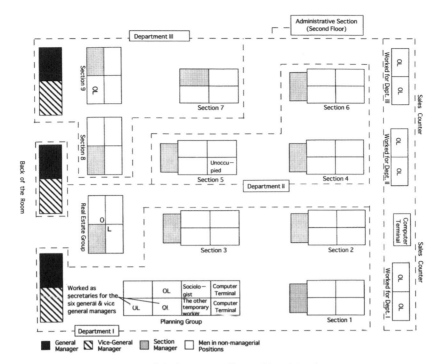

Figure 6: Arrangement of desks in an office at Tōzai Bank

required close coordination with the men on the floor, physical proximity was considered necessary. An OL came from the other department every day to help the four men. Despite working in the room
nearly all day, she did not have a desk and was forced to use whichever
of the four men's desks happened to be free at the time. Altogether, as
many as sixty-two company employees, including eleven OLs, worked
on the floor (fig. 6).

THE OFFICE LADIES

The widely used term *office lady* is an English expression
of Japanese coinage. According to a dictionary of words of foreign origin, it is an honorific expression for a female office worker. The term
dates from 1963, when a weekly women's magazine, *Josei Jishin*, invited
suggested replacements for the then-popular expression *business girl*,
or *BG* for short; *office lady* was chosen in response to readers' votes
(Yoshizawa and Ishiwata 1979). *BG* had often appeared in journalism

during the late 1950s and early 1960s. For example, an article written in 1960 discussed the short and superficial career of BGs. It provided a list of jobs that a typical BG performed in an office:

Clean ash trays and desks in the morning; perform assistant clerical jobs such as to transcribe, make fair copies of, and send out slips; order food so that men's appetites will be satisfied at noon; be interrupted in her tasks, and be made to go buy cigarettes in the intervals of a day's work; and, from time to time, sew the buttons of a henpecked man who, when leaving his house in the morning, hesitated to ask his wife for the service; and so on. (Yamada 1960, 71)[3]

The article summarized the tasks of BGs as "simple, routine assistant jobs that are performed each time in response to an order." Another article suggested that the typical BG working in Tokyo was a woman no older than twenty-four who had graduated high school, lived at home with her parents and consequently *did not* work for a livelihood, and would marry and stop working about three years after joining a company (*Nihon* 1963).

Living with their parents who took care of daily living expenses, most BGs were able to use the money they earned as they liked. Although their pay was modest, their capacity as consumers was prodigious. Their role in the consumer market attracted much journalistic attention. BGs were said to have frequented beer halls, bowling alleys, ski resorts, movie theaters, and concerts. Many took private lessons in flower arrangement, cooking, or sewing. Together with their boyfriends, BGs played a significant part in the leisure boom of the sixties (Nagasu and Ichibangase 1963). Having both money and time, BGs were portrayed in journalism as the cheerful and innocent leaders of the new consumer society.

OLs today are still considered the leading figures in the consumer market, setting the latest fashions and trends. Many popular books on OLs introduce their values and lifestyles. These accounts do not attempt to hide the fact that OLs' jobs are mostly simple and repetitive, requiring little time to learn, and that after a while OLs are bored with their work. However, the OLs depicted in these books enjoy their "after five" lives. Far from being depressed, they are portrayed as exuberant and energetic consumers.[4]

Wishing to tap the huge "OL market," companies conduct interviews and surveys of OLs. The sheer number and the breadth of the surveys are staggering: they cover OLs' views on work, love, and marriage; their financial planning; how they spend their after-work hours and summer holidays; their preferred fashions, restaurants, sports, travel, and other leisure activities; their gift-giving practices; and much more. One food-processing company even conducted a survey on OLs' bowel movements![5] Because the majority of the surveys do not follow the rigorous sampling procedures customary in social science, we must be careful of what we deduce from them. However, some help us understand the lives of OLs.

Research conducted by a life insurance company is particularly relevant for our purpose, for it focused on OLs working in the headquarters of large companies located in the central business districts of Tokyo (Chiyoda-ku, Chūō-ku, and Minato-ku) in 1991 (Fukuhara 1992). The OLs studied were limited to single women between the ages of twenty and thirty-five. The effective sample size was 575. We do not know how many OLs refused to answer the questionnaire, which was to be filled out and returned to the insurance company. The average age of the OLs studied was 24.4, and the average tenure was 3.5 years. According to the survey, the average monthly gross income of the OLs was a little less than two hundred thousand yen.[6] The OLs replied that they could use as much as seventy thousand yen as they wished each month. The study attributed the large amount of money the OLs had at their disposal to the fact that three-quarters lived with their parents and thus did not pay rent or utility fees.

How did the OLs spend their money? At least two or three days a week, almost two-thirds of the OLs spent time after work shopping for items other than daily necessities, dining out, and going to movies, theaters, and concerts. A little less than half the OLs replied that they visited hot springs two or three times a year, and 40 percent went skiing at least three times a season. One-third of the OLs traveled abroad every year.

Surveys also revealed their complaints. What the OLs were most dissatisfied with in the workplace was the company uniform. The second most frequent complaint was that their jobs made poor use of their talents, followed by discontent with their bosses' management capability and lack of men in the office whom they would like to date. It is noteworthy that few OLs objected to the unequal treatment of men and women in their companies. As for future plans, almost three-quarters of the OLs intended to leave work upon marriage or childbirth. Approximately 15 percent of the women hoped to continue work after marriage and childbirth, and 6 percent replied that they would continue work after marriage but have no children. The last 4 percent wished to remain single. The findings indicate that the overwhelming majority of OLs intended to marry. In fact, the number one reason for the OLs to save money was to prepare for marriage.

Let us now examine the profiles of OLs in Tōzai Bank and compare them to the survey data. I became well acquainted with not only the eleven OLs working in my office but also four women of a nearby department who ate lunch with us everyday. Appendix C summarizes age, marital status, educational background, tenure, and other information about these fifteen OLs.[7] The average age of the fifteen women was 26.9 at the start of the study. If we exclude four women who would not be included in the study because of their age and marital status, the average age was 24.9, approximating the average age of the OLs in the survey data.

Except for one thirty-one-year-old and one forty-four-year-old, all the women were in their twenties. Six women were between the ages of twenty and twenty-four, and seven were between the ages of twenty-five and twenty-nine. This group of OLs was younger than the average age of all female employees of the bank (thirty-one years old)—primarily because women working in regional branches tended to stay longer in the company than those in large cities. The explanation often given for women's lengthier tenure in regional branches is that, in rural areas, the bank's policy of offering uniform compensation despite regional differences gives it a competitive advantage in hiring over lower-paying local companies. It is said that quite a few women in regional branches continue working even after marriage and childbirth. Although women working in rural areas fall outside the scope of this study, it is worth noting that OLs' work lives potentially differ by geographical area.

Of the fifteen OLs, six were university graduates, five were two-year college graduates, and four joined the bank immediately after finishing high school. The bank stopped recruiting men and women from high school ten years ago, and all four OLs with only high-school education had been with the company ten or more years. The relatively high concentration of high-school-only employees was reflected in the OLs' rather long average tenure of six and a half years, compared to a tenure of three and a half years in the survey data.

Three women were married at the start of the study. One of them, the thirty-one-year-old OL, took maternity leave for her first child during my study. After her leave, she returned to work in the bank. The other two married women were younger and did not have children. The forty-four-year-old woman was separated from her husband and had two children. Among the eleven single OLs, only two lived by themselves. The rest lived in their parents' home, as did the majority of the OLs covered in the survey data.

Two of the eleven single women became engaged during my study. Another two, one of whom was already engaged, got married and eventually quit the bank. One of these women married a colleague in the bank. Because the company did not allow both marriage partners to continue working, this OL—following the custom for women in her situation—gave up her job, while her husband continued his career in the bank. The other woman married a man outside the organization and continued working in the bank for a short time, until her husband was transferred to another city. That four out of fifteen women either became engaged or got married and left the bank during the study suggests the high turnover of OLs in the bank as a result of marriage.

Before I examine the daily lives of OLs in detail, I would like to clarify my use of the term *OL*. It is a much-used expression in present-day Japan; not a day passes without the word appearing in magazine or newspaper headlines, and it pops up frequently in conversation. However, the exact definition of the term is unclear.

The word has no place in government statistics. It does not appear in many of the standard Japanese language dictionaries. People seem to use the word as it suits them. Some limit OLs to single women in their twenties who work as clerical assistants. Others hold that women employed in a company are OLs, whereas still others suggest that all working women are OLs. Even among the authors of books on OLs, the definition varies.[8] Therefore, it is not exactly certain whether OLs include saleswomen in large department stores—or, for that matter, whether a woman who is fifty years old and works as a clerical assistant in an office would be called an OL.

This study defines an OL as a woman working regularly in an office who engages in simple, repetitive, clerical work without any expert knowledge or management responsibility. Besides being the most generally used, this definition helps to focus the present research. I believe it is only at this level of specificity that distinctive features shared by women justify treating them together under the type of single study intended here. Any broader definition, such as all working women, does more harm than good by lumping together women working under vastly different conditions.

Because OLs portrayed in journalistic accounts typically work in a large, prominent company, many saleswomen working in well-known department stores call themselves OLs. I have not included them in

this study, however, following government statistics that distinguish between clerical and sales workers. Although the word *OL* usually brings
to mind an image of a young woman, I include in this study women of
all ages who conform to the preceding definition, because there is no
consensus on the age at which a woman is too "old" to be called an
OL. Being an "old" OL has implications vital to any study of OLs, as
discussed in chapter 2.

THE TWO-TRACK SYSTEM

At Tōzai Bank, men and women were recruited immedi-
ately from colleges and universities for two different positions: *sōgōshoku*
(integrated track) and *ippanshoku* or *jimushoku* (clerical track). Those
in *sōgōshoku* were trained to become managers, and *ippanshoku* employees worked as their assistants. The deceptively gender-neutral terms
cloaked the fact that integrated-track employees were almost all male
and clerical workers were without exception female. In recent years,
the bank recruited 50 to 80 university graduates each year for the integrated positions. Among them, only a handful were female. In addition, 100 to 150 women were hired as clerical workers. About half of
the women recruited for clerical positions had university diplomas, often from the same institutions as the men in the integrated positions.

The sex-discriminatory policy was reflected in the number of managers in the bank: at the time of the study, there were less than ten female managers out of a total of about two thousand (less than one in
two hundred). All eleven women on the floor where I worked, as well
as four women in the nearby department, were clerical workers.

Recruitment of female university graduates for both *sōgōshoku* and *ippanshoku* was virtually unknown before the implementation of the Equal
Employment Opportunity (EEO) Law in Japan in 1986. Before implementation of the law, the only women the bank officially employed were
junior-college graduates. (Incidentally, the two-year degree program offered in junior college is primarily for female students. There are few
junior colleges for male students.) Women graduating from university
were penalized for their overqualification: only those with "personal
connections" to the bank, usually through their fathers or relatives, were
hired, with the agreement that they would be treated as junior-college
graduates.

Even at the time of the study, the bank did not value university education for its clerical staff. A woman who had graduated from univer-

sity and been with the bank for two years was ranked and compensated the same as a junior-college graduate who had been with the bank four years. This was an improvement over the old policy in effect before the implementation of the EEO Law, which treated the same university graduate as a junior-college graduate who had been with the bank two years. It is clear, however, that the new policy still failed to pay for the price of higher education that the university graduate received. A junior-college woman earned money while her university counterpart paid tuition and was nevertheless compensated at the same rate as a university graduate of the same age.[9]

Until shortly after 1982, the bank recruited men and women directly from high school. In the older generation of employees, a number of these people remain. I was told that when the two-track system was introduced, all white-collar male employees, including those with only a high-school education, became integrated staff, whereas all female workers were designated as their clerical assistants. At the time of this study, only one such woman had been subsequently promoted to the integrated position. When the bank started recruiting female university graduates for clerical positions, this resulted in the often strained combination of a university-graduate assistant and a boss who joined the bank immediately from high school. However, on the floor where I worked, there were no men with only a high-school education.

Although people within the bank and the Japanese public in general talked of the two-track system, in reality there was a third category of employees in the bank: *shomu* (miscellaneous jobs). *Shomu* consisted entirely of male employees who worked as company car drivers, messengers, mailmen, bookbinders, building receptionists, and the like. The bank stopped recruiting employees for *shomu* some years ago and began filling these positions with part-time workers in their fifties and sixties who had retired from their primary jobs. Another small group of *shomu* regular employees were physically disabled men.

Shomu workers were present in the everyday life of the bank. For example, one had to pass the receptionist's desk to enter or exit the building, and the mailman came to our room to deliver and pick up mail each day. However, they were curiously absent from the minds of *sarariman* and OLs. People in the office used the words *men* and *women* to denote *sōgōshoku* and *ippanshoku* workers respectively. *Shomu* workers were usually left out in their reference to *men*. OLs had few contacts with *shomu* workers and generally knew little about them. One OL, for instance, stated that they were all part-time workers. I later found out that the man who sat at the nearby receptionist desk was a full-time employee who had been working in the bank for almost thirty years. When I told the OL what I had learned, she was genuinely surprised.

It was not only *shomu* workers but women in the integrated track who were ignored in the dichotomy between *men* and *women*, the most salient categorization of people in the company. After the implementation of the EEO Law, the bank adopted the gender-neutral terms *integrated* and *clerical* in its official documents. In everyday life, however, people in the office continued to talk and think in gender dichotomy: a man often asked an OL before picking up a transferred phone call whether the caller was a "man" or a "woman"; what he wished to find out was whether the caller was an integrated staff member whom he must answer with respect, or whether the caller was an ordinary OL. Similarly, OLs frequently replied to a customer's call apologetically, "There's no man on the floor at the moment who can answer your question."

When I called the personnel department of the bank before accepting the job, a woman answered the phone and explained their recruitment policies in a competent manner. When I asked her a further question, however, she said abruptly, "Let me transfer this call to a man." It was apparent from the way she said it that I was to interpret *man* as "someone in a more responsible position to answer your questions." Indeed, because there were still few integrated-track women in the organization (less than twenty among approximately seven thousand employees), people seemed to feel little inconvenience in treating them as an exception to the men-women dichotomy.

In accord with the perception of the overwhelming majority of the people in the office, unless otherwise noted, the words *men* and *women* will be used hereafter to denote *sararīman* in the integrated track and OLs in the clerical position respectively. Despite the fact that the terms reinforce sex discrimination, I use them because, to do otherwise would mask the gross unfairness of present conditions.

Office Ladies' Daily Work Lives

OFFICE LADIES AS "GIRLS"

When not referred to as *women*, OLs were often—indeed, more often—referred to as *girls* (*onnanoko*). Although they were addressed by the men on the floor by their names, to an outsider both within and out of the bank, OLs were simply "girls." Thus a man speaking to another man on the phone often said, "I'll have one of the girls go get it," or "Our girl made a mistake."[10]

Carole Pateman (1988) compares calling adult women "girls" to calling adult male slaves "boys," and argues that both usages are a graphic illustration of a perpetual nonage that women and slaves cannot cast off. The words suggest "civilly dead beings." By lumping together OLs as "girls," men showed their unwillingness to recognize OLs as individuals. Indeed, respect for OLs' individuality was minimal. For instance, when a woman helped a man prepare a report, her name rarely appeared on it, even if she had done most of the work. The man for whom she worked took all the credit. In the real sense, OLs did not have names in the organization, and hence their names did not appear in the official record.

Working under someone else's name is common in Japan. Young businessmen write many reports on behalf of their bosses, and graduate students in Japanese universities often work for their professors without recognition in print.[11] The difference between the OLs and the businessmen and graduate students is that businessmen and graduate students are serving a form of apprenticeship; it is mutually understood that the boss or professor will eventually help the young person get recognition. However, no such thing can be expected for OLs. Most OLs' work will remain unrecognized forever.

Some women I talked to said that the most humiliating part of being an OL was this "namelessness." Men's individuality was respected. Each man accumulated credit and demerit marks according to his performance. In contrast, differences among individual women were more or less ignored. When a woman made a mistake in her work, the vague "Our girl screwed up" became a legitimate excuse. Seldom did men try to find out which of the women made the error, just as few men were interested in knowing which woman did a splendid job. Being treated as "one of the girls" made many OLs feel that they were mere replaceable cogs in the gigantic machine.

In accordance with the practice of lumping OLs together as "girls" was the fact that OLs in the bank were not seriously evaluated. Men were evaluated according to their performance and were graded on a scale from A to E, which determined the bonus they received. In theory, OLs were supposed to be evaluated as well. In reality, however, I was told that almost every OL received the grade of C, which indicated that she was an average worker.

That evaluation of OLs' performance virtually did not exist was brought home to me one day when two other women and I were discussing the compensation scheme for OLs. Matsumoto-san explained to me that the base payment was the same for all OLs with the same educational background who joined the firm in the same year, but bonuses could, in theory, differ according to their performance evaluations. At this point, Kuze-san gasped in surprise, "Is there such a thing as a performance evaluation?" Apparently, she did not know that OLs, including herself, were being evaluated.

Matsumoto-san informed her bewildered colleague that indeed OLs received grades that ranged from A to E. She then described the way an OL could find out how she had been evaluated by calculating backward from a compensation chart that the union distributed. Kuze-san exclaimed, "Gosh, I didn't know!" Matsumoto-san assured her colleague, "In case of women, it's mostly C anyway. Once Ueda-san [their female colleague on the floor] asked Furukawa-san [one of the board members] about women's grades, and he said that unless there's something gravely wrong, women get Cs." The fact that Kuze-san, who had been with the bank for at least three years, was unaware that there was a performance evaluation attested to its negligible status. Because the performance evaluation did not function properly for OLs, they were oblivious of its existence.

Management's lack of enthusiasm to earnestly evaluate OLs' work was also apparent from the aforementioned organizational arrangement, under which OLs seated at the sales counter reported to a section manager on the second floor of the building who knew little of their actual work. According to this agreement, the men for whom OLs worked were not the people who evaluated their performance. As has been explained, this grouping of OLs under the section manager on the second floor was the result of managers' desire to make it easier to transfer OLs. The arrangement would have caused great inconvenience if OLs' work was to be evaluated seriously. However, since true evaluation for OLs did not exist, the awkwardness of the grouping did not seem to trouble the managers.

Men and women I interviewed confirmed that the situation was similar in other firms. Some managers pointed out that in their company, OLs' performance was reviewed, but most agreed that evaluation of OLs was taken less seriously than evaluation of men. Perhaps more relevant to my discussion is the fact that few OLs considered assessment important. Many women thought that the difference in the appraisal process was of minor significance. OLs working in various companies often used the expressions "unless there's something gravely wrong" or "unless you've done something gravely wrong" (*yohodo no koto ga naikagiri* or *yohodo no koto o shinai kagiri*) to describe to me how little it mattered to them whether they performed well. OLs in general were aware that they had few prospects for promotion. Most did not think of their present job as a lifetime career. Furthermore, references from their current bosses were seldom necessary in obtaining new jobs. There were few incentives for them to worry about the evaluation they received as OLs.

In addition to performance reviews, other customs in the workplace reinforced the notion that OLs commanded less respect than the integrated staff. Some of these practices were supported by the official rules of the company, but most of them functioned as unwritten laws. One example was the custom for a clerical-track woman to leave the company upon marrying a fellow banker. When I asked the OLs whether it was the company rule, they did not know for sure but said that it was expected. A man working in another bank spoke of a similar convention in his workplace, which, according to him, was not laid down in the official company regulation. I suspect that the rule at Tōzai was also unofficial. In practice, however, a woman left the bank if she married a coworker.[12] There was a rumor that once a woman who had married her colleague protested against leaving the company but ultimately conceded when it was hinted that her staying with the bank would "hurt" her husband's career.

Another example was marriage ceremonies. It was customary for a man to invite the general manager of his department as the guest of honor to his wedding party. However, an OL would invite a vice-general manager. "A general manager is too important to be asked to come to our parties," explained an OL.

Various day-to-day practices showed that OLs occupied a secondary position to men. For instance, when names were written on a circulation board, OLs' names were indented in the following way.

Ōbayashi (man's name)

    Ueda (woman's name)
    Kurimoto (woman's name)

Nishida (man's name)

In addition, stamps used by OLs bearing their names were considerably smaller in size than men's. They were called *mame-in* (miniature stamps). More important, OLs did not carry *meishi* (business cards), vital instruments for anyone who wishes to do business in Japan.

Perhaps what most characterized the work life of an OL in contrast to that of a *sararīman* was lack of self-control and independence. First and foremost, a woman was not allowed to manage her own time. Whereas a man might take lunch at any time he found convenient, an OL must dine at the designated time. On the floor where I worked, women alternated taking lunch so that the sales counter would not be deserted. The first group took lunch from 11:30 to 12:30, and the second group from 12:30 to 13:30. The two groups switched times weekly so that the group that took lunch from 11:30 one week would take lunch from 12:30 the next week. What greatly surprised me was the pressure that OLs felt to be punctual. Whenever we were a little late in returning to the office, women ran down the stairs to try to be on time.

It was also customary for an OL to inform fellow OLs seated nearby of every detail of her whereabouts. It was considered necessary to know where to find the person in case she was urgently needed. I could not, however, get used to the way the OL seated next to me told me she was going to the restroom every time she left. I found it hard to do the same myself, feeling that even an OL had at least the freedom to go to the toilet without having to report to someone. Dress was another aspect of OLs' life that was controlled, for they had to wear uniforms. Neither men nor women in the integrated track wore uniforms.

The difference between *sōgōshoku* and *ippanshoku* was perhaps best reflected in their levels of compensation. Because the bank used seniority to determine compensation, wages increased as an employee aged. OLs' compensation curve, however, hit a ceiling (after which there was only a slight increase) much earlier and at a considerably lower level than men's. It was well known among women that an OL who graduated from university must work diligently until she was fifty-one years old to receive the same compensation as a man with the same educational background who had been with the bank for only four years. The women said that if the OL took a maternity leave, her compensation would never reach the level of a man who had been there five years.

Although I was unable to collect precise income data for the employees of the bank, there is a survey conducted by the government on incomes of employees in large banks with one thousand or more employees. Comparison of average annual gross income curves by age for men and women supports the OLs' claim that there was a large dif-

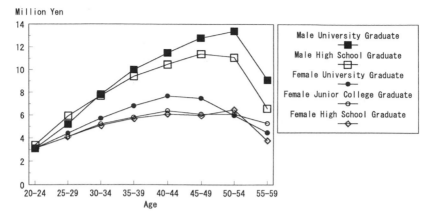

Figure 7: Average annual gross income in large banks with one thousand or more full-time employees, 1995. *Source: Rōdōshō, Chingin kōzō kihon tōkei chōsa* (Basic survey on wage structure), 1996.

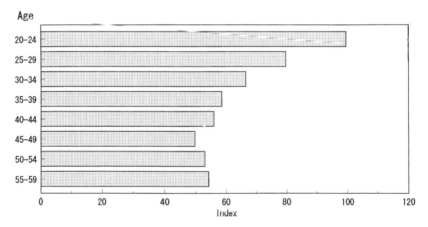

Figure 8: Wage differentials by sex (male = 100) in large banks with one thousand or more full-time employees (annual gross income base), 1995. *Source: Rōdōshō, Chingin kōzō kihon tōkei chōsa* (Basic survey on wage structure), 1996.

ference in the payment received between the two sexes. Incomes for male university and high-school graduates rise steeply as they grow older, whereas those for women increase only gradually regardless of education (fig. 7). Wage differentials by sex are the largest among people in their late forties, when women, on average, receive less than half as much as men (fig. 8).[13]

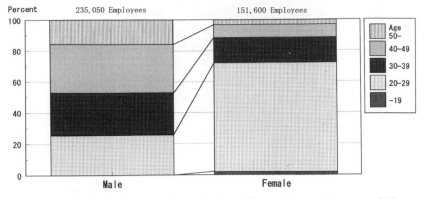

Figure 9: Employees by age in large banks with one thousand or more full-time employees, 1995. *Source: Rōdōshō, Chingin kōzō kihon tōkei chōsa* (Basic survey on wage structure), 1996.

The bank's policies concerning the treatment of women were typical of many large corporations in Japan (Lam 1992; Lo 1990; McLendon 1983; Rohlen 1974; Saso 1990). The excuse that is often provided by the companies for adopting discriminatory policies is that women's tenure with a company is too short. Because most women quit the firms at marriage, childbirth, or when their husbands are transferred to another part of the country, women do not fit the male pattern of "lifetime" employment and promotion. Figure 9 illustrates the skewed breakdown of female employees by age in large banks. Whereas the percentages of male employees in their twenties, thirties, and forties are more or less the same, with a slightly smaller percentage above the age of fifty, as much as 70 percent of female employees are in their twenties. Companies invariably profess that women are an "unreliable" workforce not worth seriously training.[14]

Why is OLs' work evaluated less seriously than men's work? The foremost reasons seem to be that OLs' length of service in a company tends to be short and managers rarely intend to promote them. A director of Itōchu, a trading company, who is in charge of personnel management, is reported to have said that because women's tenure was limited, the firm did not feel it necessary to assess their work and thereby distinguish among them. Management hoped that women would get along more harmoniously without appraisal. Apparently, management felt that evaluating women would do more harm than good by encouraging competition and thereby disrupting relationships among them (*Nihon Keizai Shinbun*, 26 September 1994).[15]

In this regard, it is noteworthy that evaluation means different things for (mostly male) white-collar workers in the integrated track in Japan and their counterparts in the United States. Whereas work appraisals are tied to annual discussion of employees' compensation in most American firms, in many Japanese companies a significant portion of employees' salary is negotiated by the corporate union. Japanese *sararīman* usually do not talk about their compensation with supervisors on an individual basis in the way that many American workers do. Appraisals are instead important for *sararīman* to determine who in the long run should be promoted into the next rank of managers and when. In the words of a man working in a bank:

In our bank, we are always rank ordered unofficially among our *dōki* [those who joined the organization in the same year]. For example, that you rank about xth among 100 *dōki*. Such ordering is not a gross estimation of placing people into high, middle, and low groups. Instead, we are given an exact rank. However, no difference is made in the salary we receive up until we are about thirty-five years old. Managers wait until we are about thirty-five years old. By then consensus is built [concerning each employee's evaluation], and so they begin promoting from among those that are given high evaluation. This way, people will consent to managers' decisions, thinking that it's only proper that those ranked high get promoted first.

As described by this banker, appraisal for white-collar men (and some women) in typical Japanese firms is primarily a means by which to select employees to be promoted into ranks such as *kachō*. It is an instrument to screen workers of high caliber, and its effect becomes apparent only after many years. This, of course, does not imply that men can take appraisal lightly. As the interviewee illustrates, men in his bank are constantly given detailed evaluations. It is just that the result does not become official until the first major promotion. Until then, there is little difference in the amount of pay *dōki* workers receive. The first selection usually does not take place in large Japanese companies until employees have worked for about ten or more years. Given that OLs' length of service is usually short and that management rarely intends to promote them, evaluations of OLs lack major objectives.

In contrast, the majority of blue-collar women in Japan must work under strict surveillance. Scrutiny of their work is usually considered necessary to control factory-line productivity. When a worker is slow, her productivity affects the efficiency of the entire line, which may consist of both male and female workers. On the shop floor, the sex of a worker does not normally exempt her from strict evaluation.

In response to the recent slump in the Japanese economy, many companies are attempting to cut costs. Whether corporations can continue to afford the luxury of frivolously evaluating OLs' work remains to be seen. This issue is taken up again in the conclusion of this book.

OFFICE LADIES AS "OFFICE WIVES"

Rosabeth Kanter writes in her study of women in an American business organization that the marriage metaphor was used to portray the relationships between secretaries and bosses:

[The marriage metaphor] was . . . implicit in the way many people at Indsco talked about the relationships between secretaries and bosses. Over time, a serious emotional bond could develop. One executive secretary promoted into management described leaving her old boss as a "divorce." . . . For the first few months after her promotion, she stopped in to see him every morning, hanging her coat in her old office instead of the new one, and finding herself concerned if he had a cold or looked unhappy. (1977, 89–90)

Similarly, many OLs at the bank spoke of themselves as "wives," often half in jest. Japanese critics also frequently likened OLs to "office wives."[16] The marriage metaphor was a popular characterization of the relationships between men and women in the office both in the United States and in Japan.

There was, however, a significant difference between American secretaries and Japanese OLs. Whereas many American secretaries worked for specific managers, few OLs did. Among the fifteen OLs at the bank, only one OL held a job that was supervised by one man. Other OLs usually worked in pairs for a group of anywhere from six to fifteen men. Even the two general managers who were members of the board did not have personal secretaries. They had to share the services of two OLs with four other general and vice-general managers. This arrangement is typical among Japanese companies. Rodney Clark reports that there were few secretaries in the Western sense of an assistant to a boss at the Japanese box manufacturer where he conducted his research (1979).

Unlike their Japanese counterparts, American bosses were more likely to exercise personal preference in the choice of their female assistants. Whereas some American secretaries were hired by the men they worked for, all OLs, including those working as secretaries for top executives, were hired by the personnel department, which later appointed them to their respective offices.

Because of the working arrangement and hiring procedures, the one-to-one relationship characteristic of American secretaries and bosses that promoted the use of the marriage metaphor in Kanter's case study did not exist in Tōzai Bank. Therefore, what prompted people to refer to OLs as "office wives" could not be the kind of intense bond that existed between American secretaries and bosses. Instead, it seemed to concern the nature of the tasks performed by OLs.

The OLs on the bank floor were assigned all kinds of miscellaneous jobs. They picked up mail from the basement mail room, sorted it, and distributed it to the appropriate addressees. They sorted and distributed various memoranda and notifications. They stored important materials by putting them in order, punching holes in the margins, and filing them in binders. They addressed envelopes. They copied documents and sent them by fax or by air-shooter. They printed out deposit balances. They typed letters and documents. They sent telegrams of condolence and congratulation. They bought gifts for customers. They served tea when customers came. They constantly picked up telephones and transferred calls to the appropriate people.

The OLs were also often summoned to fix paper jams and add paper to copiers and fax machines. They were sometimes even asked to paste together papers that had been mistakenly torn apart by men. A woman would, upon being called, jump up from her desk and scurry over to a general manager's desk, only to be asked to fetch him an eraser or refill his stapler. One OL sewed a button back on a general manager's suit.

The term *office wives* compared the OL's role to that of a wife who takes care of her husband at home. The reference emphasized the fact that offices were not all that different from the Japanese home. In each place, woman catered to the needs of men. The metaphor also seemed to comment ironically on men's dependence on women both at home and at the office. It is said that because a wife looks after his daily needs completely, a Japanese man often does not know where to find his socks and handkerchiefs when she is away (Iwao 1993; Lebra 1984). Similarly, in the office, men were often at a loss if OLs were not there to help them.

Without OLs, men on many occasions did not know where to find documents and files, could not fix paper jams or add paper to copiers, and did not know how to operate word processors.[17] Many could not make transportation arrangements for business trips and did not know how to get their expenditures reimbursed. Some men also seemed unsure of the details of paperwork. Men were in the comfortable position of having these nuisances taken care of by OLs, but their comfort was bought at the expense of becoming dependent on women.

The tasks delegated to OLs were simple and mechanical. They were often considered valueless compared with men's jobs. However, no matter how seemingly insignificant, these tasks were essential in that they had to be performed. Even if a man succeeded in negotiating a difficult bargain with an important customer, the contract would not materialize unless an OL completed the necessary forms and saw to it that they went through the required procedure. If a man had not taken time to learn the process himself, he had to rely on OLs to perform a job that was vital for the success of his business.

Several men I interviewed expressed this feeling of dependence on women. For example, a man working in a real-estate company, who supervised five salesmen and a woman assistant, said he felt that he must take especially good care of his female assistant. He thought he would be in more trouble if the assistant quit than if one of the salesmen did, for he himself could replace the salesman, but he could not replace the assistant. A man working in a general trading company summarized succinctly, "Women do jobs that you yourself can't do."

TEA POURING

It is appropriate to consider one aspect of OLs' work—tea pouring (*ochakumi*)—at length because it has attracted attention as a symbol of the drudgery that OLs must endure.[18] Tea pouring helps us understand what it means to be an OL, because it was the task the OLs at the bank detested most.

Customers often visited the departments, and tea had to be served each time. When customers came, the man in charge of their accounts would tell an OL working for his department the number of cups of tea he required and which cubicle to bring them to. The OL had to drop whatever work she had been doing and rush to the kitchen. She would set cups and saucers on a tray, pour Japanese tea, and bring them to the designated cubicle. Some customers, upon being served, murmured "thank you," but more often her service was ignored both by the customers, who were almost always male, and her male colleague. Nevertheless, she would bow politely and retreat with the tray.

When the customers left, the man was supposed to ask the OL to clear up the table for future use. But because he often forgot, the OL had to keep an eye on the cubicle or the man's seat to make sure that the meeting was still going on. When clearing the table, she had to change ashtrays, because many Japanese businessmen smoke. On the floor where I worked, the temporary staff had to clean dirty cups and ashtrays piled in the kitchen sink and were also often asked to serve tea by OLs, who relayed the request made by men.

When an important customer had to be attended by the general or vice-general managers, one of the three general managers' rooms located on the second floor was used. OLs did not particularly enjoy serving tea on the second floor, not only because they had to climb stairs but because the group was usually large and many cups of tea had to be balanced on the tray. The serving order was important, and an OL needed to gauge the hierarchical ranking among the guests the moment she entered the room. This was usually done mechanically, taking the cue from the seating arrangement. When I confessed that I had never served tea before, many OLs looked surprised. One of them quickly drew a diagram for me and taught me the rule of thumb in interpreting men's importance from the seating arrangement (fig. 10).

Serving tea was a major source of OLs' complaints. They often grumbled that they had to pour tea too many times. During lunch, they soothed their feelings by sharing their annoyance. They were invariably irritated when they had to change ashtrays because a single cigarette had been smoked, or when they had to clear cups of tea that had not been touched. Unfinished cups of tea invited their displeasure by making them feel that their labor was wasted.

To an outsider, typing a letter and serving tea might seem equally tedious and unpleasant tasks, but for an OL, there was a world of difference. Women were far more offended when asked to serve tea than to do other jobs. No matter how many times they had poured tea, OLs said they could not help feeling irritated every time they were asked for the service. I heard many women use the expression *muttosuru* (gets on one's nerves) to describe their annoyance when asked for tea.

One OL working for a food-processing company explained the difference between serving tea and other tasks:

Sure, what we do are all simple things—serving tea, making copies, typing documents. After all, our job is different from men's jobs. But that doesn't mean we feel all right to be ordered to bring tea. I mean, an OL has her own way of doing things. You think of the procedures, for example, that you'd make copies first, then type this letter, and next that document. In the middle of all that, you're suddenly told to bring tea, and you're supposed to smile cordially and say, "Yes, I'm coming." Every time you serve tea, you interrupt your job and serve for others. It may sound funny to talk about *your* job, when all the jobs are ordered by men. But once you accept them, they become your jobs.

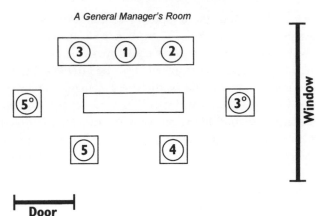

A General Manager's Room

$\left(1 \right) \sim \left(3 \right) \left(3° \right)$ if present) =   the guests. They are asked to take seats farther away from the door than the bank members.

$\left(4 \right)$ = the highest-ranking bank member in the room (often the general manager). He sits farthest from the door among the bank members, but nearer than his guests.

$\left(5 \right)$ = the second-highest-ranking bank member in the room (often the vice-general manager).

$\left(5° \right)$ if present = other bank members.)

Figure 10: Diagram drawn by an office lady indicating the proper tea-serving order

OLs detested serving tea because it emphasized their subordinate position. In typing letters and making copies, women usually had the latitude to decide how and when to do a job. Because OLs were scarce resources, a man could not ordinarily order OLs to type a letter or to make copies immediately, except at a truly pressing moment. It was only in serving tea that women had to put aside whatever they had been doing and follow the orders of men. Tea pouring reminded women that they did not have control over their time.

It was also probable that OLs felt tea pouring was more demeaning than other tasks because it called attention to their subservient role. Susan Pharr (1990) has applied Erving Goffman's definition of "status rituals" to her study of Japanese female civil servants' rebellion against pouring tea. She argues that the asymmetry of the sexes is "ritualized" in women's deferential act of serving tea to male colleagues. She further notes that in order for such status rituals to have meaning for those performing them, the deference behavior must be warmly rewarded by reciprocal conduct. Indeed, OLs at Tōzai had a favorable view of a man who said "thank you" when served tea. An expression of gratitude undoubtedly helped women think well of a certain man. I speculate therefore that the distastefulness of the job would alter somewhat if the emphasis on servile status in pouring tea was weakened by men regularly offering their thanks. The nature of the task—which recalls the domestic, serving role of women—was as much a reason for OLs to dislike the job as the fact that it had to be performed immediately.

OLs frequently mentioned that they would appreciate men's help in serving tea. Many agreed that their burden would be greatly alleviated if men would return dirty cups and ashtrays to the kitchen. Yet it was OLs themselves who made such help unlikely, insofar as they clearly marked the kitchen as women's domain.

The kitchen was called *ochashitsu* (tea room), and OLs took turns tidying up the room. The room was used predominantly to prepare tea for customers, but it was also a place where women touched up their makeup and brushed their teeth after lunch. Despite the fact that they were given a separate space and lockers, women kept their personal belongings in the tea room: the shelves were full of items such as brushes, pins, and cosmetics. In addition, it was a place where women got together to talk privately.

Understandably, men seemed to feel awkward in stepping into the kitchen. Once when I was working in the *ochashitsu*, a man came to the room and asked for a glass of water. My first reaction was to say, "Why don't you open the cupboard, and help yourself to a glass?" But I thought better of it and handed him what he had asked for. By the way he stood uneasily at the doorway, it was apparent that he felt he dare not intrude into the room.

As we have seen, women account for approximately 40 percent of all employees in Japan. One-third of all female employees are clerical workers, and the overwhelming majority of women who work in the office are OLs. Given their numbers, their male colleagues' dependence upon them for essential if simple tasks, and their irritation at chores such as tea pouring, why is it that OLs rarely engage in formal protest against discriminatory company polices such as their exclusion from managerial ranks, the gender-dichotomized two-track employment system, and frivolous evaluations of their performance? This is the subject of the next chapter.

2

Why Office Ladies
Do Not Organize

As we have seen, office ladies in Tōzai Bank and in other large corporations face intense sex discrimination. In spite of their ability and education, they are treated as low-level clerical workers. The companies, expecting them to leave within several years, are generally reluctant to invest in their training. As a result, their opportunities for promotion are severely limited. It is difficult to imagine how well-educated, intelligent women can put up with this situation, and many Western observers look for vocal protests by OLs against company authority. However, protest movements among OLs are rare. None of the women I worked with at Tōzai Bank could remember any direct protest. When I asked my interviewees about protest movements in their offices, many just shook their heads and said, "Those things don't take place."[1]

Given this quiescence, some scholars claim that OLs are largely content with their position in the workplace despite the stark structural inequality. For example, in her participant-observer study of a Japanese electric and electronic equipment manufacturer (1990), Jeannie Lo depicts OLs as childish and submissive workers who had no choice but to accept whatever the company required of them. She describes how her male boss summoned OLs by addressing them as ——*chan* (a filial term for an inferior) and then dismissed them with a quick wave of his hand. Although Lo admits that she felt insulted, she decided to keep her thoughts to herself because other women did not seem to mind this treatment. Similarly, Mary Saso (1990) writes that, except for a few professionals, Japanese women appear passive and seem to accept discrimination.

Scholars who claim that Japanese women passively accept discrimination take comfort in the assumption that this supposed passivity results from women being bound by traditional roles. They postulate that women will stand up and protest once they are liberated from "premodern" ideas. In short, these scholars argue that overt sex discrimination and women's acquiescence are the results of Japanese culture lagging behind Western nations, and judging from the speed with which Japanese society has been Westernized, discrimination and acquiescence will soon disappear.

Although the hypothesis seems compelling, it does not fit the data: critique of male authority abounds in OLs' discourse. Insofar as the critique does not take the form of open protest movements, it goes undetected by the cursory observer. James Scott argues persuasively that lack of open rebellion does not necessarily imply that subordinate groups consent to the existing power relations (1985; 1990). Based on his own fieldwork among peasants in a Malaysian village as well as various source materials on serfs, untouchables, slaves, laborers, and prisoners, Scott maintains that because the oppressed face formidable constraints in voicing open rebellion, they resort far more frequently to offstage resistance. Onstage, the subordinate groups show self-protecting compliance. However, to take their onstage compliance as "mystification" or "false consciousness" is to overlook the "hidden transcript," because the powerless clothe their resistance with the public language of conformity.

Similarly, OLs frequently hide critical, observant eyes underneath their demure attitudes and feminine smiles. To interpret the seeming conformity of OLs as wholehearted willingness to serve men would be to overlook their ability to penetrate the prevailing ideology (Kelsky 1994).

However, I do not agree with Scott's contention that there is no explanatory power to ideological domination and that subordinate classes are not constrained at the level of thought and ideology. The ineffectiveness of ideological hegemony is not demonstrated by the fact that weaker parties speak ill of the powerful and express anger behind their backs. The OLs at the bank often voiced discontent at specific kinds of treatment from men. Yet they rarely discussed, even among themselves, whether the basic structure of the arrangement between men and women should be changed. OLs often got angry and criticized a man who arrogantly requested their services, but they did not necessarily question women's role in providing assistance to men.

William Sewell (1992) notes that a society has multiple structures operating in different modalities and that these structures vary in depth; the deepest structures are pervasive and tend to be taken for granted. From this point of view, discontent voiced about a surface-level structure does not prove that people's conceptions are untainted by the workings of power at the deeper level.

Scott also asserts that fear of retaliation causes subordinate groups to defer and consent to the powerful while cultivating a dissident subculture offstage (1990). Such a view of power as simple repression is problematic when studying Japanese OLs. The depressingly coercive context in which peasants, serfs, untouchables, slaves, laborers, and prisoners lived is different from that of late-twentieth-century Japanese corporations. Fear and terror created through routine repression may have inhibited open defiance among the powerless described by Scott, but OLs in contemporary Japan do not face such naked exercise of power. Furthermore, power is not as arbitrarily exercised in rational bureaucratic organizations as it was against those whom Scott studied.

In contrast to the stark oppression and exploitation found in class relations, the deployments of gender are often more subtle and complex. Although their positions within a company differ, Japanese men and women working for the same company belong to similar socioeconomic groups. Often they marry someone in the same company, which accounts for the widespread usage of the term *shanai kekkon* (marriage to a colleague in a firm). According to a survey of more than two thousand random-sampled couples who wed in 1995, almost half replied that they first became acquainted in the workplace (Bic Bridal 1996). Under such circumstances, women may not perceive themselves as positioned below men, but rather parallel to men. The belief that women are equal but different is a prevalent theory that masks structural relations of inequality by guaranteeing the sexual division of labor and differential gender characteristics (Weedon 1987).

If such is the case, the threat of the exercise of power does not explain OLs' seeming acquiescence. In this chapter I investigate why OLs seldom organize to rebel. I argue that multiple, crisscrossing lines of division among OLs and pressure to bid farewell to "OLhood" by moving on to the next step in their lives undermine the solidarity necessary to stage a formal, organized movement.

Although I point to OLs' weak solidarity in order to explain their failure to organize, I explicitly argue against the views that women are apolitical, that they are incapable of uniting, and that they have difficulty in cooperating for the collective good. There is a general belief among the Japanese public that women's "comradeliness" is somehow inferior to men's. The frequently used phrase *otoko no yūjō* (male comradeship) has no counterpart for women. *Otoko no yūjō* is highly prized for its beauty, whereas friendship among women is considered to be either shallow or untrue.[2] Sadly, women are themselves often skeptical of the sincerity of their friendship. For example, one OL I talked to suggested that jealousy, which she considered to be inherent in woman's nature, made it difficult for women to unite.

Contrary to such views, this chapter shows that solidarity among OLs is weak because of the unfortunate company policies that divide them. Specifically, hiring women with different educational backgrounds for the same type of jobs creates resentment and undue tension. In addition, emphasis on early retirement promotes feelings of loneliness. As a result, most women seek solitary solutions to their problems at work instead of organizing formal, social movements. They believe that joint efforts to redress their current situation would be unreliable and unrealistic. In light of these findings, women's failure to organize rebellion should be attributed to company policies that undermine solidarity rather than to women's supposed inherent lack of cooperation.

I begin by examining the relations among the OLs at Tōzai Bank. By analyzing their language, acts, and behavior, I review the tenure-based hierarchical associations among the women. Next, I look at other lines of division, which often contradict the hierarchy created by tenure. Then I examine what "OLhood" and early retirement mean for OLs. I conclude with the impact these factors have on the solidarity among women.

Divisions among Women

Anyone new to the office would have thought that the OLs on the bank floor were on extremely good terms with each other. They always seemed to be doing things together: they ate lunch together; they took their tea break together; and they went places together. I heard men use the expression "girls flock together" more than a few times.

I thought the OLs got along very well until one day one of them admitted that she sometimes tired of chiming in with the other women's conversation. She confessed she read TV columns in the newspaper every morning so that she would know the storylines of popular dramas. This way, she said, she was able to follow other women's conversation without actually watching the programs.

TV programs, travel, and men were definitely the OLs' most popular lunchtime topics.[3] I had naively assumed that they liked to talk about these matters. However, the woman's remark made me realize that they might not enjoy talking about these things, or being in each other's company, as much as it seemed at first. I began to observe the relationships among them more carefully.

Dōki, Senpai, and Kōhai

The OLs' relationships were structured hierarchically according to the length of their employment with the bank: the longer the tenure, the higher one's position in a group. Because all the OLs at Tōzai Bank were recruited as new graduates, those with the same tenure had joined the company in the same year. The year a person entered the firm was considered important, and this importance was reflected in people's ongoing concern to identify one's *dōki* (those who joined the company in the same year). The word was used frequently by both men and women to describe their relationships to one another. Anyone who was not one's *dōki* became either *senpai* (one's senior) or *kōhai* (one's junior), valued terms not only in the bank but also in Japanese society in general.

A strict hierarchy among the OLs was shown by the deference *kōhai* paid *senpai*. An OL showed deference to her senior OL by addressing the person by her last name with a suffix *san*, or speaking to the person in polite terms such as ——*desu* and ——*masu*, and sometimes even in honorific terms such as ——*nasaru* and ——*sareru*.

In turn, a senior woman spoke in casual terms and addressed her junior OL either by her nickname without any suffix or by nickname, last, or first name with a suffix *chan*. The OLs assessed the relationship between two persons by their choice of words. This was reflected in a conversation between two OLs concerning another woman they did not know well. "You know this woman with long hair? I think she's Kei-chan's *dōki*," said one woman. The other replied, "I see, you heard them speak on equal terms with each other."

Of course, other factors besides tenure affected the deference shown to a person. For example, how well one knew a person was also taken into account: the more intimate one was with a person, the less elaborate the formality. Therefore, a woman often chose to use both honorific and polite terms *gozonji desuka* when asking a many-years-senior OL with whom she was not well acquainted whether she knew something. In contrast, an OL who was senior by only a few years, with whom one was on friendly terms, was usually asked the same thing by using only the polite term *shittemasuka*, whereas a junior OL was asked in the casual term *shitteru*.

Language was not isolated from other ways in which deference was shown. I became aware of this when the other temporary staff member, who began working at the bank after I did, adamantly insisted on letting me walk in front of her whenever we proceeded through the narrow aisles between the desks. I started to observe the way women walked through doors, got on elevators, and took lunch.

I noticed that most of the time women walked through a door in order of seniority. When getting on an elevator, it was usually the junior woman who stood by the buttons and pressed them to keep the doors open or to shut them. At lunchtime, when most people on the elevator headed for the cafeteria on the eleventh floor, the person at the buttons held the doors open and let everybody else get off first. I also observed that it was usually the senior woman who announced that the lunch break was over and it was time for everyone to head back to the office. The rules, however, were not rigid. A woman would not wait at the door for a senior OL who was walking three yards behind her. Similarly, a junior woman would not push her way through the crowded elevator to reach the buttons.

In her study of a shop floor in a small, family-owned factory in Tokyo, Dorinne Kondo finds that "awareness of complex social positioning is an *inescapable* element of any utterance in Japanese, for it is *utterly impossible* to form a sentence without *also* commenting on the relationship between oneself and one's interlocutor" (1990, 31). Similarly, it was impossible for the OLs not only to talk, but also to walk through doors and aisles, get on elevators, and have lunch without first sorting out the hierarchical relationships among them. Therefore, one of the first questions the women asked a new acquaintance was when she joined the company.

I also came to understand that the *senpai-kōhai* relationship was something different from being a friend. The women's conversation revealed that they found it both awkward and funny when an outsider mistook as friends two women, one of whom was six years senior to the other. A similar distinction between being friends and being *senpai-kōhai* was made by an ex-OL of a general trading company. She commented, "If you become very intimate with your *senpai*, you become friends. But if you don't, then she remains your *senpai*." Although it is possible for *senpai* and *kōhai* to become friends, they are not necessarily friends.

Sources of Tension

EDUCATIONAL BACKGROUND

If tenure were the sole criterion that determined one's position in the bank, the relationships among the OLs would have been more straightforward than they actually were. Unfortunately, the OLs' world was complicated and strained by the existence of other criteria, and, to make matters worse, these criteria did not correspond neatly to tenure. One major source of tension was the difference in their educational backgrounds.

As readers may recall, an OL's official rank at the bank was determined both by length of employment and level of education. In terms of compensation and promotion, the university graduate who had been at the bank two years was regarded as equivalent to the junior-college graduate who had been there four years and the high-school graduate who had been there six years. This official rank usually corresponded to one's age.

Consider, for example, the relationship between the two OLs profiled below:

	OL X	OL Y
Tenure	4 years	3 years
Education	Junior college	University
Official rank	Grade 6	Grade 7
Age	24	25

Because OL X has longer tenure, she is OL Y's *senpai* and is paid deference accordingly. However, because of the difference in their educational backgrounds, OL X ranks lower in terms of the official grade. As a result, both OL X and OL Y tend to feel that they are being treated unfairly: OL X resents that her pay is lower than that of her supposedly "junior" colleague; and OL Y finds it unpleasant having to yield to a *senpai* with less education.

At the bank, high-school and junior-college graduates thought university graduates in general were stuck-up, whereas university graduates tended to think that they were unfairly bullied by *senpai* who had only finished high school and junior college. An incident the OLs called the "open bank book case" took place in a different section of the company a few years before I arrived. A junior-college graduate supposedly remarked to her university-graduate *kōhai* how nice it must be to receive a large paycheck. So tenacious was the *senpai's* insistence upon this point that the university graduate finally had to show the *senpai* her bank book in order to convince her that the difference in their compensation was not as large as her *senpai* thought it to be.

Similarly, a university graduate remembered a nasty remark made by a senior OL who had graduated from junior college. A male employee received a letter in English and asked the senior woman to translate it into Japanese because he had difficulty with the foreign language. The woman looked at the junior OL, who happened to be standing nearby, and suggested that he ask her instead, since she was a university graduate. Although everyone in the workplace knew that the man had also graduated from university, he had to remind her of the fact. For the senior woman, the man's university diploma was not a target for sarcasm, but the junior OL's was.

One wonders whether a similar tension exists between male high-school and university graduates. (There are very few junior colleges for men in Japan.) Although uneasy feelings often exist between these two groups of men, there is little direct conflict. One of the reasons for this seems to be a general understanding that, in large established companies, male university graduates are far more likely to be promoted over men with only a high-school diploma. As an ex-personnel manager of a bank explained:

Although everybody has a chance to advance, university graduates tend to be promoted faster than high-school graduates, because they have deeper knowledge and more extensive experience. But there are some exceptionally capable high-school graduates who are in no way inferior to university graduates. These people are promoted—perhaps not with the same speed as the university graduates—but they nevertheless advance, and some even make it to the position of branch manager.

Similarly, another man working for a shipping company told me:

When university graduates join a firm, high-school graduates of the same age have already been working for four years. Naturally, they [high-school graduates] know more about the job and are paid respect accordingly. But both university and high-school graduates know that in several years their positions will be reversed, with the university graduates in higher offices. It would be unwise for high-school graduates to put on airs with university graduates because retaliation would be easy later on. So they don't do such a thing.

Both men's statements show that education has priority over tenure in determining the relative importance of men in the organization.[4] Therefore, men with different educational backgrounds usually do not engage in an obvious struggle over their positions. In contrast, positions among women are much more ambiguous.[5]

On the one hand, seniority according to tenure makes sense for women whose company service is bound to be short. As the man working for the shipping company pointed out, it is during his early career that a man's tenure counts more than his educational background: only after several years do university graduates overtake high school graduates. Many women do not stay with a company long enough to see educational background gain potential importance over tenure.

On the other hand, even if women did stay long enough in a company, it is doubtful whether much importance would be attached to their educational backgrounds. Because one does not need a university diploma to serve tea or to type letters, and because women are tracked into such jobs, there is really no rational reason to value women who are university graduates more than women who are junior-college or high-school graduates. Indeed, male managers of Tōzai made no attempt to assign university graduates more complicated tasks than other OLs. If anything, difficult jobs tended to go to OLs with longer tenure. In spite of these facts, the official ranking was determined in part by woman's educational credentials, which meant that an OL with longer tenure who was working on more difficult assignments did not necessarily receive greater pay.

The OLs at Tōzai suffered as a result of the management's indecisive attitude toward recruiting highly educated women. The bank, along with many other large Japanese corporations, began hiring female university graduates on a regular basis after the implementation of the EEO Law. The management hired these women partly because of the pressures against sex discrimination but failed to provide them with the types of jobs and positions that they rightly deserved. Reluctant to use the women's talents, the bank gave these overqualified women jobs that they could have done without higher education. The bank also compromised in the amount of compensation that female university graduates obtained: the company did not pay for the investment that these women made in gaining higher education, yet it did not treat them exactly the same as junior-college graduates.

Because they deserved better jobs and positions, it was only natural that women with university degrees felt mistreated. Many resented being given the same tasks as junior-college and high-school graduates. However, from the point of view of junior-college and high-school graduates, it was unfair that university graduates should receive better pay when all were doing the same job.

AGE

Age is one of the major determinants of seniority in Japanese society at large. Generally speaking, the older one is, the more respect one is paid. Japanese frequently ask a person's age, because without the knowledge, they cannot decide on the proper way to treat the person.

It is important to note that among OLs of different educational backgrounds, seniority based on tenure contradicts with that based on age. In the case of OLs X and Y on page 50, we see that because of the difference in educational background, OL Y is older than her supposedly "senior" OL X. Because this goes against the general custom that she is used to in larger society, OL Y feels discomfort in having to look up to a *senpai* younger than herself.

The inconsistency between the two criteria of seniority surfaced often among the OLs at Tōzai. It was a source of tension among the women, as reflected in a lunchtime conversation between two OLs with nine and a half and one and a half years of tenure respectively. The *senpai* OL advised her *kōhai*, "You should experience as many things as possible. Love . . . work . . . everything." I remember her words well, because they sounded like those of an old woman offering her "philosophy of life" to a young, inexperienced granddaughter. Obviously, the *senpai* OL considered it appropriate to give the somewhat presumptuous advice to the *kōhai*, because she had been on the job much longer. It soon became apparent that the *kōhai* had other opinions, for she pointed out casually that the age difference between her *senpai* and herself was actually quite small. Despite considerable discrepancy in the length of employment, their ages differed only by four years because the *senpai* was only a high-school graduate and the *kōhai* was a university graduate.

LENGTH OF SERVICE IN A SECTION

Length of service in a section sometimes contradicted the hierarchy based on length of tenure with the bank. Two women with the same educational background and the same length of tenure with Tōzai worked together for a department. They talked in casual terms with each other, but one OL was often ordered by the other to do things in a certain way. One day, after having been given instructions by the other woman, the OL explained to me that because the woman was her senior regarding work, she had to respect her ways: having transferred to the section only three months ago, she had to learn how things were done. Since the two women were *dōki*, they talked in casual terms. But when it came to work, one had to look up to the other as her superior.

It was evident that the one who had been given instructions did not particularly enjoy giving way to her *dōki*. She confessed that she sometimes wished she had been able to stay in her former section. If she had, she thought she would have been the boss of the section whom everybody would rely on and respect. She said, "Being taught how to do things is OK when you're young, but it's hard at my age."

At the bank, as in many Japanese corporations, job rotation was valued as an important opportunity for men to accumulate the extensive knowledge and experience necessary to become competent managers. Transfer was thus quite frequent and routine among men. However, among women, it was less so. Women were transferred mainly to balance the number of OLs among certain departments.[6] Unfortunately, transfer did not confer any positive value on OLs. For OLs, "extensive knowledge and experience" were unnecessary. What was important was to know, for example, whether a certain document was contained in a red or blue file, or whether the file was in alphabetical or numerical order.

Indeed, one of the men I interviewed working in another bank told me that they speak of *onnanoko oboe* (girls' way of remembering):

What women do every day involves pieces of a job that must be processed quickly without any mistake. They don't know how a certain job fits into the entire picture, or why they must do the job. We men would hate it if we didn't know the meaning of the jobs we were doing. So, among us, we call it *onnanoko oboe*. They just memorize mechanically what to do if a certain item is marked X and if another is marked Y. I guess their [different ways of learning] do not really reflect differences between men and women, but are more related to what the company expects from us. But people tend to think that women cannot make sound and comprehensive judgments.

When rote memory is all that is expected of OLs, knowledge that an OL accumulates in one department is wasted in a job transfer. The OL has to start all over again, which gives her a weak position in the new department.

CONTRADICTIONS AMONG CRITERIA

Given the potential contradictions among age, educational background, tenure at the bank, and tenure in a certain section, solidarity among the OLs at Tōzai was difficult to achieve. Although length of tenure at the bank was the primary determinant of seniority, the other three factors caused tension among the OLs.

On the bank floor, there were four pairs of OLs who worked together. After a few months, I realized that only one of the pairs was on truly good terms. Unlike other pairs, all of the potential criteria for determining seniority between these two OLs were consistent. In other words, the "senior" OL was senior in all the important factors: she had longer tenure in both the bank and in the section and was older in age. The level of their education did not contradict, for both were junior-college graduates. In contrast, the other pairs who did not get along all suffered from inconsistencies: one pair consisted of junior college-graduate *senpai* and university-graduate *kōhai;* another pair included a woman with an unusually long tenure of twenty-five and a half years with the bank, but the woman was a high-school graduate and her considerably younger partner was a university graduate; the women in the third pair, already introduced in the preceding discussion, would have been on equal terms with each other except for length of tenure in the department.

I was surprised by the severity of the discord between women working in pairs. An OL confessed during lunch that she often dreamed of being scolded by her *senpai* partner. She recounted how her *senpai* used to summon her into the kitchen and admonish her, for example, to pick up the phone more quickly. Another OL told me that she had to "dump" her university diploma in order to get along with other OLs. She said she no longer felt any pride in having graduated from university. If she clung to such pride, she thought she would never get along with women who had junior-college and high-school diplomas. Gradually I began to understand that it was not men's potential disapproval that made women run down the stairs after lunch in order not to be late, but the fear of female colleagues' critical looks. As one OL summarized, "You don't care so much what men think about you, but you must watch out what other girls might think."

Divisions among OLs were not confined to the bank but occurred in many large Japanese corporations that hired women with different educational backgrounds for the same type of jobs. The uneasy relationships among women with different levels of education were often disclosed during my interviews. The exceptions were OLs employed at electronic giants, where education, rather than gender, determined one's position within the organization. In these companies, female university graduates received treatment equal to or nearly equal to that of male university graduates, whereas female junior-college graduates worked as their assistants. Junior-college graduates working under this system also voiced discontentment, but their hostility was not toward female university graduate as in other companies. Instead, they showed strong dissatisfaction with company authority, which denied them the opportunity to do more than simple clerical work. A junior-college-graduate OL working under the more gender-neutral arrangement commented: "I don't have any grudge against university graduates, really, but I do have complaints against the company system. There's really no hard feelings between junior-college and university graduates in our department, or in other sections of the company that I know. It's probably because we don't do the same job." In companies such as Tōzai, it may be that the frustration experienced in the workplace by junior-college and high-school graduates was directed at university-graduate OLs because they were clearer and more accessible targets than distant company authority, which treated all women as low-level clerical workers.

Meaning of "Exit"

EMPHASIS ON EARLY RETIREMENT

It has often been pointed out by the Japanese public that OLs are one of the richest groups in the society. It is said that because most OLs live with their parents and rely on them to pay for their living expenses, they can spend all their earnings on luxuries. Indeed, the majority of the unmarried OLs I came to know at Tōzai lived with their parents and seemed to lead comfortable lives.

For example, many OLs enjoyed traveling abroad. In the year that I worked at the bank, two OLs went to Hawaii, another two went to Paris, one went to Australia, one to Canada, one to Tibet, and another to Hong Kong. Even those OLs who decided to stay within the country took vacations in remote places like Okinawa (the southernmost island) and Hokkaidō (the northernmost island). In addition, many enjoyed long weekends at ski resorts or hot springs in the winter and by the seaside in the summer.

However, the OLs did not consider their generous spending on travel to be a permanent phenomenon. They would often justify their current luxuries, saying, "It's only for now." One woman, who went to Hawaii in the summer and Singapore in the winter of her second year at Tōzai, who visited Hokkaido in her third summer, and who was planning to go to Hawaii again in the winter and San Francisco in the summer of her fourth year, explained her extensive travels: "People like my parents get half disgusted and say, 'You're going again?!' but I feel I should take this chance and travel while I can." This woman and many others believed that their carefree lifestyle was permissible only for a few years while they enjoyed their "OLhood." In fact, all the while they appeared to be having a good time, they seemed restless, waiting for something to happen. There was a feeling, especially among the unmarried women, that being OLs was only a temporary arrangement and that they were somehow not yet their real selves.

Youth conferred positive value on women in the Japanese marriage market in general, but it was also rated highly in the workplace. Many people, both men and women, used the expression *chiyahoyasareru* (puffed up by others' attentions; danced attendance on) to describe how young women were waited upon by their male colleagues. A woman who worked in a general trading company explained what was meant by *chiyahoyasareru*: "It means to be invited incessantly to play tennis, to go skiing, to attend parties, and so on by men [in the company]. Even if you don't try hard, you're invited to some sort of a gathering on Friday evenings."

However, such invitations stop coming after a few years, because men characteristically turn their attention to the fresh supply of young women who are brought into the organization each year. An OL of a food-processing company described how older women were usually no longer able to attract men's attention: "When you go to a drinking party, it's only the new women who are paid attention by men. Other women are treated as though it didn't matter whether they came or not. Men don't even look at you." A banker expressed his sympathy for older women, many of whom had to go through the bitter experience of being abruptly abandoned by men in the workplace, and explained why younger women tended to be more popular: "Younger women are more popular, because they are new to the workplace. People get tired of being together all the time. When a new woman joins, men are curious to find out what sort of a person she is." The man added, rather hesitantly, that younger women were also likely to be prettier.

The situation becomes increasingly intolerable for older OLs. One day, when I was chatting with my fellow temporary worker, who had worked as an OL at a prominent general trading company for eight years before her marriage, I asked her why she had quit the job with the firm and become a temporary worker. It was obvious that she was making much less money than before, and, as a temporary worker, she was now at the bottom of the office hierarchy, doing bits and pieces of work, often bossed around by OLs when she herself used to enjoy OL status. To my surprise, she was amazed that I needed to ask: "Do you really find it strange [that I chose to be a temporary worker instead of continuing as an OL]? It's difficult working as an OL when you grow older. The way people look at you and treat you—you begin to think it's better if you quit." She explained that, on the surface, people in the office treated older OLs in the same way as younger OLs. However, when she went drinking after work, she heard many people say nasty things about old women. From the moment she joined the company, she had heard such things said repeatedly and had been determined not to stay for too long.

It was ironic that many OLs dreaded growing old and at the same time paid deference to older women as their seniors. Despite solemnly observing the seniority rule, women, both young and old, were keenly aware that a reverse-seniority system was at work for women in their relationships to men: younger OLs were generally more popular than older OLs. It goes without saying that this reversal of the rule of seniority further complicated the already complex and difficult relationships among the OLs.

The marked appreciation of youth in OLs is related to the jobs they do. Because OLs are assigned simple, repetitive work, the skill, experience, and knowledge that usually come with age have less value for them than for men. Being young and attractive becomes one of the primary criteria by which they are judged.

The small group of single women who remain in the organization beyond what is regarded as a marriageable age are sometimes looked down upon by both men and younger women as those who failed to get married. Men usually cease to treat them gallantly; for instance, they no longer bother to escort them home after late-night parties as they do younger women. If older single women truly enjoyed their work, perhaps they would not be disdained by their *kōhai*. However, monotonous clerical work without any hope for career development did anything but make their lives look attractive. As a result, many younger women at Tōzai talked behind their backs and said that they definitely did not want to be "like them."

Up to a certain age, the older an OL, the more likely it was for her to feel that her time was running out. One thirty-four-year-old, unmarried OL working in a real-estate company lived with her parents and made a handsome salary; she had no immediate complaint about her comfortable life. However, she felt acutely uneasy about her future. When I inquired about her plans, she sighed deeply.

Future? That is the biggest problem. When I joined the company, I expected to work for only four years or so. I thought about quitting. For instance, working as a temporary. But that's only keeping up appearances and deceiving yourself. You quit because you want to get away from the inquisitive eyes at your workplace that accuse silently: "She can't get married," and "How long does she intend to stay on?" I feel lonely and helpless going on working like this. I didn't intend things to turn out this way. It's especially painful when your *dōki* quit.

The woman's story vividly tells us that working as an OL may be a comfortable way of life for a limited period but can eventually distress a woman who, for some reason, fails to follow the expected path.

Understandably, the marriage of one of their members was a primary concern for the OLs at Tōzai. Young OLs expressed uncomplicated interest in the fiancé, but older OLs had mixed feelings. Although they unanimously congratulated the bride-to-be, some of them could not help feeling left behind. After hearing that one of the women on the floor was soon to marry and resign, an OL with almost ten years of tenure murmured sadly, "The time you feel lonely and desolate being an OL is when one of your fellow workers marries and leaves."

In some companies, an OL leaving to get married paid farewell visits on her last day to all the people she had come to know through her daily business, handing out handkerchiefs or sweets as tokens of gratitude. Such a woman wore her best dress. Parading through the building in festive attire, she was instantly identifiable as "a girl who is leaving to get married." At the end of the day, she was given bouquets of

flowers by her colleagues and went home in a taxi that the company ordered specially for the occasion (*Nihon Keizai Shinbun*, 9 November
1992).

At Tōzai, there was no such ceremonious display of "marriage retirement," but one of the women I interviewed reported a similar custom in a general trading company where she used to work. According
to her, a bride-to-be proceeded happily and proudly from the top to the
bottom of the office building, wearing a diamond ring. My interviewee
felt that the ceremony promoted the feeling among women that "marriage retirement" was the happiest outcome for them. "When you're in
the company, you're led to think that the greatest happiness for a girl is
to be able to show off her happiness and be the first to bid farewell to
her *dōki*." She added, "You feel superior to your fellow OLs when you
can say good-bye to them because you're getting married and leaving
the company. It's silly, really, because the sense of superiority lasts only
for a moment. But for that one moment of superiority, you quit the
company. . . . If you have to send off so many women year after year,
you'd begin to want to marry any man! I think the ceremony puts pressure on women to get married."

She also thought that solidarity among OLs was difficult because
women were, in a sense, competitors in the race for marriage: "There's
always the fear that you'll be left behind. Especially when your *dōki*
start to leave one by one, you begin to feel the pressure. You certainly
don't want to be the last one to go! You also compare the social standing of your fiancés—which company he works for, for example. If his
company is not well known, you feel a bit embarrassed. Marriage to a
man of good social standing becomes the most important goal of your
life." In their study of American women in college, Dorothy Holland
and Margaret Eisenhart (1990) found a similar high-pressure peer system that drove female students into the world of romance, where their
attractiveness to men carried most weight.

Perhaps because Tōzai lacked the custom of an elaborate display by
the departing bride-to-be, competitiveness among the Tōzai OLs did
not seem as strong as among women in the general trading company
previously described. Another factor that might have diminished rivalry
among the bank OLs was that there were no young men on the floor.
Male graduates entering the bank were usually assigned to branches
first, and by the time they were transferred to the headquarters, most
were older and married.[7] It is important to note, therefore, that the degree to which OLs felt themselves to be contenders differed according
to the particular circumstances of the workplace.

Married women were spared the fear of being left behind and the disgrace of lacking suitors. In recent years, an increasing number of Japanese women have continued working after marriage. At Tōzai, so long as the husband was not an employee of the firm, a woman was able to stay. When I began working at Tōzai, there were two married women in my office and one in the department nearby. Married women's commitments to the company were thought to be temporary; it was assumed that the women would leave after childbirth or upon intervention of other family matters, such as the husband's transfer to another part of the country. Because staffing had to be planned in advance, managers plagued married women with subtle questions about their future plans and sometimes asked them outright when they expected to have babies.

The social standing of a married woman within the company became ambiguous if she remained for many years. It was less disturbing to see young OLs do menial jobs. When young women provided services to men, it did not position them as inferiors to men in the broader context of Japanese society because the young OLs' low-grade jobs were in part justified by their junior status. Indeed, most young businessmen also start their careers in Japanese firms by doing clerical work. But as they accumulated tenure, men were assigned to more important positions, whereas OLs were not. The unfair treatment usually did not become conspicuous in the individual workplace because most women did not stay long enough to actually experience it. However, it became obvious and problematic if a respectable married woman—especially one with children—continued to work as an OL: she was generally believed to have more important commitments at home than in the labor market, and the fact that she continued to work meant either that she found her job extremely fulfilling or that she was a member of a lower class who must work full-time even after marriage.

Under the influence of Western feminism, people in Japan have gradually acknowledged that some women continue working for a sense of accomplishment and personal happiness. However, they are also aware that OLs' jobs provide little satisfaction. If a woman continues working as an OL, people wonder whether it is for economic reasons.

This explains the ambivalent attitudes of the OLs on the floor toward Yamada-san. Yamada-san, a woman in her forties, had been with the bank an unusually long time. She was highly respected for her experience and knowledge; some younger women even said they were afraid to speak to her. But, at the same time, the women whispered behind her back that she was separated and had to work to raise two children. It was also said that she often drank after work with different men because she was lonesome. It was apparent from the way the OLs talked about Yamada-san that they did not particularly envy her life.

My fellow temporary worker shared the view that properly married women should not continue to work as OLs. Comparing herself with Yamada-san, she thought that she was lucky she could live on what her husband made and did not have to work full-time: "It's a privilege to work temporarily, and not something that you should be ashamed of. It might be a little unpleasant being asked to do odd jobs here and there by other women, but it's only a side job. The fact that I'm married is much more important." The temporary worker was able to justify her low-level position in the workplace because she was a woman success-fully married to a dependable husband. According to this view, what counted most for a woman was not the type of job she held, but her marital status.

One of the most important demographic changes currently taking place among Japanese young people, especially in metropolitan areas, is that they are deferring marriage until later in life. By 1995 the average age at first marriage rose to the historic high of 26.3 years old among women and 28.5 years old among men (up from 24.4 and 27.2 years old respectively in 1960). Deferment of marriage is particularly notable among women; the ratio of never-married women in their late twenties to all Japanese women in their late twenties rose almost ten percent in just five years. In 1995 there were almost as many women in their late twenties who had never been married as those who were married. Ac-companying the increase in the average age at first marriage is the in-crease in women's years of service in a firm. Women worked on average 7.9 years in 1995 (up from 4.0 in 1960).

This evidence may seem to suggest that OL status is no longer a temporary "way station" on the road to marriage or, alternatively for those who have failed to find a husband, a "blind alley" as James McLendon has argued (1983). It must not be forgotten, however, that the overwhelming majority of OLs envision themselves getting married (see chapter 1). Equally important when considering whether OL sta-tus has ceased to be temporary for most Japanese women is career tra-jectory or, to be more precise, the lack thereof for OLs.

As McLendon describes vividly in his study, the OL position was in the past explicitly regarded by the majority of companies as only a short-term arrangement for the young woman prior to marriage and child-birth. Now, even though Japanese women's expectations about mar-riage and work are changing, few aspects of OLs' work have altered.

Even if more women wished to continue working after marriage or childbirth, the OL job provides them with minimal career prospects.

OLs may have more years to enjoy their leisurely lifestyle than before. Yet the fact remains that few embrace "OLhood" as a lifetime career. Therefore, many high-spirited OLs venture into new jobs, perhaps in *gaishikei* (foreign-affiliated companies) where opportunities are believed to be more egalitarian, or go study abroad as Karen Kelsky reports (1994). The formerly close link between marriage and early retirement is disappearing as women wait longer before marrying. Yet the pressure many OLs feel to move on to the next step in their lives seems no less intense than before.

At Tōzai, preoccupation with the next stage of their lives undermined OL solidarity for yet another reason. When OLs thought of their married life, they were reminded of the likelihood that their future *sararīman* husbands would eventually transfer to offices outside of Tokyo, making it impossible for them to commute to their present workplace. It was customary for Japanese firms to transfer male employees without considering the impact on their families. It was also generally understood that a man must prepare to face a heavy penalty if he refused to transfer. Many OLs understandably felt it pointless to organize and ask for desired reforms when it was highly probable that they must quit after marriage.[8]

Mary Brinton has shown the remarkable consistency with which social institutions in Japan are male-dominated, a situation that creates a tightly linked system that perpetuates traditional gender roles (1993). She therefore predicts: "Change in Japanese gender stratification will not come about mainly as a result of Japanese women protesting discriminatory labor practices" (1993, 327). The present study similarly illustrates how difficult it has been for OLs to reverse the vicious cycle of gender stratification through group efforts. Even if a certain organization agreed to adopt a more gender-neutral policy, OLs would still have to retire from the workplace unless firms where their husbands were employed also changed their practices.

"EXIT" OR "VOICE"

In his study of how individuals may express dissatisfaction, Albert Hirschman (1970) identifies two options: withdrawal from the unhappy situation, which he calls "exit," and protest against the authority concerned, which he calls "voice." He argues that the presence of the exit option serves to restrain the use of voice, because whereas exit is simply an either-or decision, voice is an art and, therefore, must be learned and developed. For Japanese OLs, the aspiration to resort to voice seems to be weakened by the existence of exit. As we have seen, few women consider working as OLs their lifetime occupation. Instead, many perceive it as only a temporary job. On the one hand, the thought that what they do is temporary helps to make their unsatisfactory work more tolerable. On the other hand, the expectation that they will quit the job soon diminishes the need to exercise voice.[9]

Exit was extremely tempting for the women at Tōzai. One OL wondered how good it must feel to resign from work. For her, quitting would make the statement that she would be fine even without work and that the job was a small part of her life. "Men are tied down to the company, but we can say good-bye. That's a nice feeling," she said. Exit promised women a release from the monotony and boredom of everyday OL work. Marriage, one of the proper ways for them to retire, brought them pleasurable attention as attractive women with suitors.

Although exit was a desirable solution for an individual OL, it considerably weakened the solidarity among the women at Tōzai. As suggested by the woman who felt lonely when she learned of her colleague's "marriage retirement," togetherness was greatly undermined by the sight of fellow workers making happy exits and leaving others behind with the tedium. Under the circumstances, many OLs felt pressure to seek their own options for exit rather than trying to voice protest to the company authority.

It is disheartening that OLs' exits have not motivated company authorities to redress the current situation. The authorities are not hurt by women's desertion. Quite the contrary, they *prefer* women to exit, so that they can replace them with younger workers. A man working in the personnel department of a bank boasted that very few OLs in his company "stray from the proper path of marriage and remain at work."

Before the implementation of the EEO Law, many firms overtly prompted OLs to resign after several years of service. This custom was called *katatataki* (tap on the shoulder), because male managers would typically approach the OL from behind and tap her on the shoulder, suggesting that it was time for her to quit. Most companies have ceased to rely on the notorious custom of *katatataki* since the implementation of the EEO Law. However, many corporations still successfully engage in what Hirschman calls "conspiracy in restraint of voice" by exerting pressure on older women to leave the company (1970, 61).[10]

Companies in general preferred OLs to leave after several years of work, for both direct and indirect economic reasons. It was costly to employ older women, because women's wages rose gradually with age. Longer service also implied that the firm must pay a larger retirement allowance, which was usually calculated by multiplying the length of service by a certain fixed amount. Because many companies did not expect OLs to do anything more than simple clerical work, it was more economical to employ younger—and therefore cheaper—women than experienced and skilled but more expensive workers (Ōsawa Machiko 1993; Ōsawa Mari 1993).

It was also generally believed that younger women worked more enthusiastically. As mentioned earlier, the logic was that, being newer and junior members of the organization, younger women felt less distaste for menial jobs. It was easier for them to justify their service to men in terms of their inexperience and junior status. However, as women accumulated tenure, they became increasingly dissatisfied doing the same, low-grade jobs day after day, year after year, when the men who joined the company with them began to rise in importance.

On the floor at Tōzai, men were older than women, except for the OL with twenty-five and a half years of tenure. (Only men with a certain tenure were transferred to the departments on the floor.) Older women talked of the day when finally the youngest men on the floor would be their *dōki*. They apparently did not welcome the idea of having a male *dōki* on the floor and hoped to resign before that day came. At first I did not understand why they did not want to work with their male *dōki*, but I began to see that serving tea or making copies was easier to do when the order came from someone senior to them, rather than their *dōki*.

Preferring younger women as cheap and docile labor, some companies encouraged OLs' "harmonious separation" (*enman taisha*) from the workplace. I was told that a woman at Tōzai was given a maternity allowance if she retired upon childbirth. An OL explained that in the general trading company where she worked, a premium was paid on the retirement allowance for women who left at the end of April or May after a smooth transfer of work to the new recruits. In fact, there were many Japanese companies that customarily offered a monetary incentive to women who chose to retire upon marriage or childbirth (Saso 1990; *Nihon Keizai Shinbun*, 15 December 1993).[11]

Companies not only offered inducements to retirement but sometimes actively discouraged OLs from continuing to work. A banker related a rumor that one of the most important jobs of a branch manager at a rival bank was to persuade married women to retire. Another man working in a different bank said that he had been told by his boss to be kind to a "problem OL," acting as her big brother, listening to her complaints, and getting her to quit as soon as possible.

Even systems that supposedly made it easier for women to continue working did not always function in the expected way. Many firms in Japan are now equipped with fine systems that, if utilized, would assist women to work after marriage, such as a fourteen-week maternity leave and a year-long childcare leave.[12] However, at Tōzai those systems were difficult to use. For example, because no special arrangement was made to help the section when a woman went on maternity leave, the burden of making up for the temporary shortage in the workforce was imposed on other women. During the period of my research, a woman in a nearby section took maternity leave, which was extremely inconvenient for her three fellow OLs. On witnessing their trouble, several OLs on the floor declared that they themselves had no intention of taking a maternity leave and continuing to work after childbirth. They agreed that although a woman had the right to take a maternity leave, she nonetheless would be under great pressure to avoid causing so much annoyance to other OLs. An OL said, "You can't help feeling ill at ease for annoying other OLs, and I don't know if this job is worth all that trouble."[13]

Even fewer women took childcare leave. One woman who succeeded in taking the leave remembers the great pressure exercised against her. She was summoned by her boss many times and was asked to come back after taking only a maternity leave. She refused somehow: "Now that I think of it, I don't know how I was able to stick to my plans!" The woman was certain that although the system was there, the company authorities did not want OLs to use it; they preferred OLs to quit so that they could hire younger women. Although in the end she managed to take the leave, she described the time as a dark period that she would like to forget.

The woman's story indicates how difficult it was for an OL to actually take a childcare leave that, in theory, every woman had the right to take. In addition, when the OL returned to her workplace, she faced criticism: she was said to have selfishly pursued her own interests and to have "disgusted everyone" by taking childcare leave. No wonder few women took childcare leave at the bank.

According to a recent survey conducted by the Ministry of Labor, 95 percent of companies with five hundred or more employees claim that they allow mothers to take childcare leave (*Rōdōshō* 1994). However, among working women who gave birth in 1992, only half actually took the leave. In addition, 60 percent of the women who took the leave resumed working after six months, although most companies state that women may take up to a year's leave. These findings illustrate that having the system and actually using it are two completely different matters.

Sometimes a company attempts to discourage a woman from continuing to work by transferring her to another section or assigning her a difficult job. An ex-personnel manager of a bank described this practice in a typically convoluted Japanese way: "At a convenient moment such as after the return from a maternity leave, the company might transfer the woman to a section where it's not easy for her to manage work. Then it's more likely for her to quit. After all, we cannot fire employees, and so if we can have the person quit in a natural way through such personnel relocations, it's better for the company. Yes, I must admit it isn't true if we say that the management doesn't have such intentions at all."

At Tōzai, a married woman, who strongly expressed her intention to take a maternity leave and continue to work, requested a transfer to a suitable section to carry out her plans. Her request was granted— halfway. She was transferred, but the new section was much busier than the previous one, which made it even more difficult for her to take a maternity leave. Although we have no way of knowing for sure, the OLs on the floor where I worked decided among themselves that it was in effect *katatataki* (the tap on the shoulder suggesting retirement).

Conclusion

During my research at Tōzai, I became acquainted with many OLs. Some of them I came to know so well that they shared their current problems and future dreams with me. Similarly, in answering my questions in interviews, OLs of various large corporations disclosed their present worries and future plans. Women at the bank and other OLs I interviewed both commented that they did not talk about these matters with their colleagues at work. True to their words, the lunchtime conversation among the OLs at Tōzai centered around TV programs, travel, and men. Each woman generally had a few good friends, usually among her *dōki*, to whom she would confide her innermost feelings. However, relationships among the OLs in general seemed sadly superficial.

Weak ties among OLs produced an environment that was not con-
ducive to formal protest movements. However, women's lack of strong
solidarity was not the result of "inherent female nature" but rather the
result of company policies that created complex lines of division among
the women. In many offices, OLs who had longer tenure in the workplace were given more important and difficult assignments than junior
OLs, regardless of their educational background, and were respected
as *senpai*. However, because many companies took into account both
tenure and educational background in determining official ranks and
wages of their female clerical workers, an OL with longer tenure was
not necessarily the one with higher pay. She might also be younger in
age than her supposedly junior OL. The relationship between women
with contradictory seniority status was usually strained.

Overt emphasis on early retirement for OLs also weakened their solidarity. Working as OLs of large corporations and often living with their
parents, many women lived comfortably. However, OLs enjoyed this
carefree lifestyle only for a short period. Because it was easier to justify
young OLs' engagement in menial jobs, older women faced prejudice
when they continued to work. Many OLs felt pressured to graduate
from "OLhood" and move on to the next step in their lives. Watching
their colleagues make happy "marriage exits" from the company was
painful, especially for older OLs, who felt left behind. Preoccupation
with early retirement in effect undermined solidarity among the OLs.

Contrary to Hirschman's prediction, OLs' "exits" from the organization did not deter companies that discriminated against women. Instead, finding the OLs' early retirement convenient, many firms employed various measures to encourage them to quit after several years
service and replaced them with a new and younger workforce. Because
the companies had in most cases no plans for promoting women even
if they stayed on, they were thus spared the embarrassment of having respectable middle-aged women continue to do menial jobs. The
feelings of unfairness about the fact that men get promoted but few
women do were greatly alleviated by employing older male managers and younger employees of both sexes, rather than having an equal
distribution of both men and women in all age brackets. Those few
women who did not quit were often labeled as either social failures who
could not marry or social inferiors married to husbands who could not
support their families.

Encouraging OLs to make early exits conveniently masked for the
firms the stark inequality of their treatment of men and women. Hir-

ing young women for clerical jobs and having them quit for marriage allowed the firms to stress that women have roles "different" than but not necessarily inferior to those of men.

According to James Scott (1985; 1990), subordinate groups suffering from class-based domination are restrained from engaging in open protest because of routine repression and severe coercion. OLs in contemporary Japanese corporations are also discouraged from organizing formal protest movements, but their reasons differ from those of Scott's examples. They are inhibited from voicing open rebellion by a lack of solidarity caused by divisive company policies. In my opinion, many observers erroneously judge OLs as being largely content with the current discriminatory treatment because the observers do not appreciate the strained relationships among the OLs or the pressures they face to quit after several years. Where there is no direct exercise of power to repress open protest, it is easy to mistake a subordinate group's silence for acquiescence.

Unfortunately, the reasons for the seeming acquiescence of women in various relations of subordination have often been complex and less lucid; they are not always or merely a response to force. I believe this is what makes gender-based domination a grave, complicated, social problem. In the next three chapters, I examine women's manipulative strategies to resist male authority.

3

Gossip

Never did I dream that talking behind someone's back was so prevalent among office ladies. Hardly a day passed without someone putting down another worker. The target was almost always a man. OLs also talked about other women, but unless they were close friends, they usually refrained from belittling women. Instead, they discussed who was getting married, what her fiancé was like, and how the two met.

Lunch break was the ideal time for OLs to gossip about men's annoying behavior. An OL typically complained to other OLs of some unpleasant incident that morning or the previous afternoon.

OL 1: I'm really furious with Kataoka!

OL 2: Which one is Kataoka-san?

OL 1: The young one. He joined the company in the year sixty [1985], so he should be about twenty-nine. Anyway, when things get busy, he just stops listening to what other people have to say. And then afterward, he annoys us with persistent questions. He asks, "What? What? What's going on?" and makes a big fuss out of it. Just this morning, I found out that Matsuda *buchō*'s [general manager's] schedule was all screwed up because of him. You know, [he's] a type we've got plenty of in this bank.

OL 2: Yeah, I know what you mean. Is he single?

OL 1: Yes. There seem to be good reasons why single people remain single. Good guys get snatched up first.

OL 2: Yeah. There's always something wrong with a single man one way or another.

OL 3: When Kataoka talks to you, he places both of his hands on your desk and sort of looks into your face, doesn't he? It always makes me feel sick—makes me say, "Get away from me!"

OL 4: [*Giggling*] Do you really say that?

OL 3: Yeah, when I'm busy, I do.

OL 1: I know exactly what you mean. I always do *this* when he comes [*bends herself back exaggeratedly*]. I hold something in my hand to put between him and me. You know, as if to say, "Don't you dare get any closer!" Did you know that Kataoka was invited to Nishimura *kachō*'s [section manager's] home because he looks like Wally [a cartoon character]? Nishimura *kachō*'s kids loved him for it.

OL 3: He does look like Wally!

OL 1: Doesn't he? Shall we call him Wally from now on? No, I guess not. Wally's too cute for him.

The OL who had to sort out Matsuda *buchō*'s schedule because Kataoka-san had forgotten to cancel appointments indicated her anger first and foremost by neglecting to add suffix, *san*, to the man's name as she normally would.

By gossiping about these unpleasant experiences, OLs seriously damaged the offender's reputation among the female staff. In the preceding case, both OLs 2 and 4, who have little daily contact with Kataoka-san, are given an unfavorable impression of him. OL 1's story may not determine the way the others view Kataoka-san, but it will undoubtedly influence their opinion. As an OL explained, "If one of us talks badly about a man, all the women who hear the story begin to take a dim view of him."

A man's reputation is not determined overnight. It is evident from the conversation that this was not the first time Kataoka-san offended OLs 1 and 3: every time he did something "wrong" in the eyes of the OLs, he became the target of their reproach, until finally his reputation was thoroughly trashed. Women's dislike of a repeat offender often escalated into physical aversion, at which point his bad reputation was almost impossible to change. Both OLs 1 and 3 disliked Kataoka-san so strongly that they detested his physical proximity. Indeed, many OLs I interviewed said there were one or two men in their office whom they preferred to keep at a distance.

When a man repeatedly annoyed OLs, the gossip about him became less logical and more emotional. Whatever the man did became the possible target of criticism. One woman who worked in a pharmaceutical company described how the OLs grew to detest an unpopular man's habit of wiping his hands with a handkerchief as he emerged from the rest room. She added, "The same conduct could have been considered cute if done by somebody we like."

As OLs recognized, behavior that would not normally draw attention was criticized in detested men. From the point of view of men, this was problematic, because it increased the unpredictability of OLs' accusations. Because similar innocuous behavior might become the focus of OLs' censure, men understandably felt that OLs got angry unreasonably and at random over trivial matters. Some men were wary of women's gossip because of its unpredictable nature. The following sentiments, voiced by a man working in a research institute, are illustrative:

I care a lot about how I treat women. It's because women tend to complain about petty things—like someone is slow in answering the phone, or that he doesn't clear the table—that sort of thing. When women get together, trivial things are made into big issues. And they spread. Men also speak badly of another person, but we don't make a fuss out of small things. I often hear my male colleagues grumble that they were accused unreasonably by a woman.

Indeed some men expressed confusion and anger because they thought they had been unjustly condemned by women for unimportant things. For example, an unpopular man on the bank floor was reproached by an OL for throwing garbage into her wastebasket instead of his own. The man complained that it was the first time he had ever been criticized for putting garbage in a garbage can! Another man working for an electric wiring company was at once indignant and perplexed because he had been blamed for giving the same instructions both verbally and in writing. He did so because he thought it was easier for the OL to understand what he wanted her to do, but he was accused of slighting her. The man asked for my opinion, so I agreed that it was rather strange for the woman to have reproached him, but asked him how they had been getting along before that. He admitted that they had not been on good terms.

Because men usually did not have access to OLs' lunchtime gossip, they were unaware that bad reputations were built gradually. A man became aware of women's antipathy to him only after he had accumulated many accusations. By this time, anything he did was likely to appear distasteful. I noticed, however, that four main criteria recurred in women's backstage talk and were particularly important in the early stages of the OLs' evaluation of any given man.

Office Ladies' Criteria for Evaluating Men

First of all, an arrogant man was disliked, whereas a courteous man was praised. A man was considered arrogant if, for instance, he asked for tea to be served to his customer by calling out, "Four teas to room one!" Such a man's commanding tone was contrasted to the politeness of another man who said, "Sorry to disturb your work, but would you please bring four teas to room one?" One man enraged women on the bank floor by saying curtly, "Necktie." He wanted an OL to take out a black necktie that was kept on hand in a cabinet for male employees who needed to attend a funeral. "What was *that?* Who does he think he is? He could have at least said, 'Could you hand me the black necktie?'" fumed the OL. "There are a lot of ways to say it, and all he says is the noun!" agreed another woman. Because men often angered OLs by the way they spoke, both women were convinced they could easily write a manual for men on "good and bad uses of language."

In contrast, some men were popular among OLs because they were courteous. In addition to speaking politely when making requests, these men thanked the OLs when they brought tea to their customers and apologized when they caused trouble. Polite words, however, were not primarily what the OLs sought: they wanted a man's opinions to match his courteous behavior. In general, they believed that behavior reflected inner thoughts, but they were quick to sense when a man's attitudes were at odds with his actions; they knew whether the man was really sorry to bother them with tea serving, or whether he thought it their inevitable duty to serve him. They believed they could detect the conceited man's belief that he can lord over women.

OLs who had graduated from university were especially sensitive to men's views of women's role. "He thinks women exist to provide miscellaneous personal services to men," "He treats women as mere messenger girls," and "He thinks women's place is in the home," these women complained. One university graduate contrasted a "liberal" man to a "conservative" man and admitted that she worked wholeheartedly for the former but shirked tasks for the latter. She particularly detested her deputy-general manager, who joined the bank after finishing high school. She judged the man to be "conservative," because she heard him say under the influence of liquor things such as "Silly women are cute" and "Women who go to university are thoughtless, obstinate, and unfeminine."

The second recurring criterion was related to the first: men who treated OLs as fellow human beings, who indicated care and concern for their lives, and who showed empathy with the type of work they did, were immensely popular. In contrast, those who seemed to regard OLs as machines that provided services at the touch of a button were loathed.

One section manager was much admired by OLs on the floor because he asked them what the matter was when they looked troubled. Another man was liked by many OLs because he remembered to tell them the results of a business matter that concerned them. An OL explained: "If you become involved in something, you naturally want to know how things turn out—whether it works well for the man and the company or not." This particular man often remembered to tell OLs how things turned out and to thank them for their help. It was nice, said the OL, to be told that what they had done had helped. The considerate man was compared with a man who made a lot of fuss when he asked for OLs' help but neglected to tell them the outcome once the business was settled. Such a man gave women the impression that they were regarded as nothing more than unfeeling machines.

Though all this sounds reasonable, OLs' wish to be treated nicely sometimes assumed a different aspect because of the nature of their positions within the organization. For several reasons, OLs in general did not feel that they owned their work. For one thing, the company did not evaluate their performance seriously and treated them together as "girls." For another, the work they performed was often piecemeal, and therefore it was difficult for them to cultivate a sense of their own jobs. Pouring tea for customers, copying documents, and typing manuscripts tended to be regarded as services provided for men, rather than professional work that they were paid to do.

In addition, OLs were often asked to do jobs that seemed personal rather than professional. They sometimes made vacation travel arrangements for managers, and I witnessed a woman purchase and wrap prizes for a golf tournament that a group of men planned for pure entertainment. Although these examples clearly indicate an abuse of authority, there was a large gray zone where the line between business and personal tasks blurred. This was because at Tōzai, as in most other Japanese companies, there was no clear job description for OLs. As a result, whenever men asked women to perform tasks, they tended to "ask for favors" rather than make official requests based on their authority. OLs became used to being asked to do favors and increasingly lost the sense of fulfilling professional responsibilities even when they were engaged in what could be regarded as their proper jobs.

Women's weak sense of professionalism was reflected in their word choice. Work, for them, was seldom something that they simply "did" (*shigoto o suru*), but rather was "done *for* somebody" (*shigoto o yatte-ageru*). Similarly, a boss used different phrasing to recognize work done by men and work done by women. He usually used *gokurō-san* (I appreciate your effort) when speaking to a male subordinate. Although it was possible to say *gokurō-san* to a female subordinate, it was more common for him to say *arigatō* (thank you). *Arigatō* expresses gratitude for the service provided, whereas *gokurō-san* indicates acknowledgment of the work performed without expressing a strong sense of gratitude. By thanking women more often than men, a boss suggested that women worked differently from men.

OLs in general believed they were entitled to thanks for the various jobs they did for men. When a man failed to express his gratitude for their work, they criticized his lack of appreciation. He was condemned for assuming that he deserved to receive their services.

Some men were aware of OLs' weak sense of responsibility toward their work and treated them accordingly. For example, a man working in a real-estate company explained how he regarded male salespersons and female assistants differently:

I clearly differentiate between salesmen and assistants. When a female assistant complains about her work, I say, "There, there, don't make a fuss. I'll listen to what you have to say." I regard her as somebody I must attend to—someone I must soothe and calm. Of course, a salesman sometimes complains about his work too, but this I see only as a sign of temporary confusion. Superficially, I say that salesmen and female assistants are equal, but in reality, I rank them. I don't expect much from my female assistants, and so I indulge them. I don't expect them to assume responsibility for work.

Men who did not distinguish women's role in work from men's and treated them in a strictly businesslike manner often incurred their displeasure. It was ironic, for these men were condemned by women precisely because they would not discriminate against them. A man who worked for an electric wiring company analyzed the reason he lost popularity among women in his office:

Because there were many transactions to be made, women's contribution was critical. It was absolutely necessary to gain their cooperation, and so men in the section were careful not to offend them. It was generally thought in the office that a man's job was to soothe and humor women's various complaints and get them to cooperate. You can call it a sort of discrimination, I think. That is, women were regarded as something different from men— people who must be lured into doing work by offering bait. Women, on their part, seemed to think that men would soothe them whenever they fretted. I was the only man in the section who was indifferent to their fretting. And so I became the target of their censure.

Both of these statements indicate that when men and women are not regarded as equal business partners, treating women nicely may be a form of discrimination. In the words of a man working in a heavy electric equipment company, men have to attend to women who are "almost like spoiled children."

A man's business capability was the third criterion in determining OLs' attitude toward him. Women at Tōzai talked admiringly of able men and despised those who were slow-witted and inefficient. There was a very practical reason for OLs' preference for capable men. An incompetent man often annoyed women with extra work: he pestered them with silly questions and unreasonable requests; he issued unclear instructions; he often gave wrong directions and later asked for many revisions; and he made requests at the last minute, which sometimes required OLs to work overtime.

The fourth criterion was whether a man was generous or stingy. When an OL gossiped about a man, one of the important pieces of information she provided was how generous he was to women. This was brought home to me when an OL described her present and previous direct supervisors. She did not like her former boss very much, because he was particular about details. He asked, for example, for a copy to be reduced to 93 percent. It was difficult for the woman to work with such a meticulous man. However, she added, he was generous. When she and two other OLs in the section had to work overtime, he often treated them to dinner. On a rare occasion when he had to leave earlier than they did, he bought them fruit sandwiches for them to eat after work. Upon his transfer to another section, the three women gave him a small wallet. In return, he sent them each a large box full of gorgeous muscat grapes, which they thought must have cost a fortune. Her present boss, in contrast, did not care about small matters and was fun to work with. However, she emphasized, "He has never treated us to lunch or anything." The woman repeatedly said that her current supervisor had never given her a treat, as though it was the only defect he had in his otherwise perfect character. It was also apparent from her comments that, for her, her previous boss's faults were somewhat offset by his generosity.

OLs regularly exchanged information about men's generosity. They talked about which restaurants men took them to for lunch and dinner, what souvenirs they received from overseas business trips, how much money they were given to buy themselves cakes and sweets, and what White Day gifts they received. (On White Day, men reciprocate women's Valentine's Day chocolate gifts. Valentine's Day and White Day gift-giving customs in the office are discussed in the following chapters.)

It was common for an OL at Tōzai to ask a man to buy her and her fellow OLs pastries or to take her out for lunch. I witnessed a woman practically force her direct supervisor to treat her and me to lunch. On that day, the other six women who usually had lunch with us were either on vacation or had other appointments, so the woman and I were the only ones left to have lunch together. She decided it was a good opportunity to go outside of the bank to one of the restaurants. (Because it was difficult to secure seats for eight women during the crowded lunch hour, we usually ate in the company cafeteria.) When her boss came back from an early lunch, she asked him rather bluntly, "You wouldn't think of going out to have lunch for a second time, would you? Since there's only me and Ogasawara-san, I was thinking of going outside and was hoping that perhaps you might give us a treat." The supervisor did not have any choice but to give us lunch tickets worth about four thousand yen, which we used in the company cafeteria. I later heard the poor boss grumble that a man must be rich in order to supervise OLs.

At first I did not understand what made OLs so bold. One incident, however, led me to realize that they thought they deserved treats from men because the men were better paid. On that day, a man who was decidedly unpopular among the women on the floor took a can of juice from an office refrigerator and drank it. The juice happened to belong to an OL. It was immediately evident that something out of the ordinary had happened: all across the open office, the OLs got together and talked among themselves in twos and threes. After a long whispering session, they came back to their seats, several saying things such as: "He's a thief!"; "I cannot believe it!"; and "What does he think? That a can of juice grows in a refrigerator like a plant or something?"

The women continued to talk about the incident in their seats so that even men could hear them say, "It's the same as stealing cans from a vending machine," and "It's unforgivable to take a can of juice that a girl has bought with the little money she has." Yet it was obvious that the man did not intend to "steal" the juice; rather, he had absentmindedly taken it—as, he innocently admitted, he had taken two other cans in the past.

Initially, I was shocked by the vehemence of the women's rage over a mere can of juice, which led them to condemn the man as a thief. However, this man was disliked by the OLs before the incident, and the OLs would probably not have made such a big fuss over a can of juice if someone else had taken it. The difference between the man's interpretation and the women's interpretation of the incident suggests that the man and the women had contrasting views of *uchi* and *soto* (inside and outside) (Bachnik and Quinn 1994). The male employee might have been treating the refrigerator contents, and hence people who stocked it, as his *uchi*. From his point of view, he was only *amaeru*-ing (asking for indulgence) when he took the juice. The OLs, in contrast, saw most men in the office as *soto*, who should not ask for this kind of indulgence.[1] (See the latter part of this chapter on how women view their male colleagues as strangers.) However, I also came to understand that the OLs' anger stemmed in part from the fact that men were paid considerably more than they were.

Men's better pay was one of the unpleasant facts of life for OLs. They often speculated about how much money a certain man must be making. Such speculation invariably led them to grumble at the large difference in the amount of compensation that men and women received. The more incompetent a man seemed, the more they felt the difference in pay was unjustified. Therefore, it seemed natural to many OLs that men should treat them occasionally. Yet it was unthinkable that a woman would have to pay even one hundred yen to buy a man a can of juice. Although women were aware that they might have larger discretionary incomes than men, since most men had to support their families, this did not seem to influence their attitude toward "treats." It is interesting in this regard that three ex-OLs of large Japanese companies, now married to businessmen working in similar institutions, said they thought it utterly unjust that their husbands had to treat OLs, whom the wives considered far better off than themselves, but they had felt it only right for men to treat women when they were working as OLs.

OLs' attention to men's generosity cannot be considered separately from the company's compensation policy that discriminated against women. OLs were acutely aware that men's pay increased rapidly with accumulated tenure, whereas their own stayed relatively stable, which resulted in a widening gap in pay between the two sexes. It was whispered among them that even Uchida-san, the man who took the can of juice from the refrigerator, must be making at least double the amount they made. Many women regarded the inequity in pay as a just reason for OLs to be given treats, and thus OLs' concern over men's generosity was, in this sense, a critique of discriminatory company policies.

Similarly, the three other main criteria OLs used to distinguish a good man from a bad one were also related to discriminatory company policies. As we have seen, women often demanded that men give them special attention. Because the sexes were not on equal terms, men had to assume the responsibility for women's work as well as their own. Many OLs thought it was the men's job to ensure that OLs were happy with their work. If an OL was dissatisfied, she had the right to protest, and a man must attend to her complaints. Those men who thought women had the obligation to work and failed to show proper appreciation for the jobs OLs performed were severely criticized. Such criticism expressed the women's refusal to assume equal responsibility and obligations as businesspeople when they were not given corresponding rights.

However, OLs disliked men who considered themselves above women and assumed arrogant attitudes. The company justified its discriminatory policies by insisting that women had different roles and priorities in life from men, which implied that women were not necessarily inferior to men. OLs reproached men who lorded it over women.

Finally, although there were practical reasons for OLs to dislike incompetent men, this criterion was also related to discriminatory company policies. From the OLs' perspective, it was almost a breach of contract for men to be incompetent. Many OLs were discontented with the discrimination they faced. It was not fair that men should be selectively promoted and considerably better paid. Women's discontentment was somewhat alleviated if the man who was promoted and highly paid was capable and, therefore, apparently deserving of the advantageous treatment. In a sense, women could perhaps reluctantly accept a man being given favorable treatment if he was an astute businessman. In contrast, OLs had little tolerance for incompetent men. Many of them found it nearly unbearable to work as assistants to such men and to provide services such as making copies and serving tea.

The four recurring criteria in OLs' gossip about men all relate to discriminatory company policies. For many women, it was "part of the deal" that men be courteous to them, be attentive to their needs and complaints, be competent managers, and be generous. A man who failed to meet any one of these criteria was often reproached for not carrying out his responsibility. He was criticized for unfairly profiting from the system without doing his share of work. OLs were disgusted by a man who conveniently alternated between upholding and neglecting discriminatory policies as they suited his purpose.

OLs sometimes stated explicitly that the company's discrimination against them meant that men had to shoulder certain responsibilities. An OL on the bank floor vented her anger during lunch: a man had mildly complained of his busy schedule and talked enviously of the woman who could leave work early. Hearing her story, the OLs agreed that it was not fair for the man to say such a thing to her, because their positions in the company were completely different. One of the OLs protested, "He says such a thing only when it's convenient, and other times treats us as 'girls'!"

Most OLs had little sympathy for busy men. The employees of the bank were allowed to take fifteen days off in addition to one-week vacations in the summer and in the winter. Women took turns taking at least a day off every month. Men, however, seldom took a day off. When I pointed out the difference to an OL, she replied, "Why, of course. They're that much better paid. I would get really furious if they were able to take as many holidays as we can." At another time, a man was strongly condemned for leaving work early to play mah-jongg while his female assistant stayed overtime to type his report. An OL expressed her feelings succinctly, "If they're going to discriminate against us, they should at least protect us."

Because OLs' gossip seemed unreasonable and capricious, men tended to view angry women as "creatures of impulse" and despise their gossip. However, OLs' criticisms of men are not without reason. OLs may not stand up and advocate equal treatment. They may not even use the term *discrimination*. But their gossip shows that they are in most cases strongly aware of the unfairness they face. Gossiping women are not "merely" carried away by emotion; through gossip, they assert that if men are to take advantage of discriminatory policies, they must shoulder the accompanying responsibility. OLs are quick to identify any man who evades men's responsibility and yet makes the most of the inequitable system. Such a man meets strong opposition from OLs for "taking a free ride."

The Effects of Gossip

As we have seen, OLs' gossip makes it costly for men to discriminate against women; it ensures that men pay their "dues" for such discrimination For gossip to be truly effective, however, reputation must be important to men. In large Japanese firms, this indeed seems to be the case.

In order to climb the organizational hierarchy, a man must prove his competence as a manager. One of the key requirements of a manager is the ability to supervise his subordinates, including OLs. Failure to gain cooperation from OLs is often regarded as a sign of a man's weakness as a manager. A man's potential as a manager is questioned by company executives and personnel directors if he has a bad reputation among women.

A man may, therefore, try to give the impression to his boss that he is on good terms with OLs. One OL at Tōzai told me that even though she and her immediate supervisor quarreled often, the man never mentioned this to the vice-general manager or complained of her disagreeable attitude. In fact, she had often heard him praise her work in front of the manager. The woman suspected that this was a calculated move to indicate to the manager that the man got along well with his assistant.

Men seemed to fear that the personnel department would hear of their bad reputation. Unlike human resource departments in typical American companies, personnel divisions of Japanese firms usually wield considerable power because they single-handedly do the hiring for the entire organization. They also keep track of all employees' performances and evaluations and assign jobs and positions. If the personnel department suspects a man of being a poor manager of OLs, that man has little chance of promotion. In her study of a large American company, Rosabeth Kanter found that a secretary's opinion of her boss did not affect his fate in the company (1977). This is not true in Japanese companies. What OLs think about their superior often matters to the man's future in the firm.

I do not argue that reputation is not a matter of concern for OLs. On the contrary, most women, especially for the sake of finding marriage partners, preferred to have a good name rather than a bad name among their male colleagues. Many wished to be considered attractive and feminine. Some flirted. A number of women I interviewed said that there were quite a few such women in the workplace and indicated contempt for them by calling them *burikko* (a woman who exaggerates femininity by acting "cute"). Reputation, however, was not as directly linked to women's marriage prospects as it was to men's promotions. A woman did not necessarily look for a husband in the workplace, whereas a man had to "make it" in the company. Moreover, unlike the majority of men who were tied down to the company they worked for, many women thought that if worse came to worst, they could leave the workplace. Therefore, maintaining a good name in the office was ultimately more important for men than for women.

For OLs' gossip to damage a man's reputation as a competent manager, that gossip must disseminate. And disseminate it did. Men feared the way women's gossip spread like wildfire. As a form of entertainment all OLs could participate in, gossip circulated fast and wide. As discussed in chapter 2, OLs spend long working hours together but are not necessarily close friends. Their relationships are frequently superficial, and they rarely disclose their innermost feelings to any but their few intimate *dōki*. Under such circumstances, gossip concerning men becomes a handy topic in which all women can participate. The following sentiments, voiced by a woman who used to work as an OL in a general trading company, are representative: "There wasn't any overt hatred between us university graduates and junior college graduates. But I'm sure both sides felt a little uneasy with each other. That's why gossiping about men is popular. It's the safest thing to talk about. It's one thing we can all talk freely about. We can relax when we say bad things about men. We feel the togetherness." In contrast, she thought that gossip about women was taboo except within a truly close circle of friends. She explained, "We can't gossip about women. It's too scary. You don't know how the story might leak." When I asked her whether this meant that it was all right for gossip about men to leak out, she responded that it was in fact good for a man being gossiped about to hear the story so that he could change his attitude accordingly.

Because men were such a safe and handy topic, gossip about them was frequent and enthusiastic. The OLs at Tōzai tirelessly repeated whatever story was current that day whenever a new listener joined the group. As a result, word spread rapidly, so that usually by the next day, all the women on the floor and perhaps many more knew how a man had offended an OL.

Men sometimes discovered what OLs were gossiping about at lunch because women continued to gossip during regular business hours. OLs seldom reproached a man to his face, but they did not refrain from talking even when other men were within hearing distance. When the victim was not a general or a vice-general manager and, therefore, not too powerful, women sometimes deliberately let the man know that he was being gossiped about.

Having overheard women's talk, many men I interviewed could point out one or two men in their offices who were unpopular among women. A man working in a machine-tool manufacturing company described the situation to me:

I'm sure there are men who are liked and others who are disliked by girls. I can tell because I often hear them complain that this man does such and such a thing, or that man's such and such a habit makes them sick. When I hear them say these things, it makes me realize that although girls usually smile, they say what they want to say behind our backs. I heard them say things like they felt disgusted at a man who tapped them on the shoulder from behind, or that a man had made an unreasonable request. That sort of thing.

Similarly, a banker told me that women could not care less about being overheard by men. He added, "When I hear them say terrible things about men, I just hope I won't become the next target of their criticism. I try not to do things that will offend them. I think it's only natural for a man to think so." By talking in front of men, OLs wittingly or unwittingly made some men think twice about their attitudes toward women.

In addition to damaging a man's reputation as a competent manager, gossip interfered with a man getting his work done by making it difficult for him to gain the cooperation of OLs. OLs often stopped cooperating with a man they did not like, as the following statement from a man working in a home electronic manufacturing company indicates:

Girls work according to their likes and dislikes. They keep smiling at you, but once something goes wrong between you and them, that's the end of it. When a girl says, "I don't like that man," that means she won't cooperate with him. There's no such a thing as distinguishing between private feelings and work. The girl becomes very emotional, and it takes a hell of a time to restore the relationship.

Another man working in a research institute observed, "Women work as the mood takes them. They will do a very tedious job for men they like, but for those they don't like, they either postpone doing the work or they don't do it at all." Although none ever refused entirely to cooperate, OLs at Tōzai often made a wry face when a man they did not like requested their assistance. Many men said women's displeased looks made them hesitate to ask for their help again.[2]

Naturally, men feared the spread of gossip. As we have seen, OLs who heard a bad story about a man began to take a dim view of him. Many men agreed that being disliked by one OL was the same as being disliked by all the OLs. A man working in a general electrical and electronic products manufacturer noted, "It's really something how women are connected with each other. For example, girls always eat lunch together. If you offend one OL, you'd better be prepared to receive queer looks from all other OLs." A banker described a similar situation in his office: "If one girl decides that this man is no good, then all the girls start thinking in the same way." Because being gossiped about increased the likelihood that a man would lose the cooperation of many OLs, men feared women's gossip. They knew that the climate of opinion formed by gossip frequently encouraged OLs to resist in other ways (see chapter 5 for further discussion).

Critical and Persistent Gaze

Gossip was a form of entertainment for OLs. Therefore, it was not limited to men's unpleasant behavior but also included reports on their pleasant characteristics, their chances for promotion, funny stories, and other information about them. Any story about men was a safe subject that all OLs could enjoy. Besides, in the mundane worklives of OLs, there were not that many new things to talk about at lunch day after day. Under the circumstances, any tale concerning men was bound to have some value.

One of the distinctive features of OLs' gossip was that a man was seldom assessed by himself but was customarily compared to another man. For example, when OLs put down X-san who never gave them a treat, he was at the same time compared with Y-san who took them out for lunch occasionally. Y-san's pleasant behavior was thus mentioned and admired in OLs' lunchtime talks.

This comparison made women's criticism more powerful. Contrasting "bad" and "good" examples indicated that their criticism was well grounded and that it was more than just idle complaint. If no man ever indulged OLs, then perhaps the demand that women be indulged by men was unreasonable to begin with and their complaints groundless. However, if OLs could point to men who did give them treats, then their accusation that a man was stingy became more credible.

Men seemed to find this comparison one of the most irritating aspects of women's gossip. The vague charge that he was stingy did not embarrass a man as much as the claim that all the men had bought OLs souvenirs from overseas trips except him. OLs at Tōzai were well aware of the effect of comparison and frequently used it to their advantage. They made elaborate displays of presents given and let other men know that they had received treats. One OL described how souvenirs from overseas trips had escalated into expensive presents such as handbags because of the "competition among men." Reports about men's good characteristics were, therefore, as important as information about their unpleasant attitudes. Women annoyed men by constantly comparing them to each other.

OLs also entertained themselves by gossiping about men's performance records. Because they were excluded from the competition for advancement, they could afford to be irresponsible onlookers. OLs on the bank floor had access to surprisingly confidential data. For example, a woman was typing a chart one day that contained personal information on employees, including position, occupational grade, educational background, and the year of joining the bank. The OL explained to me that every woman in the clerical track became secretarial grade II in ten years counting from the time she finished high school, regardless of whether she joined the firm immediately afterward or went on to receive higher education. In the case of men, however, the difference in their speed of promotion increased as they accumulated tenure. She showed me the chart she was typing, pointed at three men's names, and informed me that they had all joined the bank in the same year. One man was already *buchō* (general manager) with the councillor III grade, the next man was *kachō* (section manager) with the councillor II grade, and the last man did not have any title. It was evident that the OL felt she should not discuss such matters openly, for instead of calling the names, she pointed at them silently and asked suggestively, "See?" She then added, "I bet there's a large difference in their compensation, too."

I later learned that OLs enjoyed using their knowledge of personnel data. The man without the title was looked down upon by women and secretly given the nickname "Makkun." They referred to the man considerably older than themselves with the suffix *kun*, a term customarily given to an inferior male.

OLs coolheadedly observed men's serious struggle for promotion. They knew that there was a strict hierarchical relationship among the three general managers and that the lowest-ranking general manager always made sure he was the first to get in a company car and wait for the other two managers to appear whenever they went out together. An OL also noted that the manager customarily took the least honorable seat, the one next to the driver. She commented, "It's not an easy business being a man. Even if he has become a general manager, he must still try to please those in higher positions. There seem to be no limits." When they witnessed the harsh realities of being the "company warriors," many OLs seemed somewhat glad not to be part of the game.

OLs made the most of their privilege of observing peacefully men's often desperate struggle to survive the race for promotion. During lunch one day, the OLs gossiped about a section manager who used to work on the floor. He was known to be hard upon his male subordinates. The OLs narrated how his first victim stopped coming to work; finally, a vice-general manager had to visit his house and persuade him to return to the office. Uchida-san, an unpopular man among the women, became the boss's next target. They remembered how the manager tore up Uchida-san's reports in the presence of other people. They entertained themselves describing the way Uchida-san bent his head and stood in an upright posture without daring to make the slightest move while his boss reproached his work. "He wouldn't answer a phone even if it rang. He'd just continue standing in the same posture. So one of us used to pick up the phone and say he was in a meeting or something," explained an OL. The manager was infamous for "killing" his male subordinates but was never unkind to the OLs. Therefore, they could amuse themselves by watching in detail from a safety zone as men, especially those that they disliked, suffered at the mercy of the tyrannical boss.

OLs' attitudes as bystanders were reflected in their words. They called men in their twenties and early thirties who did not yet have any title "those young ones" or "the young people." These phrases make sense if used by older men in higher positions to refer to people considerably younger than themselves. It was rather strange, however, for OLs who were younger than the men to use such expressions. Instead of referring to the relation between the men and themselves as one would normally do, OLs expressed the men's objective position within the organizational hierarchy. This shows how easy it was for women to detach themselves from the office hierarchy and assume the neutral stance of onlookers.

Furthermore, OLs entertained each other by sharing funny stories about men. They narrated how a man in a hurry to inform people that a colleague's mother had passed away caused confusion by mistakenly saying over the phone that the listener's mother had died. They convulsed with laughter over the tale of a general manager who had to change his attire to attend a funeral; one of the OLs brought him a black necktie, then left, and he began to change in his private room. Remembering that she had forgotten to inform him that a car was waiting, she returned. Her voice from behind the door caught the manager by surprise, and he answered in great confusion, "W-w-wait! D-d-don't come in yet!" Long after the manager had left for the funeral, the OL, still giggling, said, "Oh, it was so-o-o funny. The way he was upset and all! He was so cute. We're making a laughingstock out of the general manager, aren't we? But, you know, we all like him." Apparently, the OLs enjoyed the very human reaction of the usually sober and dignified general manager. Needless to say, the story was passed on to other OLs during lunch.

The general manager's story was told for pure fun. However, a humorous story was sometimes told to make fun of the man concerned. This happened more often with unpopular men. For example, one man was said to sweat freely. According to the OLs, he used eau de cologne in such abundance that it was possible to detect his presence from the smell. If they came into a room after he had left, they could tell at once that he had been there. In this way, minute details of men's behavior were turned into comical stories by the women. Their incessant gaze directed at men was sometimes kind but more often critical.

OLs exchanged information on men that seemed trivial and insignificant to an outsider. That a man keeps a picture of his pet cat in his wallet or that a man's daughter went to Australia on a school excursion may be utterly uninteresting for someone who does not know the men concerned. However, this information interests the OLs who work with these men day after day. Any story concerning their common acquaintances was worth being told to break the monotony of the OLs' worklives. However, I suspect that the stories were also interesting because they revealed that the stern-looking man adored a pet cat, or that the stingy section manager sent his daughter to an expensive private school. By disclosing the personal lives of men, gossip enabled the OLs to imagine characteristics the men did not reveal at work.

Many researchers have documented how a Japanese *sarariman* is expected to put his company and work before his relationships at home (Allison 1994; T. Lebra 1981; Ōsawa Mari 1993; Rohlen 1974; E. Vogel 1963). It is said that as *kaisha ningen* (company people), men work so hard that they spend little free time at home. The assumption is that unless they commit themselves intensely to work, they won't be promoted. The wives' role is to provide various domestic services to husbands who have little time to take care of themselves at home and not to distract them.

Because a successful businessman is expected to give himself wholeheartedly to his work, men at Tōzai were keen to present themselves as "company persons" and downplay their private lives and roles as husbands and fathers. As Erving Goffman notes, "A performer tends to conceal or underplay those activities, facts, and motives which are incompatible with an idealized version of himself and his products" (1959, 48). Men often boasted of how late they had worked the previous night and were in general reluctant to talk about home and family. Anne Allison (1994) similarly observes how a Japanese white-collar worker turned his absence from home into evidence of hard work and made it the subject of competition among his colleagues.

OLs were an audience for men's performance as "company people." They suspected, however, that the character a man projected at work was not all there was. When a man inadvertently revealed a part of himself that he took care to conceal, OLs found it amusing in part because it was inconsistent with his usual performance. They were eager to know that a man adored a pet cat or that a manager sent his daughter to an expensive private school because such details confirmed that the supposed "company person" indeed had a personal side, just like the OLs.

Ojisan kaizō kōza

OLs' gossip and other aspects of their lives that have hitherto remained closed to outsiders are being made public through books published recently in quick succession.[3] Many of these behind-the-scenes stories of OLs are written by women working in a company, although not necessarily as clerical assistants, and are based on information collected from women working as OLs in various firms. For example, the editing groups Onēsama Company for *Tonari no OL zubari 36 gyōkai* (OLs next door in thirty-six industries speak frankly) and Nippon no OL Kenkyūkai for *Nippon no OL tachi* (Japanese office ladies) each distributed questionnaires to one thousand OLs in an attempt to delineate ideal typical OLs.

A book that introduces various well-known companies to prospective OLs, *Shin OL zukan* (The new OLs' pictorial book), also gathered data from women working in those companies. The focus of this volume is not on major business activities of the companies or sales and profit figures, as is usually the case with recruitment books consulted by job-seeking graduates, but is instead on the daily working lives of OLs. *Shin OL zukan* discloses whether OLs are responsible for mopping the floor and wiping the office desks, whether men make their own copies, whether OLs can make private phone calls, and how prevalent marriage between employees is. The authors consider this information vital for any women interested in working at these companies.

Many of the books quote OLs extensively. The name of the woman quoted is not usually disclosed, but her age and the type of company where she works are indicated. The overall impression conveyed by the use of quotes is that the book tells the true stories of OLs. One volume, *OL jutsu* (The art of being an OL), consists entirely of interviews with more than a hundred OLs.

Many authors expect their books to be read by men as well as by women. *OL jutsu* explains on its cover page that the book is intended for men working in a company: "How do women sitting nearby observe you every day? Please read this book laughingly, angrily, and, if possible, seriously" (Group Nagon 1990). Gotō Ukiko, the editor of *All That's OL!* and *It's OL Show Time!*, is reported to have attributed the recent demand for books on OLs to men who wish to better understand women: "Women have come to account for over 40 percent of the working population, and their work style has changed. As a result, it is no longer possible to manage personnel without considering women. Men are taken aback at this change and want to know the true nature of women" (*Nihon Keizai Shinbun* 2 December 1991). In fact, according to the same article, the four books, *All That's OL!*, *Imadoki OL daizukan* (The encyclopedia of contemporary OLs), *Saigo ni warau OL wa dareda?* (Who is the last OL to laugh?), and *Tonari no OL zubari 36 gyōkai* (OLs next door in thirty-six industries speak frankly), had each sold approximately ten thousand copies as of December 1991, and 80 to 90 percent of their readers were men. In this respect, it is revealing that one book states explicitly in the title that it is written "for men who can no longer understand women" (*Josei ga wakaranakunatta ojisamatachi e*).

Among the most successful and most influential books on OLs are those in the series *Ojisan kaizō kōza* (Lessons for transforming men), which are based on a popular two-page column published in the weekly magazine *Shūkan Bunshun*. The column started in 1987, when two women, Shimizu Chinami and Furuya Yoshi, came up with the idea of reporting on ordinary OLs' views of the male middle managers with whom they worked. They formed the "Committee of Two Hundred OLs," a clublike group, to distribute questionnaires to OLs working in different companies, asking their opinions on male middle managers. Statistical data and quotes were published, along with funny and frank comments by Shimizu and Furuya. Among the wide range of topics discussed in *Ojisan kaizō kōza* (hereafter *Ojisan*) are men's poor taste in everything from ties, socks, undershirts, and casual clothes, to briefcases; repellent physical characteristics such as bald heads, dark eyebrows, flabby buttocks, and long little fingernails; annoying habits such as thinking aloud, boasting, making gross noises while eating, and lowering their trousers in public in order to tuck in their shirts; and desperate efforts to be promoted.

Although the column was initially scheduled to appear only ten times, it became such a smash hit that it never ended; it was still going a decade after its start, in the winter of 1997. The membership of the "OLs' Committee" continued to grow, reaching 1,200 by the end of 1989. The columns were compiled in six books and adopted for television and film, as I learned from interviews with Shimizu and the editor, Sasamoto Kōichi (Shimizu and Furuya 1989).

Coauthor Shimizu emphasizes that when she and Furuya started *Ojisan*, they did not intend to publish in a magazine, much less become famous figures in Japanese journalism. Shimizu was working in a tedious job as a software programmer in a leading electronics company. To kill time, she began using a fax machine, because "it looked like you were doing work." She and her friend Furuya faxed simple questionnaires to friends working in different companies, asking such things as "Is a man in your office sometimes laughed at because he is wearing a funny tie?" They collected as many as two hundred answers within a week. She attributes the ease with which they were able to collect answers to OLs' latent desire to amuse themselves with matters regarding men in their offices. She says, "OLs wanted to have fun with things concerning men. Once we put a little system in place, it spread rapidly."

Ojisan indeed seems to be a slightly exaggerated version of OLs' gossip. For example, *Ojisan* discusses how men make desperate efforts to please their superiors, quoting the following reports from OLs:

When I handed out sweets in my office, Noguchi *kachō* [section manager] first said he did not want one. But, on learning that the sweets were a gift from *buchō* [general manager], he came to me hurriedly to receive one, and said in a loud voice that everybody could hear, "I really like sweets."

Buchō called from the meeting room next door, "Hayashi ku-un." By the time I turned around, Hayashi *kachō* had already rushed to the room. (Shimizu and Furuya 1989).

Ojisan exposes OLs' distaste for the leather shoulder bags that were popular among businessmen at the time: "Anything is better than leather shoulder bags. Men with shoulder bags look bad: the bag bites into the shoulder, crumples the suit, and exposes a fat belly. It is a miserable sight. Some shoulder bags are discolored and look as if they stink. They may be expensive bags, but they certainly make men look shabby" (Shimizu and Furuya 1989). Sasamoto Kōichi, the editor of *Shūkan Bunshun* when the series started, believes that *Ojisan*'s success was driven by men's shock upon learning the OLs' views. When a man read the column, he realized that OLs observed him in great detail and often with malicious intent. Sasamoto says that *Ojisan* made public the secret, whispered talk of OLs.

Things that are difficult to say directly to the person concerned can be expressed through *Ojisan*. Many men did not know that OLs thought leather shoulder bags ugly until the series reported this opinion. According to Sasamoto, quite a few men in his company stopped using shoulder bags altogether when the column was printed. He thinks men care very much how they appear in the eyes of OLs.

Sasamoto was ultimately responsible for deciding to publish *Ojisan* in *Shūkan Bunshun*. He says that he changed little of the original series proposed by the two women. The only major modification was the title: the authors initially named the column *Ojisan kaizō keikaku* (A plan to transform men). Sasamoto softened the title by replacing *keikaku* (a plan) with "*kōza*" (lessons). He thought it more appealing if the title emphasized the idea of teaching men rather than laying out a plan to transform them.

One of the key concepts of the column, Sasamoto maintains, is the word *ojisan*. For lack of a better expression, I have translated the word as "men," but it means much more than that. According to a Japanese dictionary, *oji* with the suffix *san* indicates an unrelated, middle-aged man (Kindaichi, Saeki, and Ōishi 1984), which is contrasted to the female counterpart, *obasan*. Although the word is generally employed in a neutral sense, it is at once very awkward and sarcastic when used by OLs to refer to their bosses and other male coworkers. In Japanese offices, subordinates, including OLs, usually call their superiors by their titles, such as Tanaka *buchō* and Nakamura *kachō*. It is therefore decidedly out-of-the-ordinary for an OL to refer to her boss as *ojisan*.

Sasamoto presumes that the term *ojisan* became popular because it appropriately stressed the way young OLs in their twenties looked at men in their offices. The word suggests that OLs do not see men as their fellow workers, but regard them as unfamiliar objects to observe. It illustrates that OLs think of men as strangers who lead completely different lives from their own. The word left a very strong impression on Sasamoto and was a dominant factor in his decision to publish the work.

I suspect another reason for the word's popularity among the general public is that it aptly captures OLs' ironic indifference to office hierarchy. Although OLs are officially at the bottom of the organizational hierarchy, they have, in another sense, an existence that transcends it. They remain aloof from the office hierarchy because they are excluded from the race for promotion. It makes small difference to them whether Tanaka-san is a *buchō* or a *kachō*. Indeed, for that matter, he is just a plain, middle-aged man, or *ojisan*, to them. Rodney Clark argues that the use of standard ranks in Japanese companies to address people and to refer to them gives the ranks immense social significance, for "neither a rank holder nor those he deals with can easily forget his status relative to theirs" (1979, 106). By calling a man *ojisan* and thereby removing his title, OLs demonstrate that they can indeed forget his status. The word *ojisan* shows how women can strip away all the authority that cloaks a man and treat him as a mere middle-aged duffer.[4]

I would like to point out that OLs' indifference to office hierarchy does not result from an inability to appreciate rank and order. Women's disregard for authority has often been wrongly attributed to their weak business sense. Women ignore office hierarchy, it is held, because they do not appreciate the importance of maintaining order in a large bureaucratic organization. Moreover, women's disrespect for the boss is frequently taken to be proof of their overly emotional character. Whenever OLs find something unpleasant about a person, it is said, they put on a long face regardless of their relationship to the person. Such women, the argument goes, are not professional businesspeople (*Nihon Keizai Shinbun* 17 February 1994; 15 June 1992; 5 January 1991).

The idea that women are emotional and unfit for serious business on the ground that they show little respect for office authority ignores an important aspect of OLs' worklives: women rigidly observe seniority among themselves. As we saw in chapter 2, a woman pays respect to a senior OL in various ways. She uses polite terms or, in extreme cases, honorific terms when speaking to her. She gives way in walking through doors and narrow aisles. In elevators, she offers to stand behind the buttons and press them. In fact, I suspect that the discord among OLs caused by contradictory index of seniority would not be as strong if hierarchy were taken lightly. Therefore, it is not appropriate to interpret OLs' disregard for male authority as indicative of their general inability to respect organizational hierarchy.

Let us return to analysis of why *Ojisan* became so popular. In addition to attributing the success of the column to the shock that men felt upon learning the malicious intent of OLs' gaze, Sasamoto points out how well the column fit the magazine. As a weekly magazine, *Shūkan Bunshun* is unique in that it is widely read by women although its major readers are businessmen. According to Sasamoto, the ratio of male to female readers of *Shūkan Bunshun* is approximately 6:4, whereas most other magazines in Japan are read almost exclusively by one sex. That the magazine has both male and female readers ensures that the column is read by both sides—those who accuse and those who are accused. It would not be half as fun, Sasamoto maintains, if *Shūkan Bunshun* lacked either men or women as readers: OLs' accusations would lose their sting if there were no *ojisan* to read them, and *Ojisan* would not be able to reflect an increasing number of OLs' voices if there were no female readers to offer feedback.

Coauthor Shimizu states that there are in general two different types of humor in columns such as *Ojisan*: "liable to be true" and "not liable to be true." The former amuses a reader who finds a remark true to life. "Yes! Yes! This definitely happens!" is the reader's reaction. In contrast, the latter is so incredible that it is foolishly funny. "No, this cannot be," the reader responds. Although Shimizu tries to include both types of humor in the column, she thinks *Ojisan* is popular predominantly for the "liable to be true" type of humor.

Although OLs energetically accuse men in their office of various transgressions, Shimizu warns that their lively criticisms do not necessarily empower them. By participating in *Ojisan*, OLs effectively renounce their claims and responsibilities toward work. It is only because they have abandoned all such rights and duties that they can speak out in the way they do. Shimizu says that OLs do not stand in the same "ring" (*dohyō*) with *ojisan*. She explains with the following example:

Let's assume that there are two buildings standing across the street. A phone rings and your boss is summoned to the building across the street by his superior. It's funny, isn't it, to watch him rush to the building, ignoring the red light. But if you were yourself a *kachō*, you might do the same thing. Or, let's suppose the president of your company looks like an octopus. You and your colleagues laugh at him and secretly call him "that octopus." But if you must curry favor with the president because your whole family depends on the money you make, then you might stop calling him "octopus."

Shimizu adds that in Japanese society, women never have to stand in the same ring as men.

Sasamoto holds similar views. He points out that *ojisan* and OLs are not on the same footing: An OL who makes an accusation remains anonymous, whereas an *ojisan's* right to defend himself is not guaranteed. OLs are in a stronger position than *ojisan*. Sasamoto suspects that it is this reversal of real-life positions that makes the column amusing. This relative unfairness is permissible because the topics covered by the series are not usually serious. *Ojisan* seldom discusses "big issues" such as sex discrimination or the Equal Employment Opportunity Law. Instead, its favorite themes are men's tasteless attire and their peculiar habits.

Conclusion

Many OLs watch men's every move day by day, hour by hour. In so doing, they are particularly alert to men's disagreeable behavior, which they report to each other during lunch break. Although OLs rarely discuss discrimination directly, many are keenly aware of the situation in which they work and have a clear sense of their rights and responsibilities as well as those of men. Men and women have unequal rights in the organization, and most OLs think that responsibilities should reflect this discrepancy. For instance, they often believe that it is men's responsibility—not their responsibility—to make sure that work gets done, because it is men who ultimately enjoy the fruits of the labor. Men must, in this way, pay their dues for treating women unequally. Those who do not pay are criticized as "free riders." Such men include those who are arrogant, those who remain indifferent to OLs' needs and complaints, those who do not provide generous treats, and those who demonstrate little aptitude for business. According to women, these men have acted unfairly according to the rules of the game.

Certain men earn a bad reputation among OLs, to the point where anything they do is likely to meet with OLs' disapproval. Women's dislike of a man frequently culminates in physical aversion, which gives men the impression that women's criticism is unreasonable and emotional. Most men are careful, however, not to invite the hostility of women, because a bad reputation among women can harm a man's prospects for promotion. A bad reputation often means that OLs will not cooperate readily with the man's requests, which raises doubts in the minds of company directors and personnel managers about the man's ability to supervise OLs and about his overall competence as a manager. In chapter 5, I discuss how the climate of opinion thus generated frequently encourages women to resist in other ways.

Japanese OLs whom I came to know are similar to American secretaries described by Kanter (1977), in that both have limited access to formal means of control within the firm and use gossip to gain power. Where they differ is the reason why gossip enhances their power. For Kanter's secretaries, gossip is a way to use their privileged access to information. Informal communication through secretaries is so important, according to Kanter, that bosses sometimes use secretaries to get an inside reading of a situation. Few Japanese OLs, in contrast, occupy such a central position in information exchange. Except for executive secretaries, most OLs do not work closely enough with a specific man for them to gain knowledge that is useful and important to other men. Unlike the gossip of American secretaries, the gossip of Japanese OLs is primarily a way to destroy a man's reputation and thus his success in the firm.

Japanese OLs described in this chapter are like Kanter's American secretaries in that gossip makes their day more interesting. OLs not only discuss unpleasant characteristics of men but also their more pleasant aspects, their performance records, funny stories, and almost anything else about them. In fact, practically everything a man does is observed, evaluated, and reported on. OLs often eye men critically, from head to toe.

A number of studies examine the relationship between gender and the power to look. For example, in his discussion of European nude painting in which women were the sole subjects, John Berger (1972) argues that men act while women appear and that men look at women and women watch themselves being looked at. Similarly, Rosalind Coward maintains, "The ability to scrutinize is premised on power. Indeed the look confers power; women's inability to return such a critical and aggressive look is a sign of subordination, of being the recipients of another's assessment" (1985, 75).[5] OLs' gossip is subversive because it is the product of women staring back at men. OLs assess men and judge men. It is men in turn who are embarrassed and irritated by women's persistent gaze.

Ojisan kaizō kōza, the popular column in a weekly magazine, has successfully brought to light OLs' everyday gossip about men in their offices. The column is widely supported because many people find "true to life" the situations that it describes. In particular, the word *ojisan,* originally used to refer to a middle-aged man to whom one was unrelated, has become a new fad word used by OLs to refer to their bosses and other male colleagues. The word emphasizes women's view of men as strange objects to observe. It also expresses women's ironic aloofness from office hierarchy.

Although many OLs energetically review and comment on male behavior, this criticism is possible only because they do not compete with men for promotion. Women can laugh at men making desperate efforts to please their superiors because OLs usually do not have to do the same to support themselves and their families. Only they can afford to observe calmly and coolheadedly men's funny, pathetic, and sometimes ugly struggle for promotion.

OLs therefore face a serious dilemma in their efforts to exercise power. They must resist the existing social order within the terms available to them as "office ladies." Their various demands, such as to be given attention and generous treats by men, and their spirit of criticism, manifested in *Ojisan,* take advantage of their unique position within Japanese corporate organizations: they are excluded from the race for promotion. Their resistance to male authority is premised on the condition that they remain outside of the serious business world.

Nevertheless, in spite of severe constraints, many OLs have challenged existing male authority. They have observed, reviewed, judged, and commented on men's behavior. By scrutinizing and criticizing men, they have called into question conventional understandings and customs in the male business world. In her discussion of OLs in Tokyo, Karen Kelsky observes that "the OL position is . . . an economic tool that enables some young Japanese women to participate in a larger, empowering OL culture. While OLs may not challenge men directly, in the Western legal/political sense, they do so indirectly, through the language, work patterns, and play patterns of their subculture" (1994, 10). I have found in my own research that OLs often question male authority without taking actions that stand out in their routine worklife. They laugh at men who make desperate efforts to please their superiors, and thus they highlight how funny and pathetic—indeed, how abnormal—"company people" really are. By exposing the hitherto taken-for-granted work attitudes of many men, OLs call into question the basic values of *sararīman*.

As Shimizu, the coauthor of *Ojisan*, says, OLs' challenges may not be effective in bringing them into the same "ring" as men. But perhaps they may help create a new, completely different ring, where women are not only spectators but also participants. This is not a fantasy far removed from reality, because women's voices seem to have triggered discussion among men. As a banker said at the end of an interview, "Women in the company are perhaps to be pitied. But women have the home. My daughter, for instance, is very to close to her mother. I make efforts to join the family by helping with household matters, but it's difficult when I have to spend so much time away from home. . . . The company is a place where lonely men are compelled to throng because they have been shut out from the home and have nowhere else to go."

Another man working for a manufacturer of heavy electrical equipment told me that he misses his family. Because his work keeps him in the office until late at night, his small daughter, who sees her father only infrequently, begs him to "call again," thinking that he lives somewhere else. Men are becoming increasingly aware that their company and work are depriving them of a decent human life. Kathleen Gerson (1993) has found that a significant proportion of American men would actually prefer to work less and parent more. She therefore argues that economic and occupational structures are more firmly divided by gender than by the preferences of individual men and women.[6] Similarly, some Japanese men, contrary to the stereotype of being work-obsessed, voice their desire to spend less time at work and more time with their children. They may wish to renounce long-established male privileges and claim new rights to care for their children.

4

Popularity Poll

Unlike the American holiday, when men and women ex-
change gifts, Valentine's Day in Japan is an occasion for women to give
gifts to men. The men reciprocate on White Day, which falls exactly one
month later. The office ladies at Tōzai Bank, where Valentine's Day was
a major event, placed little emphasis on the romantic aspects of the holiday; nonetheless, their preparations for the day started much earlier
than February fourteenth. Weeks in advance, OLs examined a catalog of
gift chocolates to determine what they would give to the men in their
departments. Some went to department stores to inspect chocolates in
the basement food halls. There was an obstinate insistence that chocolate was the appropriate gift for the occasion. A man's popularity could
be measured by the chocolate that he received. This chapter examines
women's practice of giving Valentine chocolate to male colleagues and
bosses—and of giving farewell flowers to men being transferred to other
workplaces.[1]

A Break from the Monotony

On Valentine's Day, it was customary for OLs on the bank
floor to give chocolate jointly to all the men in their respective departments. Two OLs in Department II made it a rule to give chocolate to
all the men who at the time of the holiday belonged to the department
as well as to all those who used to be members of the department but
had left since the last Valentine's Day. Because there were many job ro-

98

tations during this particular year, they gave chocolate to eleven men who had been transferred to other sections, in addition to sixteen men who were currently with their section. They even intended to airmail chocolate to those who had moved to overseas offices such as New York and Hong Kong. "Postage costs more than the chocolate itself," one of the women said.

Some OLs enjoyed choosing chocolates. Early in February, two women went to a department store during lunch for a "preliminary inspection" of chocolates. A week before Valentine's Day, an OL went shopping for chocolates that were to be distributed to the male colleagues in her group. At about two o'clock on the afternoon of the day, it was announced that the chocolates were on display in the tea room. The three of us women working nearby dropped our work immediately and went to see them. In the tea room, the OL proudly displayed her choice of chocolates. They were colorfully wrapped in the shapes of various animals. There were all sorts of animals, so that none of the twenty-seven chocolates were the same! We marveled at the elaborate wrapping and enjoyed the break from our monotonous office work.

About two weeks before Valentine's Day, a memo was circulated in the bank, asking employees to avoid using the bank's internal mail for private use. It added that each year Valentine's Day put an extra burden on the system, which prevented it from operating smoothly, and called for special restraint. Despite this request, OLs used internal mail to send chocolates to men working in distant branches. Incredibly thin chocolates were bought, wrapped double in company envelopes, and smuggled out with other mail.

The day before Valentine's Day, OLs busied themselves during lunch wrapping gifts and writing cards that were to be given to men in their respective departments. Women in Department I worked on putting a rice cracker and a chocolate in a colorful paper bag and sealing it with a sticker. The cost of one gift was only 450 yen, because the cards, the bags, and the stickers were provided free by the store. The same sentence was written on all the cards. It read, "You must be tired from hard work. Please take a break and enjoy the sweet chocolate." Those for the general and the deputy managers were written with even politer phrasing. An OL in Department II put an animal-shaped chocolate and a card for each man in a small plastic bag decorated with many hearts and wrapped it with a ribbon of red, pink, or gold. The women in Department III were not with us at the time, but I was told that they bought cute chocolates molded into the shape of beach umbrellas.

Chocolates that were to be systematically distributed in the departments were thus prepared openly, but those that were to be given indi-
vidually were prepared in private. Women made lists of men to send
Valentine chocolates. One day, I ran into two OLs discussing Valentine's Day chocolate in the tea room. One woman held a memo pad.
On top of each page, she had written the name of a man she planned to
give chocolate to, and following that, she had entered the names of
women with whom she intended to give chocolate jointly. The woman
asked, "How about Aoki-san?" The other woman's name would be
added to the list if she wished to give chocolate jointly to the man with
the rest of the women on the list. After having gone through the list
with her colleague, the other woman said, "I'd better make my list, too.
I promised Chie-chan I would join her in giving chocolate to a number
of men, but I'm beginning to get confused about who they are."

On the morning of Valentine's Day, the tea room was full of colorfully wrapped gifts waiting to be presented to men. The "official" chocolates that women gave to men in their respective departments were
distributed at about noon, when most of the men were out of the office
for lunch. When men came back from lunch in groups of twos and
threes, they found the chocolates on their desks. Many of them quickly
read the cards attached to them and came over to the women's desks
to express their thanks. None, however, seemed to open the package,
much less to sample the contents. Most of the chocolates were swiftly
put away in briefcases or in desk drawers.

All through the day, there was a flurry of activity in the office, for
OLs came in and out far more frequently than usual. OLs working in
different sections of the building whom I rarely saw on normal days
came to the floor, usually in twos, to present gifts to men. If the sought-
after man was there, women handed out the gift and left after a short
exchange of words. If he was not present, they left the gift on his desk.
These presents were usually decorated with red and pink hearts all over
the wrapping paper and tied with brightly colored ribbons. Because of
this, they stood out in the normally sober and subdued office. When I
happened to walk by a manager's desk with another woman, she quickly
detected a fine box of chocolate on the vacant desk. The OL whispered, "Look! There's a box of Godiva chocolate on Sonoda manager's desk."

OLs on the floor left the office to deliver gifts to men working in
other sections of the bank. A woman near me sat huddled at her desk
and made rustling noises for a long time, busily putting chocolates in
company envelopes. After a while, she left the office, holding a paper file

and a shopping bag full of the brown company envelopes. When she came back, the shopping bag was empty. She repeated the process many times, each time departing with a shopping bag full of presents. Toward the end of the day, a telephone rang at her desk. I heard her reply, "I'm almost through. . . . No, I haven't gotten to the fifth floor yet." It was apparent that the call was from another OL, with whom she was jointly presenting chocolates, asking whether the gifts had been successfully distributed.

Despite the extensive celebration, the company authorities did not recognize Valentine's Day as an official bank event. It existed only because OLs chose to give chocolate to their male bosses and colleagues. Considering the inconvenience it caused the bank, it was surprising that such large-scale gift-giving among employees was tolerated by the company authorities. As one woman commented, "You can't get things done on Valentine's Day." In addition to the loss of worktime, the holiday consumed company property such as envelopes and clogged the internal mail system.

Yet the company authorities tacitly approved Valentine's Day—perhaps because it was initiated by OLs. Rosabeth Kanter (1977) describes how the presence of secretaries represented the "human side" of American corporate bureaucracy. For example, it was secretaries who remembered birthdays, "lending a legitimate air of occasional festivity to otherwise task-oriented days" (1977, 69). In a similar manner, Japanese OLs added a personal touch to rationalized organizations. Men could converse idly with OLs and enjoy a brief break from serious business. Women could spend time and effort on gift-giving within offices, thereby fostering the harmony of the workplace. It was considered legitimate for women to initiate Valentine's Day gift-giving, whereas men, the professionals, were allowed only a passive role, that is, to return gifts to women on White Day. (See chapter 6 for discussion of White Day.)

A Barometer of Popularity

Although Valentine's Day gift-giving within offices thus appears to provide fun and merriment that relieves the monotony of work, there is more to this quasi-holiday. For example, vice-general manager Hase was very popular among OLs on the bank floor. He did not have an arrogant attitude toward OLs. He was attentive to their complaints and tried to solve their problems. He also treated them from time to time. And he received a vast amount of chocolate.

A few days before Valentine's Day, I learned that a group of OLs intended to give the manager chocolate. This was in spite of the fact that he would also receive the "official chocolate" from them as a member of the three departments. The chocolate bought especially for him was much more expensive than the official chocolate prepared for all the men on the floor. For some time, OLs talked about the manager, speculating on how many chocolates he would receive on Valentine's Day. One OL said she looked forward to seeing just how many women in his former offices would send him chocolate. Another OL agreed that any woman would feel like presenting him with chocolate on Valentine's Day.

Valentine's Day chocolate, especially the "nonofficial" chocolate given voluntarily, conveyed messages such as "I feel grateful to you" and "I like you." Consequently, both men and women felt the number of chocolates a man received measured his popularity among women. A woman who had worked in a general trading company explained:

A man is evaluated by the number of chocolates he receives on Valentine's Day. Some people receive not only from their sweethearts but from someone like me who gives to express her gratitude. If a man is a wonderful guy, there would be many girls like me and he would receive many chocolates. You don't give [a personal gift of chocolate] to a man you don't like even if he's your boss. . . . [The number of chocolates] is like a barometer of popularity.

OLs at Tōzai also believed that the number of chocolates a man received indicated his popularity among women. For example, one woman liked her previous boss very much. Whenever he happened to pass by in the company cafeteria, she waved at him. One day, long before February fourteenth, when she gave him such a greeting, another OL asked her whether she intended to give him chocolate on Valentine's Day. She replied with an emphatic yes. True to her word, on Valentine's Day, she and her friend left the cafeteria earlier than usual during lunch to give the man chocolate. Another woman encouraged them, "Don't let other women beat you! Be sure to hand him the chocolate yourself." I asked the OL whether he was that popular, and she replied, "Oh, yes! You should see it yourself. There's always heaps of chocolates on his desk." I was told that, although he was married, he was more popular than most single men.

Indeed, the difference between a popular and not-so-popular man was shamelessly exposed in the open office environment, as the former was showered with chocolates that could fill a huge cardboard box, whereas the latter received only a scanty number of "ultra-obligatory" chocolates (*chō-giri choko*). Even among the ten men whom I interviewed, the unevenness of the number of chocolates received was evident: the most popular man received as many as twenty-one gifts of chocolate, whereas the least popular man received only one.

Valentine's Day is a touchy topic for some men, which is why a number of male informants seemed reluctant to talk about the holiday. During the interviews, several of them repeatedly reminded me to keep the data confidential. One man working in a stock brokerage agreed to be interviewed only after he made doubly sure that I would destroy the tape of our conversation. In spite of all my assurances, he gasped with apparent annoyance when I asked him how many chocolates he had received: "Gosh, you want me to answer such a question?" In sharp contrast, none of the women were concerned about confidentiality.

Describing the dangers that Brahmin in ancient India faced when they accepted the king's gifts, Marcel Mauss writes that "to receive from kings is honey at first but ends as poison" (1967, 58). Mauss interprets the reluctance of the Brahmin to accept gifts from the king in terms of a temporary dependency relationship the gifts create between the donor and the recipient: "The bond that the gift creates between the donor and the recipient is too strong for [the Brahmin]. . . . The recipient is in a state of dependence upon the donor. It is for this reason that the Brahmin may not accept and still less solicit from the king" (1967, 58). Gifts are dangerous to accept, because they render the recipient dependent on the donor.

Japanese Valentine chocolate is similarly poisonous. Because chocolate measures a man's popularity among women, it matters to a man whether he receives chocolate. Men's vulnerability to chocolate is reflected in the response of many male informants whom I asked how it felt to receive chocolate. Using the same phrase, they made the same humbling admission: "I knew that it was only an obligatory chocolate, but I still felt good to receive it." Valentine's Day in Japan is not just a merry, joyous holiday, because men in positions of authority become symbolically dependent upon women.

Resistance through Chocolate

Some OLs enjoyed Valentine's Day by playing pranks on men. An OL at the bank described how she and her fellow OLs had given to a man working in a different section one of the chocolates left over from those they distributed to every man in their department, pretending that it was a gift bought especially for him. She said, "He gave us gorgeous presents in return for it. Aren't we clever?" Another OL, giggling, agreed, "Ignorance is bliss!"

OLs enjoyed being mischievous: the degree of "I like you" is always unclear; it could even mean "I love you." A man who receives chocolate, even if it is jointly given, cannot help but wonder for a moment whether the chocolate was given with a message of love. One of the single men I interviewed, who worked for an automobile manufacturer, thought he had received at least three chocolates with a love message. He said, "You're suspicious that there might be a [love] message there, but you don't know for sure. I mean you can't tell by the chocolate itself. You guess from the way she has been treating you all along."

A married man working in a pharmaceutical company confessed that he made conscious efforts to convince himself that the chocolates were given as an "extension of everyday communication" and that "there was nothing more to them." Women enjoyed watching men getting confused or trying not to get confused. If a man misinterpreted the chocolate and acted in a strange way, a woman could get back at him and say, "Are you kidding? It was only an obligatory chocolate!"

Some OLs used the holiday to settle old scores with men, as a woman who had worked as an OL in a manufacturer of electric household appliances explained:

I think a man who didn't get any chocolate should think about why he didn't. He should reflect on his conduct. I think it's good for things to become clear. [But why should there be a day for men to reconsider their behavior and not a day for women to do the same?] That's because there are men in the office who consider women inferior. Some men think they're superior to women, and they should rethink that. I mean, some men think women are there to work for men, and treat us like maids. There are men like that and these people need to reconsider thing . . . . There's a darn good reason if a man can't get any chocolate, and he'd better change!

Another woman and her friends who worked in a mortgage company contrived to give their boss, whom they disliked, fewer boxes of chocolate than other men in the section. She described how the six women secretly discussed how many chocolates they should give to each man in their section. Their conclusion was for each woman to give a box to each man except the boss, and for three women to give a box jointly to the boss. In other words, the boss received only two boxes, whereas each of the rest of the men received six. Their revenge on their boss was subtle, because they decided to spend an equal amount of money for the boss and for each of the other men—the boss's chocolates were more expensive than those given to the others. However, she emphasized, "On Valentine's Day, the number is definitely what matters." She derived considerable satisfaction from the fact that the boss, unaware of the women's malicious feelings contained in the gifts, took simpleminded delight in receiving them.

Still another woman working in a construction company described to me what she called the tactics of "delayed spiking" (as in volleyball), in which she and her friends gave chocolate very late in the afternoon to a selected number of men they did not like, whereas other men received their chocolates early in the morning.[2] "This way," she explained, "those who don't receive chocolate until late will think that maybe they won't get one." The woman and her friends relished keeping the men in suspense.

The same woman and her female coworkers also gave broken pieces of chocolate to their boss, whom they disliked. "We wanted to do something more fun than just not giving him any chocolate. We pressed the chocolate bar with our fingers all over the wrapping," she explained. She suspected that the boss had understood their message, because the chocolate was broken into such little pieces that it was apparent the damage was not the result of an accident. "Of course, he said thank you, but I'm sure he realized. . . . You can call it a childish act, but we enjoyed it!"

Thus Valentine's Day is an opportunity for some OLs to manifest a spirit of resistance. They get a chuckle out of the fact that men can be made happy by trivial boxes of chocolate. They also take delight in devising various tactics, such as giving fewer boxes, delaying the time to give, and presenting broken chocolate, to further "poison" their gifts to men.

What is equally if not more important than women's temporary empowerment is the fact that the holiday provides otherwise divisive OLs an opportunity to unite. As we have seen in chapter 2, OLs in general lack solidarity. It is rare for them to form a united front on issues such as the Equal Employment Opportunity Law and discriminatory company policies. However, we have also noted that OLs join together to gossip about men, and indeed enjoy doing so. In preparing for Valentine's Day, women often gather to discuss whether to give chocolate to a man. Just as with gossip, the holiday provides an occasion for OLs to jointly assess men.

Valentine's Day also enables OLs to unite in taking revenge against men they do not like. They plot retaliation, becoming conspirators in concocting their plan. They indulge their rebellious spirit, coordinating their efforts in order to give fewer boxes, delay the time of giving, or present broken chocolate. Sharing the secret message conveyed by the chocolate, they feel close to one another. In this way, Valentine's Day encourages women to share their opinions of men and overcome discord among themselves.

Anonymity and Ambiguity

Why is Valentine's Day tolerated by men? Men, after all, participate in the holiday, albeit passively, by accepting women's gifts. Perhaps they tolerate the custom because of the gift-giving's inherent ambiguities.

In his remarkable studies on "weapons of the weak" (1985 and 1990), James Scott describes how subordinate groups resort to disguised resistance. He identifies two modes of concealment: anonymity, or the technique of disguising the messenger; and ambiguity, or the technique of disguising the message itself. My research on Valentine's Day gift-giving in Japanese offices shows that women's temporary empowerment is similarly successful in two ways: first, by passing judgment on men that reflects the opinions of all the women, and second, by keeping the meaning of chocolate intentionally obscure.

Giving chocolate in Japanese offices is a form of popularity poll. Because a woman gives chocolate primarily to express her admiration for a man, the number of chocolates a man receives indicates his popularity among women. The results of this poll reflect the opinions of many women: the number of chocolates a man receives is the consequence of many OLs' decisions whether to give chocolate to the man. Although each woman's decision affects the final outcome, the sum total is not reducible to an individual woman's choice. Even if a man receives only a small number of chocolates, he cannot blame a particular OL for the result. Borrowing from Scott, the bitter message that a man is unpopular among women is clear, but the messenger is unspecifiable.

Women enjoy not only the power to give the coveted chocolate but also the ability to sneak teasing and sometimes malicious feelings into the gift and get away with it. Women can do this because Valentine chocolate is understood primarily as an expression of their gratitude and ad-miration for a man. However, women sometimes give chocolate to de-clare love, to flirt, to joke, or to ridicule a man. The same medium of ex-change is used with little or no clue as to the real meaning of the gift. Therefore, as we've seen, the man working in an automobile company could not determine from the gift itself whether a woman had given him chocolate to profess her love; he had to figure it out from the way she had been treating him before the gift. Similarly, the manager who re-ceived fewer, but more expensive, boxes of chocolate than his subor-dinates could not be certain that women were expressing dislike through this subtle differentiation.

The fact that men are compelled to accept at face value the chocolate they receive explains why the men interviewed said unanimously, "I knew it was only an obligatory chocolate, but I still felt good to receive it." Even the manager who received chocolate broken into little pieces had to "thank" OLs for the gift.

It is seldom clear which potential meaning prevails in a given in-stance of chocolate-giving, and it is precisely this ambiguity that pro-vides OLs room to maneuver.[3] By keeping the meaning of chocolates unclear, women have deprived men of a way of distinguishing between gifts of gratitude and gifts of malice. I argue that malevolent gifts are accepted because the malice is often concealed under the guise of fem-ininity. The important point is that giving chocolate to profess love or to express gratitude and admiration and giving it for revenge assume the same outward appearance: both involve a woman presenting choc-olate to a man; both seem to be an act of respect and flattery paid to the man.

The intentional ambiguity of the gift's meaning is evidenced by the fact that informants chose chocolate as the appropriate gift for non-significant others—the majority of whom were male bosses and col-leagues—far more often than for significant others. Whereas chocolate-only gifts accounted for more than 90 percent of the gifts given to or received from nonsignificant others (170 out of 180 gifts), only half of the gifts to husbands and lovers were of this type. In gifts to husbands and lovers, women usually made the romantic message explicit by per-sonalizing the present. Many gave something else in addition to choco-late, such a sweater or a muffler. Some opted to present chocolate only, but made it themselves. In sharp contrast to these personalized pres-ents, chocolate given in the office was highly standardized, in line with its intentionally ambiguous meaning.

Farewell Flowers

It was not only Valentine's Day chocolate that served as a barometer of a man's popularity among women. OLs at Tōzai customarily sent flowers to male colleagues who were transferred to a new workplace. Because job rotation was prevalent among men, there were many opportunities for OLs to give such farewell flowers. One day I noticed three beautiful bouquets of flowers decorating the bare office. One with deep-red roses and white baby's breath was placed on the left-hand corner of the sales counter. On the right-hand side, there was a bunch of large, bright-colored, exotic flowers. Far in the back of the office, near the desk of a newly arrived vice-general manager, was another bouquet of crimson roses. I soon learned that they were gifts to the new manager from OLs in his former office. An OL explained, "It's really a strange custom. It's almost like Valentine's Day."

OLs' lunchtime conversation that day centered on the bouquets. OLs unanimously marveled at how gorgeous the flowers were. One woman commented on the large size of each cluster of baby's breath. Another woman thought the exotic flowers were so beautiful they could be made into a corsage. An OL summed up, "You can tell at once that they weren't given just out of obligation."

On the afternoon of the same day, a new bouquet was delivered. This one was a combination of pink roses and white baby's breath. The OL seated next to me, amazed that yet another bunch of flowers had arrived, observed, "Aren't they just gorgeous? Such large roses would each cost about seven hundred yen, so [the bouquet] must be worth at least five thousand yen." She then noticed a small slip attached to the gift by the flower shop, which read "From Yamada-sama." (*Sama* is a suffix a shop clerk attached to the customer's name to show respect.) She quickly looked up the name in the bank telephone directory and confirmed that the present was from a woman. Since Yamada-san was a member of the public relations section of the branch where the manager used to work, my colleague wondered whether the gift had been jointly sent from all the OLs working in the section.

Because the manager was out of the office at the time, the bouquet was temporarily placed on the empty desk near us. Many people stopped to appreciate the flowers whenever they passed the area. A general manager paused to look at the slip, murmured, "Mmm. From Yamada-san," and gave a meaningful smile. An OL working on the above floor came by, admired the bouquet, and added that the one they had received was also very pretty. We learned then that the manager had received yet another bunch of flowers, which he had given to OLs on the second floor. "The one on our floor is lilies, gladioli, and cymbidiums," the woman described.

OLs in the office were surprised that five bunches of flowers had been presented to the manager. One woman, who said that even three was an unusually large number, remarked, "He must have been really popular in the branch." Another was impressed that there was no bouquet with carnations, relatively inexpensive flowers in Japan. A third OL said that she felt a women-to-women message was being sent along with the flowers: Please take care of the manager that we admired very much.

Just as the number of Valentine's Day chocolates a man received measured how popular he was among women, the number of farewell bouquets indicated how well he was thought of by OLs in his former office. Therefore, OLs in the bank watched closely to see how many bouquets would be sent to the new vice-general manager and were impressed that he received as many as five. The women observed carefully what kind of flowers were being sent. The more gorgeous and expensive the flowers, the more the man was admired by his former female colleagues. As noted, it was significant that none of the bouquets the new manager received included relatively inexpensive flowers such as carnations.

As on Valentine's Day, when the difference between a popular and not-so-popular man became obvious in the open office environment, farewell bouquets demonstrated to a man's new coworkers how well he was thought of by OLs in his former office. In fact, farewell bouquets were even more conspicuous than Valentine chocolates. The flowers were usually displayed in different parts of the office, attracting the attention of whoever happened to walk by. They blossomed beautifully and gave off fragrance as though they were affirming the man's popularity among OLs.

Although there were various ways to present farewell flowers to a man, including handing them to him personally on his last day in the previous workplace, they were ordinarily delivered to his new office. This is noteworthy because, whereas the former method makes his popularity apparent only to people in his old office, the latter approach makes it evident to his new colleagues. Indeed, the flowers were often the first information that OLs received about the man. Even before he attempted to establish a relationship, they provided clues as to what sort of a person he might be. Thus farewell flowers gave a long and lasting impression of the man to people at his new office.

In addition to the two techniques of disguise—anonymity and ambiguity—identified by Scott, Japanese OLs' farewell flowers suggest a third method: refusal to engage in a customary act that pleases others. Sending farewell flowers is an act that gives pleasure to the receiver. It is supposedly done with good intentions. For example, OLs working in the branch office of Tōzai who gave flowers to the vice-general manager probably admired him very much. By sending him the bouquet, they expressed their sorrow at seeing him leave and their wishes for his success in his new assignment. It is precisely because OLs send flowers with such connotations that a man who does not receive them finds himself in an uncomfortable situation. A man without any bouquet is likely to be regarded with suspicion; he is assumed to have been disliked by OLs in his previous office. As with Valentine chocolates, women can embarrass a man by not giving him flowers. OLs' defiance thus can be found, not in the act of sending a bouquet, but in the absence of that act.

It is awkward for a man to complain that he has not received a present. Moreover, because the flowers are given sincerely, men find it difficult to reject the gift and thereby abolish the custom of farewell-flower sending. Hence, women have this third means of voicing resistance: they may safely voice rebellion by withholding a well-intentioned act. In other words, their strategy is a refusal to please the opponent, instead of directly displeasing him. A man may object if OLs cause him apparent discomfort, but he cannot complain just because they do not give him a gift.

Of course, the skillfulness of this type of defiance is evident in that OLs' refusal to send flowers is not a simple withholding of a reward. As discussed earlier, OLs in the new office observe carefully whether flowers are delivered to a man; they talk about the flowers he does (or does not) receive and compare them to those received by other men in the past. The real meaning of the denial of the reward is only to be appreciated in comparison with what other men receive. By customarily acting to please others, OLs are able to convey an unambiguous message when they do not act in this way.

That meaning is an effect of difference is well-documented in the case of language, as Timothy Mitchell writes: "Words acquire their meaning from other words, not from the accuracy with which they 'represent.' A word and its meaning turn out to be not a unique, two-sided object, but the product of interwoven relations of differences, one 'element' of which exists only in terms of others, in a weave that has no edge or exterior" (1988, 145). In OLs' gift-giving custom, not sending flowers assumes meaning only because OLs customarily send them to a man they like. The implication of inaction, therefore, lies in the difference between action and inaction. An act (including the absence of an act) can only be interpreted in terms of other acts. The meaning of an act derives not from what that singular act represents, but from relations of differences between that act and other acts.

Symbolic Gifts

I found from my interviews concerning Valentine's Day that women persist in giving chocolate to men even though many women are aware that men often do not like chocolate. A woman who worked in a general trading company said, "My brother comes home with many chocolates, but he doesn't like them. So my mother and I eat most of them. You think you might give something else because men don't like chocolate, but somehow chocolate has to go with Valentine's Day. . . . I think [a Valentine's Day gift] doesn't have meaning if there isn't a bit of chocolate in it."

Indeed, men at Tōzai did not particularly enjoy eating chocolate. One man left chocolate in his desk drawer for over a month after Valentine's Day. It was only when criticized by OLs that he apologized for his neglect and promised to take the chocolate home. Another man, overhearing that an OL was hungry, said he had something to eat and offered her the chocolate he had received from her and other OLs on Valentine's Day. It is interesting to note, in this regard, that, on normal occasions, both candies and flowers are rarely chosen as gifts for men in Japanese culture. They are thought nice gifts for women but not for men.

Both Valentine chocolate and farewell flowers are symbolic gifts. It is not primarily for their taste or beauty that men like to receive them. Rather, they are appreciated because of the significance of receiving them. It is supposed that Valentine chocolate is given to a "wonderful" man from his admirers. Farewell flowers are thought to express OLs' sad feelings to see their favorite bosses and colleagues leave. Both become the proof of a man's good reputation among women.

Were it not for the significance of receiving Valentine chocolate or farewell flowers in offices, men would not take as much interest in receiving them. The desirability of chocolate and flowers for men is created through the gift-giving process itself. Although value is often treated as a given in social exchange theories, it is an endogenous factor in the present case.[4] If a woman did not give chocolate to a man in an open office environment with the connotation that the man was one to whom she cared to send the gift, men would not care if they received chocolate and would not be dependent on women on Valentine's Day. If OLs did not observe carefully whether a man was sent flowers from his former female colleagues to indicate his popularity, men would not make much of receiving flowers. Women's temporary power over men derives from their being able to make their gifts more valuable to men than ordinary chocolate and flowers.

Conclusion

If gossiping among OLs fostered shared opinions of men, Valentine chocolate and farewell flowers made those opinions public. Because women gave gifts primarily to men they liked, both men and women gauged a man's popularity among women by the number of chocolates and bouquets he received. A man with few gifts was humiliated in the presence of his colleagues. Men found it difficult to abolish such unpleasant customs because OLs were able to assume innocence in giving gifts. OLs supposedly gave gifts to men they admired, and whoever was presented with them had few reasons to turn them down.

OLs' gift-giving was not entirely well intentioned, however; in the giving and withholding of gifts, they implicitly compared men to whom they gave gifts with those to whom they would not give anything. They delivered their evaluation of men in the giving and withholding of the gift: in not sending a present, they stated implicitly that a man was disliked. Such inaction assumed meaning not by itself, but only in comparison with action: it was disgraceful for a man not to get any chocolate or flowers because other men received these gifts. Yet a man without a present found it difficult to reproach OLs for their decision not to give a gift. Such a decision became offensive only when considered in the context of the entire gift-giving practice.

Because giving Valentine chocolate and farewell flowers was a form of popularity poll that reflected the opinions of many OLs, it was impossible for men to blame one woman or a single group of women for the results of that poll. The culprit, in other words, was unspecifiable. Some OLs enjoyed devising tactics of revenge, such as giving fewer boxes, delaying the time to give, or presenting broken chocolate, to a man they disliked. The man given such a malevolent gift was forced to receive it at its face value, because the message was disguised. He was, after all, being presented a Valentine chocolate.

Both Valentine chocolate and farewell flowers were highly symbolic gifts. Their primary significance consisted in the act of receiving them, and the presents themselves were often not particularly appreciated. Therefore, although men invariably expressed gratitude in receiving them, some left their Valentine chocolates in drawers more than a month after the holiday. This was understandable, for both chocolate and flowers were not something that men usually valued in Japanese culture. The fact that men prized gifts that they would not normally appreciate demonstrates the power and irony of symbolism.

OLs' temporary empowerment by way of chocolate and flowers may seem trivial when compared with male authority, but is certainly not unimportant. Although OLs constantly gossiped about men, such informal talk did not always lead them to agreement. Because gossip did not necessarily entail subsequent action, women did not have to consent to other's opinions. Giving Valentine's Day chocolate or farewell flowers, however, was a concrete act that required OLs to make many joint decisions. They had to agree on which men deserved to receive their gifts, how much they should spend on each gift, and what to buy. Valentine's Day and farewell flowers provided them opportunities to put their opinions into concerted action. On many occasions, their sense of togetherness increased.

OLs also collaborated on plans to exact revenge on unpopular men. Most often, these conspiracies did not result in any major change in men's attitudes toward OLs. Nevertheless, they were instrumental in bringing women together. In conspiring against men, women resolved points of disagreement, became accomplices, and partook of the secret. They united in sharing the hidden message conveyed in the gift.

5

Acts of Resistance

As we have seen, women express their opinions of men through gossip and what amount to popularity polls. Far from making light of these opinions, many men care how they are regarded by women and fear that a bad reputation makes it hard to gain office ladies' cooperation. In this chapter I investigate the extent to which these men's fears are justified. What exactly can OLs do to annoy and trouble men? How disturbed are men by such resistance? What enables women to take such action? Why do men in authority not prevent OLs from resorting to such measures? Are there limits to women's acts of resistance? What implications do these acts have on OLs' jobs and positions in the organization?

Not Taking the Initiative

As a clerical worker, I noticed that an OL always had latitude to use her discretion, however mechanical the task she was assigned. An OL, as opposed to a preprogrammed robot, could provide additional services to men if she chose to do so. The OL at Tōzai whom we met in chapter 3 worked wholeheartedly for men she called "liberal" and less cooperatively for "conservative" men. (As readers may recall, a man was considered conservative if he held traditional views of women's role.) When she typed a document for a liberal man and came across something she did not understand, she looked things up on her own accord, even if she had not been asked to do so. In contrast, for a conservative man, she did not bother to look things up but just kept typing as she saw fit, leaving it up to the man to come back to her if he found anything wrong. She said, "I know I shouldn't make such distinctions, but I can't help it." The OL thus tried to make life easier for a man she liked by voluntarily double-checking unclear points, but she refused to do the same for a man she disliked.

A banker explained why it was important to maintain a good relationship with OLs:

You're in a deep trouble if you make girls angry. As salesmen, our job is to negotiate business contracts. That's where our talent is—to strike a difficult bargain with our customers. But we tend to be a little sloppy in filling out detailed contract forms. There are really many items to fill out on those forms—the size of company capital, sales turnover, and so forth. We often forget to fill everything out. If it's a good girl, she voluntarily looks those figures up herself, and writes them in for us. But some girls return the form, saying bluntly that the document is not properly prepared.

When I asked the banker whether women differed in their attitudes according to the man they were dealing with, he replied emphatically, "Of course! It's only human for them to do so."

Many OLs I interviewed admitted that the way they worked varied according to their feelings about a man. As an OL who worked for a manufacturer of electronic communications equipment said, "If I were asked to do an ordinary, routine job, I would do work even for a man I didn't like. But let's say you see an extremely busy person. If it's someone I like or someone I respect, I offer to help. If it's someone I don't like, I pretend not to notice. I guess it's in the area of providing additional services that I discriminate in terms of how I work for a man."

A woman who worked for an electronic components trading company explained to me in detail the full discretion she and other OLs had either to act upon things they noticed, or to remain inactive about them. According to her, OLs often remembered the details of business contracts that a busy man forgot, because they spend so much time at their desks writing letters, making notes, and filing documents. It was up to the woman to remind the man of an important date, or to stay silent about it. "If it's the business of someone I don't like, I'll just let it pass. I think [what I do] makes a huge difference to the men's work," she commented.

I learned that OLs sometimes went quite far in pretending not to notice a way to help a man they did not like. A woman at Tōzai told how she knowingly placed a man in difficult circumstances. When she came back from lunch, she noticed a paper lying on the desk of a fellow OL who was taking the day off. The paper was written by a man she disliked. It read, "Urgent! Please type." She described to me how she dealt with the situation: "I caught a glimpse of the memo, but [the man] didn't say anything to me, and because it wasn't on my desk, I ignored it." Late in the afternoon, the man came over to her and said that the document must be typed at once. She told him she couldn't work overtime that day. He looked troubled but, in the end, had to be content with her promise that she would type it first thing the next morning. It was apparent from the way she told the story that she would have taken the initiative to type the manuscript if it had been for a man she liked.

Her refusal to be cooperative was bold for two reasons. First, she must have seen more than "a glimpse" of the memo because the two women's desks were situated side by side. Second, the two women worked in pairs, giving miscellaneous clerical assistance to men in three sections. If one of the women was on vacation, it was obvious that the other should make up for her absence. However, because the OL in question did not like the man who needed her assistance, she purposely ignored his memo. She knew that he would not reproach her, because the memo was not on her desk. Although the man may have sensed a certain degree of maliciousness in her act, or may have thought her careless not to have taken notice of the memo, there was little that he could do about it. (This of course raises the question of how OLs' compensation is determined. A discussion of this subject follows shortly.)

Indeed, OLs possessed a great degree of latitude to help men by taking the initiative or annoy men by not taking the initiative. This was because any instruction a man gave an OL was bound to be imperfect. Even the most capable businessman could not predict all possible events that might occur. When unforeseen incidents took place, it was up to the OL to decide what to do. In the preceding case, if the OL had been told beforehand that she should look at instructions placed on the desk of an absent OL, she probably would have found it more difficult to ignore the man's memo.

Another example of this latitude is provided by a man working for an electric wiring company, who often went on overseas business trips:

Suppose, for instance, a letter arrived during my absence. If I had a good relationship with a woman, she would check the content and send what she thinks important to the hotel where I was staying. Then I would be able to contact my customer immediately and perhaps prevent a disaster. But if I did not have a good relationship with her, she would leave the letter lying on my desk. Then there's nothing I can do about it. It would be too late to read it when I come back. I think a man can be greatly helped, or caused serious trouble, depending on the way a woman acts.

A man cannot specify all the important letters that he may receive while on a business trip, and, in any case, in the busy everyday life as a *sarariman*, he probably does not have time to give detailed directions. Discretion is left to OLs, and they can make his life easier or more difficult.

A man working in an life insurance company said he thought that an OL had many chances to exercise her discretion because it was often the person actually working on a task who noticed a better way to perform it: "For example, I ask an OL to make a chart on a computer. Oftentimes, when doing the work, she thinks of a better way to do it. Isn't it more efficient to calculate in this way? Or, isn't it better to add another column?—that sort of a thing. It makes a world of difference whether or not she voluntarily does 'something extra' that I didn't specify." He added, "It can be as simple a thing as to tell me, before being asked, that the job is complete. Then I will be able to save valuable time." A man cannot watch an OL's every move. He cannot give precise instructions about everything. The efficiency with which the job is dispatched depends upon whether an OL does only what she is asked to do, or whether she takes the initiative to do more.

Many OLs did not feel much guilt in failing to act in the strict interest of a man they disliked, because they were not neglecting their jobs. They did what they were told to do. They just did not take the initiative to do anything beyond that. OLs mentioned doing only what they were told to do as one of the measures they most frequently adopted against men they disliked. Men could not reproach OLs for failing to take the initiative, because, in the first place, they often did not recognize that OLs could have saved them trouble. If an OL remained silent, there was no way for a man to know that she knew about an approaching deadline or had thought of a better way to perform a task.

Of course, a man sometimes became suspicious of the goodwill of an OL. Although we have no way of confirming it, the man at Tōzai who mistakenly placed a memo on the desk of an absent OL probably suspected that the memo was deliberately ignored by her coworker. Similarly, a man working in a general trading company thought that when his female assistant got angry at him, she purposely refrained from informing him of mistakes he had made:

We all make mistakes, you know. Well, the woman sometimes doesn't tell me even if she notices my mistake. A word from her would prevent all the trouble, and yet she says nothing. . . . Girls rarely go out of their way to make trouble for men. I mean, they won't *purposely* write different things or tell a lie. But there *are* cases when they won't do anything even if they notice that something is wrong. They know very well that it will be a big mess if things are left as they are, and yet they won't take any action, thinking that it's not their responsibility.

As this statement demonstrates, a man sometimes became skeptical of OLs' sincerity, but there was not much that he could do about it. He had no way of proving that an OL had deliberately overlooked a mistake, that she was aware of an approaching deadline but remained silent, or that she knew a letter was important enough to forward. The most he could do was to click his tongue to suggest that the woman was a little careless.

Declining to Do Favors

Not only do many OLs refrain from taking the initiative to help men they dislike, but they sometimes decline these men's requests to do extra work. An OL working in a construction company gave the following example:

Sometimes we are asked to attend a dinner with a customer. But we think our duty is to do a good job during the day. There's no reason why we have to entertain customers after five. Besides, we aren't paid overtime. So attending such dinners is a favor that we do. Whether we'll attend or not ultimately depends on our relationship with the person who made the request. For example, if we remember that the general manager treated us to dinner the other day, we will probably go. It's almost as though general managers were currying favor with us, isn't it? [*Giggles.*] Some managers are not popular with women, and we never comply with any of their requests. They know that we won't, too, and so they rarely ask. These managers entertain their customers by playing golf instead.[1]

The OL thought that the difference in a woman's treatment of a man became most apparent in the extent to which she was willing to do him a favor.

An OL working for a general trading company said that a man had a much easier time working if he could gain OLs' support, because he would then receive various kinds of personal assistance from them:

If a woman were on your side, you could feel free to ask her to do things for you. For instance, if you had to go on a business trip, you could ask her to take care of small, day-to-day matters. Or, if you were transferred overseas, you could ask her to send you books and research materials. If you were disliked, a woman would never do these things for you. She would create an atmosphere that would make it difficult for you to ask in the first place.

Many men and women told me that it was customary for an OL to create an atmosphere that made it either easy or hard for a man to ask for a favor, depending on the man concerned.[2]

That women have the power to decline to do a favor was brought home to me one day, when an OL seated near me in the bank resisted a request from a vice-general manager of another department. The woman was preparing materials that were to be used in a meeting the following day. It was almost time to go home, and she was about to finish stapling thirty-eight copies of a thick report, when the vice-general manager called and asked her to replace a page in each report. Replacing a page meant she had to make thirty-eight copies of the new page, unbind the stapled reports, insert the newly copied pages into the appropriate section, take out the old pages, and restaple the packages. She agreed to do the job only if the manager came and helped her with it. Because he did not wish to be bothered making copies and binding packages, he withdrew his request. The woman must have felt she had acted rather boldly, because, upon hanging up, she said, "Mmm. I've taken an aggressive attitude toward Vice-General Manager Ozawa." The man seated next to her asked in a bewildered voice, "*That* was Vice-General Manager Ozawa?" Apparently, he could not believe that she would refuse a request made by someone so high in the hierarchy.[3]

Part of the reason the OL was able to decline the manager's request was because it was made considerably after the time by which men were expected to submit reports for copying and binding. Complying with his request, therefore, was not a duty but a favor. However, it was equally clear from the reaction of the man seated near the OL that if the manager had asked a man to do the favor, there would have been no resistance. After all, it was not just anybody who made the request, but a vice-general manager. Men who compete in the race for promotion must make a good impression on high-ranking managers. These men do not have a choice—they must do favors. In contrast, most OLs do not need to worry about pleasing managers because they are excluded from the competition for advancement.

The OL working for a construction company also said she was unconcerned whether the man asking for a favor was a general manager. If a general manager whom she did not like asked her to do something that she considered an "additional service," she refused politely, saying, "I'm terribly sorry, but I'm very busy right now. Would you please do it yourself?" She explained why she could take such a strong attitude even toward a man of high rank and office:

It's OK to refuse. I won't be put in a difficult position because of it. In a way, I'm turning my weakness into strength. After all, if it makes no difference to your promotion whether or not you say something, isn't it to your advantage to say whatever you want to say? Men must try hard to flatter their bosses. In our company, men get evaluated by demerit marks. They have, for example, one hundred points in the beginning, and points get deducted whenever they make mistakes. Your boss's evaluation of you is sent to the personnel department. But in women's case, we get the same grade regardless of whether we do well or not. We get promoted at the same time. You have to do something really exceptionally wrong in order not to be promoted with everybody else—like being absent from the office for months. I know only of two cases in the past where a woman was not promoted together [with her colleagues]. Such cases are really very rare, and in any event, if worse comes to worst, I can always quit the company.

Because of the group treatment of OLs and the ineffectiveness of their evaluation (see chapter 1), women were seldom called to account for their deeds, except for truly grave offenses. Moreover, because most OLs did not have a career in the company that could be jeopardized, even a senior manager had limited power to extract favors from them. Only OLs had the luxury of remaining sublimely indifferent to office hierarchy and refusing to do a favor.

Refusing to Work

The situation became much more serious when OLs refused not only to do favors but also to work. When a man she did not like asked her to perform a task, an OL might say, "Not now, because I'm busy." Or she might agree and then neglect the task. When the man asked for the completed assignment, she could say that she had been too busy to do it. OLs could make these excuses because most of them did not work for one boss; on the floor where I conducted research, OLs worked in pairs for three sections. Each section consisted of approximately five men including a section manager. Even the two secretaries worked for as many as six general and vice-general managers. Considering that two of the general managers were board members, this short supply of secretarial assistance, which was probably designed to keep personnel expenses to the minimum, was surprising.

At any given moment, few men on the floor had full knowledge of the jobs assigned to an OL. Even if a section manager knew what the members of his section had asked a woman to do, he was not usually aware of the contents of the jobs assigned to her by other section members over whom he had no jurisdiction. Therefore, it was primarily up to the woman to decide which job to do first. A man could not order a woman to do his job before others: if he did, he would be put in the embarrassing situation of having to quarrel with other section members about job priority.

Both men and women mentioned that making arbitrary decisions about job priorities was a frequent tactic used by OLs to put off doing the work of a disliked man. The following statement of a man working in a home electronics company is representative:

[Before I came to this new section,] I worked in a sales department. During the day, men work in the field while women look after things in the office. A man is in trouble if he can't get women to cooperate. I mean, it seems like a very common thing for a girl to do the word-processing or typing for a man she likes first. In our company, the ratio of men to women is about six to two, and so we must scramble for women's help. . . . Let's say a girl was asked to do a word-processing job by Mr. A, B, and C. Because she likes Mr. A, she works hard on his job, and it's finished by the time men come back from sales calls late in the afternoon. Mr. B's work is half done, whereas she hasn't even started on Mr. C's. The girl leaves the office, and Mr. C must type by himself at night. We can't ask girls to take responsibility for work. If a girl says she has an appointment that evening, there isn't much we can do. You have to type it yourself instead.

According to this man, most men hesitate to ask an OL to stay late against her will. After all, he said, she is one of the precious few OLs they have. The man added, "There are no other alternative resources. If you remember that you must ask for her help again tomorrow, you will let her leave when she wishes."

As discussed in chapter 1, men in typical Japanese organizations were dependent on OLs for the services they provided. Sexual division of labor, such as men's engagement in sales activity in the field while OLs typed documents in the office, reinforced men's reliance on OLs. Some men's vulnerability was further aggravated by their ignorance of how to handle office work.

In a sense, men could not help being ignorant of the specifics of office work because of job rotation. In Tōzai Bank, as in many other

Japanese companies, men regularly rotated jobs in order to gain the work experience and knowledge necessary to become competent managers. A man stayed, on average, two to three years on the bank floor and then moved on to his next assignment. In contrast, OLs rarely moved to different sections. Therefore, OLs accumulated detailed knowledge of how things were done in a particular office and passed this knowledge to subsequent generations of OLs, whereas a man learned from them each time anew. I witnessed many a newly transferred man trailing an OL like a student, being taught where things were kept and how things were done on the floor. From the OLs' perspective, the male newcomer assumed a lowly posture until he became used to the new environment.

The degree of a man's vulnerability was closely related to his self-sufficiency. Some men preferred to take care of themselves rather than be dependent on OLs. A man who worked for a general trading company said that although men's job was primarily to negotiate business with customers and that it was women's job to issue invoices, he taught himself how to write out slips. He thought he would be made light of by women if he did not know what they did, and, in this way, he could correct any mistake he found on a slip instead of relying completely on OLs. Similarly, a man working in another bank said he did not have to curry women's favor like some of the other men, because he made it a point to do things by himself as much as possible.

However, there were limits to a man's self-sufficiency. Even the trading company businessman admitted that a man capable of taking perfect care of himself must still ask for women's help, because "he has only one body." Similarly, a security analyst thought a man would be in a difficult position if he made enemies of OLs, because it was inefficient to try to do everything by himself: "I'm really greatly helped by OLs. They type and make copies for me. I can do these things by myself, but I ask for their help, because it's more efficient that way. They're much better at word-processing than I am. It would take me four hours to type something that takes them only an hour."

Sometimes a woman monopolized miscellaneous clerical work, thereby increasing her power within an office. An OL who joined a rubber products manufacturer a few years ago remembered how her then-senior OL refused to share work:

She was the type who thought that there needn't be two housewives in a kitchen. She liked to be in charge of everything. When she was not at her desk and men asked me where certain files were kept, I usually couldn't answer. It was only natural that everybody thought her more valuable and important. Men were more considerate to her than to me. Some men told me that maybe she did it on purpose. Maybe she tried to do everything by herself, knowing that by doing so she could get even managers to listen to her opinions.

In most offices, the workload was too great for one OL to monopolize jobs, and the dependence of men was not usually a source of divisiveness among OLs. However, more experienced OLs tended to wrestle more power from men's reliance on their knowledge than junior OLs.

Gaining OLs' cooperation was important for men to carry out their work efficiently. For those men who had not learned the basics of how to take care of themselves in the office, it was an absolute necessity. A man could be in serious trouble if OLs postponed doing his work. The OLs' ability to assign job priority according to their tastes was, therefore, an extremely powerful weapon. They felt relatively uninhibited in resorting to this measure, because they knew that men found it difficult to criticize their acts. After all, it was not that they were neglecting work; they just preferred a certain sequence of jobs over others.

In rare instances, however, an OL's refusal to work for a man was much more direct. She would refuse his request so many times, each time making an excuse that she was busy, that the man became suspicious of her willingness to help him. In extreme cases, she would simply stop doing any work for him. Although such outright resistance was much more likely to incur condemnation than the subtler method of postponing work, OLs sometimes got away with it. This was because, in many Japanese companies, it was ultimately men's responsibility to get work done. If it was necessary to ask for OLs' cooperation in the process of doing the job, then obtaining their assistance was also an important task. A truly capable manager was, in this sense, one who was able to raise the morale of his subordinates, including OLs. If a man could not get along with women, that indicated that he was an incompetent manager. In this context, an OL's refusal to cooperate with a man was equally—if not more—his fault.

A man working for an electric wiring company described how his assistant had "boycotted" him ever since they quarreled one day. He had hoped that the woman would distinguish between her private anger and her attitude toward work, but that was not the case. When he asked the OL to send a telex, she agreed to do it but then ignored the task. Asked when she would send the telex, she kept repeating that she would do it "soon." Completely at a loss, the man finally went to his boss and told him that he could not get his assistant's cooperation. Instead of reproaching the OL, the boss criticized the man for not knowing how to manage women. In the end, the man had to teach himself how to type and send a telex. "It was a bitter, humiliating experience," he said.

When he had a chance to think things over calmly, he decided the reason he had made an enemy of the OL was because, being new to the department, he had unwittingly ignored the tacit agreement that existed there between men and women. Men in the department went on overseas business trips regularly, which sometimes lasted for as long as one to two months. During their long absence, they had to rely on OLs to look after business at home:

Because you're gone for a few months, things come up that you just can't do by yourself. You have to ask women to be your hands and legs and, for example, send out a letter. You must manage women well, or else you will be hard-pressed. In order to ask women to look after things while you're away, you curry their favor. It's to your disadvantage if you offend them.

He realized that there was a peculiar atmosphere in his department: "It was almost as if men feared women. They treated women with utmost care." Because men were dependent on women to attend to matters during their extensive overseas trips, they carefully avoided offending their feelings. It was an unwritten law that men must try to please women. However, being new to the department, the man did not understand this rule. Because he frankly said things that "even a twenty-year veteran manager would not say," he thought his attitude appeared arrogant to his assistant OL and provoked her antipathy.

The assistant OL's boycott continued for more than a year. To make matters worse, the woman influenced the views of other OLs, which resulted in many women harboring hostile feelings toward the man. Eventually, he was transferred to a subsidiary company in a northern city far from the company headquarters in Tokyo. His male colleague who first introduced me to him wondered if his new appointment was, in effect, a demotion for not getting along with the women.

At the end of the interview, the man said he had learned the hard way that it was extremely important to get along with OLs. He now paid more respect to women's feelings. He changed the way he says things, in order to get his point across without inviting women's hostility:

I think one can call someone a full-fledged businessman only when he has learned how to truly manage women. In fact, one of a businessman's most important jobs may be to draw forth women's willingness to work. There are no women nowadays who obediently do what they are told to do. You must amuse women. I mean, things go better if you first have a friendly talk with them about something unrelated to work, rather than abruptly discussing business. It has an immediate effect on their attitudes toward you if you cheer up the atmosphere by talking about last night's TV program, for example. If you're able to make women laugh, then you're almost guaranteed success.

Notice that it is the man instead of his female assistants who tries to be pleasant. This is the exact opposite of what Arlie Hochschild predicts concerning emotion management between men and women (1983).

Completely refusing to work is a less ambiguous act of resistance than arbitrarily deciding job priority. I did not see any OL boycott work in the bank during the time I worked there, and it is not easy to imagine a woman taking things that far. As discussed in chapters 2 and 3, women cared about their reputation and were flattered when men in the office treated them well. A rebellious OL ran the risk of being considered unfeminine and becoming unpopular among many male workers if she openly and aggressively refused to do any work rather than subtly failed to take initiative or declined to do favors. However, the story of the assistant who boycotted her male coworker demonstrates that women sometimes resorted to drastic measures.

It is important to note that it was not the woman but the man who was penalized for her refusal to work. As we have seen, OLs were seldom held liable for work, whereas men were usually saddled with the responsibility to gain women's cooperation. A man's potential as a manager was called into question if he did not get along with women. The thinking went: Sure, some OLs might be a little spoiled. They might grumble that they did not want to work. But it was up to the men, the real businessmen, to soothe their complaints.

Given these facts, we can understand how men in authority sometimes fail to prevent women's resistance. It is dangerous for a *sarariman* to rely on his formal power in the organization to get OLs to cooperate, because the very act of doing so may reveal his lack of competence as a manager. A good boss is one who can skillfully draw forth his subordinates' willingness to work. It must appear that it is his personal charm (*jintoku*) that motivates women to work hard. In other words, OLs are supposed to work overtime because they want to help a man, not because they are ordered to do so.

Frank Upham characterizes the Japanese legal system as informal

(1987). The emphasis on consultation and consensus rather than on formal power to gain compliance helps support the "particularistic web of relationships that animates Japanese society" (207). Similarly, in a Japanese workplace where consensus and harmony are valued, it is considered abrasive to use formal power to coerce compliance. A man may have formal power, but it is power he can seldom use openly, lest his ability as a manager be called into question.[4]

Telling Tales to the Personnel Department

In many companies, it was customary for the personnel department to review workers' performance and progress once or twice a year. As part of this review, the personnel department inquired about employees' satisfaction with their work, their objectives for the future, and their requests or complaints. Reviews in Japanese companies therefore usually included "upward feedback" in the form of self-evaluation written or declared by the reviewee. In the bank where I worked, this review amounted to no more than a ritual for OLs. Although some managers asked women what they would like to achieve in the coming term, most were unconcerned with their performance and progress. An OL told me that, at one time, the progress review consisted solely of the manager querying each OL to confirm that she did not yet have any plans for marriage.[5]

In some organizations, the review was taken more seriously: the personnel department distributed questionnaires to the employees, or members of the division conducted personal interviews. Because managers feared that the personnel department might doubt their ability to supervise subordinates, they were concerned with employees' responses. Occasionally, they tried to censor the content of the interviews and questionnaires. An OL working in a leasing company remembered a rumor that spread in her workplace: "A woman wrote on her performance appraisal form that she wanted to be transferred to a different department. It was said that her boss put pressure on her to modify her comments, because they would cast doubt on his managerial capability. The woman must have talked about this to the people around her, because I heard indirectly that she was forced to rewrite [her comments]." The manager attempted to prevent the woman from recording what he judged to be harmful to his reputation, but he could not stop the rumor from spreading.

Some companies had a strict rule against censorship. A banker told me that there was an annual personnel review form in his organization, which each employee filled in. Section managers were allowed to read and attach short comments on the reviews but could not censor them. The banker's boss once confessed to him a fear of what OLs would write, because he could lose face if they wrote that they did not like him. If they did write such a thing, he was afraid he might be judged as someone with low supervisory ability. The man explained to me:

A man cannot write bad things about his boss. Writing such a thing will only do him harm. It'll only make him look bad. So, instead of writing about other people, you usually write about yourself—what you want to do in the future—that sort of thing, and it becomes a very stereotypical review. But women write whatever they want to write, because they don't have to worry about promotion.

The man then explained how a manager could be put in a difficult position as a result of his female subordinates' reviews. In his company, only general managers were allowed the luxury of having personal secretaries. A section manager, therefore, ran into trouble if the personnel department found out that he used OLs primarily to reserve a meeting room or call a taxi:

People in our personnel department say they can tell how a section manager uses women by reading those reviews. For example, it's not good if a woman writes in a column where she's supposed to describe her job that she's taking care of a section manager's various needs. It gives the impression that the manager is using the woman to provide him personal services. My section manager says the section manager in the next room is in trouble because women have written such a thing about him.

This man's story demonstrates the importance for managers of what OLs write in the annual review.

Men must be careful of what they write in reviews because it has an impact on their chances for advancement. Therefore, the comments they make in their reviews tend to be bland and routine. In contrast, most OLs can write without constraint. Having little prospect of promotion, they do not need to worry about the impact the review will have on their own performance evaluations.[6]

OLs can also embarrass managers by the way they retire from the workplace. We have seen in chapter 2 that companies stress the importance of an OL's *enman taisha* (harmonious separation from the workplace, as when a woman leaves to marry). *Enman taisha* is desirable because the personnel department is informed well in advance of an OL's plan to leave and can adjust its recruitment plan accordingly. In contrast, unanticipated resignation is a problem. A company cannot fill vacancies in the middle of the business term, and the understaffed office must endure great inconvenience for the rest of the year.[7]

Enman taisha is also desirable because it does not look awkward. In many offices, OLs are expected to retire from workplace early in their career. As we have seen, a manager is thought to have done the right thing if he encourages OLs' early marriage and retirement. It is a different matter, however, if a woman says she is resigning because she is dissatisfied with her work environment. Such termination leads people to doubt her manager's ability to look after his subordinates, because it is ultimately the manager's responsibility to ensure the happiness of subordinates with their work and with each other.

Based on his observation of work relations in a Japanese manufacturer of corrugated board and boxes, Rodney Clark describes the workplace's emphasis on harmonious human relations, whose maintenance was the responsibility of a manager. He writes that the leader "had to look after the interests of his subordinates and to see that they all got along together" (1979, 200). To this end, the company made available small sums of money to all managers so that they could take their subordinates bowling or to a restaurant.

Under the circumstances, a man would be put in an awkward situation if a number of OLs in his office quit one after another for reasons other than *enman taisha*. Thomas Rohlen (1974) compares such quitting and retirement for marriage in a Japanese regional bank and reports that if several women successively quit from the same office, the manager might be transferred and demoted.[8]

The reason for an OL's retirement often becomes known by word of mouth, but it is also usually made official in the letter of resignation she submits to the personnel department. A woman who used to work for a general trading company wrote "marriage" as the reason for her retirement from the workplace, although her true motive was to change her occupation. She explained why she had disguised her true intention: "I reported 'marriage retirement,' although I could have continued to work even after marriage and the true reason was to change my job. I figured it might be offensive to say I wished to resign because I wanted to change jobs. And it was true that I was getting married. So I made it a marriage retirement instead of something else." Because the woman did not want to discomfit her boss and others at the workplace, she gave a reason for leaving that was not exactly true.

However, OLs sometimes use the letter of resignation to convey a message to the personnel department, as indicated by a woman working in an iron and steel company: "You know, you usually just write a sentence or two in your letter of resignation that you're retiring for marriage or for personal reasons. Well, this woman who was quitting because she got into a fight with a general manager wrote an unusually long letter in which she described how unreasonable the general manager had been to her." She told me that the letter of resignation written by the angry woman was still spoken of in her company.

Men and women held different views of leaving a company, just as their attitudes toward annual reviews differed. Women could get in a fight with a tyrannical manager and quit the company, but men would endure the tyranny of the manager because they could not resign as readily as women could. The woman with the iron and steel company noted, "Men are also victims of this general manager, but in case of men, they simply persevere. If the general manager is your boss, your attitude toward him will be reflected on the evaluation of your performance. So they put up with him." A similar comparison between the reactions of men and women under unpleasant circumstances was made by a man working for a life insurance company:

A woman acts according to her emotion. There's no promotion for her. She doesn't intend to stick with the job for the rest of her life. She can quit whenever she wants to. She's not bound to the company. A man must get along with his boss even if he doesn't like him. Of course, what I'm saying is not really the difference between men and women, but the difference between the type of occupation. Anyway, a man must get a good appraisal and make his way up the company ladder. In contrast, a woman doesn't have to work for long. She can complain, and she can quarrel. . . . If you treat a woman as you would a man and scold her for her mistake, she'll say she'll quit. Or she'll turn away and ignore you. She doesn't have trouble quitting the company, because she doesn't have to earn her daily bread. But a man cannot quit.

According to this man, it was difficult to supervise OLs, because unlike men who attempt to control their emotions, women often do not suppress their anger. A manager must therefore maintain a delicate balance between not indulging an OL completely and avoiding the embarrassing situation of having her quit abruptly.

To summarize, men in general have the responsibility to support a family. Under the circumstances, they cannot resign from a company merely because they do not like the boss or because they have been treated unpleasantly. In contrast, most OLs do not need to earn a living or support a family and are therefore freer to express their true feelings. These women do not have to endure an unpleasant work environment. They can write bad things about their boss in the annual progress review conducted by the personnel department. They can quit the company. These unrestrained acts of an OL are problematic for managers who work hard to give the impression that they are competent supervisors. What a woman writes in the review and in the letter of resignation, and how she retires from the workplace, can undermine a man's position in the workplace.

Sōsukan

One of the most humiliating forms of resistance a man may meet with from OLs is what both men and women call *sōsukan* (total neglect). In this, not only the man's assistant but other OLs (often all the women in the department) join together to let him and other men know that he is disliked. In giving *sōsukan* to a man, OLs minimize the amount of words they exchange with him. If the man attempts to start a conversation with an OL by saying how beautiful the weather is, she will reply with a curt "Yes." In contrast, with other men she may smile, agree, and even add that she is planning to go play tennis after work. OLs hurry to leave the presence of the man they detest.

An OL working in a general trading company told me that in her department it was an open secret that women drew lots to decide who was to sit next to a despised man at a dinner party. The OL who had to sit next to him was said to have "drawn the winning number." However, because in a Japanese-style party people move around, the seat next to the man became vacant as soon as the opportunity arrived for the woman to leave, and remained unoccupied for the rest of the night.

Sōsukan occurs relatively infrequently because it must be supported by many OLs. It is not easy for women divided by the company's policies to agree to take this unambiguous act of resistance (see chapter 2). Nevertheless, it occurs. In fact, OLs seemed to agree more readily that a certain man should be condemned than that sex-discriminatory company policies should be corrected. As we have seen, OLs seldom discussed issues concerning the inequitable status of men and women.

They knew that their views toward the Equal Employment Opportunity Law differed, for example, according to their educational background and for the most part carefully avoided talking about such potentially disruptive topics. In contrast, gossip about men was a safe subject that all women could participate in. Everyday lunchtime gossip helped foster common views among OLs concerning men (see chapter 3).

In the office where I worked, *sōsukan* only occurred on a small scale: a man was treated coldly by all three women in his section. The man incurred the women's anger by leaving the office early several times to play mah-jongg while the three OLs worked overtime. The OLs knew he was to transfer to a new section in a few months. They supposed he took such a seemingly irresponsible attitude because he no longer cared for his present colleagues and work. Then, one day, an administrative manager came to the man and cautioned him that the three OLs in his section were putting in too much overtime. Surprised, the man went over to one of the OLs and asked her, "Why are you so busy?" His question enraged the already unhappy OL. She recounted her feelings later: "Why are we busy? He's our boss! He should know why we're busy! It just shows how little he cares about us. What kind of a boss is it that doesn't recognize how busy his subordinates are until someone else comes and tells him? Of course, he doesn't know. He's been too busy playing mah-jongg!" Needless to say, she told the other OLs what had happened. And *sōsukan* began.

The three women would not speak to the man. When necessary, they spoke to him in an extremely cold, businesslike manner. When he asked them questions, they answered curtly, "I don't know" or "It's not my business." Other times, they replied bluntly without even looking up from their desk. They handed him documents without speaking. Their cold behavior was so blatant that soon most people in the office noticed. Some men tried to soothe the women's feelings: they casually mentioned to the OLs that the man regretted his actions and assured them that he was really a good person. This had no effect. The OLs felt that they had to pack as much resistance as possible into the two months remaining before he transferred to another department, in order to let him know how angry they were.

Eventually the man moved out of the office, and one of the men on the floor took over his position. The successor had not been particularly popular among the three OLs; they were at first considerably disappointed to hear of the appointment. However, much to their surprise, the new boss turned out to be pleasant to work with. He took all three women to an expensive restaurant for lunch on the first day, and on days when the OLs continued to work after five, he always asked them why they were busy. He often offered to help them when they worked overtime, saying humbly, "I'll help you. Please tell me what I can do." When they did not leave for lunch at the designated time, he encouraged them to drop work and take a rest, asking, "OK. Whose turn is it to take a lunch break?" He also chatted frequently with them. Contrary to Hochschild's argument (1983), it was the boss, not his female subordinates, who made an effort to maintain good human relations. Although I have no way of knowing for sure, his attitude toward the OLs may have been influenced by his predecessor's punishment with *sōsukan*.

Besides the *sōsukan* that took place in a section of the office, there was a rumor that the newly transferred vice-general manager had experienced *sōsukan* in his former office. Soon after his arrival, the manager won OLs' favor in our workplace because he was considerate and kind to female workers. He lacked arrogance and always nodded acknowledgment whenever someone brought him tea. One Friday evening when he learned that a group of OLs were going skiing on the weekend, he hurried out of the office to buy them cookies and candies to take on the trip. One of the OLs later found out that he had paid six thousand yen for the sweets.

The manager also listened to women's complaints and tried to solve their problems. For example, a woman was frustrated because she was retiring from the bank soon and her successor had not yet been appointed. When a small group of men and women, including the OL and the vice-general manager, went for a drink after work, she told them how annoyed she was that she might not have enough time to transfer her job smoothly to the new person. Upon hearing her complaint, the manager promised that he would see what he could do.

It turned out that the manager could not do much to solve the woman's problem. Several days later, he came to her and apologized for his inability to help. Despite his failure, the OL was grateful that he had remembered her and had showed concern. She later recounted: "I didn't expect him to actually look into the matter. He's really busy, and anyway, we were all a little drunk. I thought he had forgotten all about it. Then he came over to me and apologized for not being able to help. I was deeply touched!" Another OL was impressed by the manager's politeness. When he had to answer a phone call at her desk, he took out his handkerchief and wiped the receiver after hanging up. "I've never seen any man so courteous to an OL," she said.

Because the vice-general manager had worked on another floor of the building before moving to a position at a regional branch and then returning to take a job on our floor, some OLs already knew him. These OLs were mystified by his current attitude. They all said that he was not such a nice manager before, and that it was as if he had become a totally different man. Soon the mystery was solved. The manager confessed while drinking with a small group of men and women that he had endured *sōsukan* from the women in the regional branch and decided to amend his attitude toward OLs.

When the woman who heard the manager's confession told me the story, I at first could not believe that OLs could influence the views of someone so high in the organizational hierarchy and, moreover, change the way he treated women. When I expressed my disbelief, the woman shrugged her shoulders and said, "But he would have gotten into big trouble if many girls said out loud that they didn't want to work with him. What if their voices reached the personnel department? He could have completely lost his credibility as a manager." Even his position as a vice-branch manager did not protect him from *sōsukan* by OLs.

I do not wish to suggest that hierarchy has no effect on OLs. In the bank, general and vice-general managers as well as branch managers and vice-branch managers had greater power to influence personnel management than employees in lower ranks. OLs knew this and behaved differently toward these senior managers than toward junior managers and other men. For instance, when none of the general and vice-general managers were at their desks, OLs would seize the opportunity to take a break. In addition, OLs rarely criticized senior managers during lunchtime gossip. It was also common for them to put higher priority on the jobs requested by senior managers.

It should be noted, however, that Japanese managers' power over personnel decisions about OLs is relatively limited compared with that of their American counterparts, who often hire and fire their own secretaries. In a typical Japanese company, recruitment and assignment of positions is the task solely of the personnel department. Tōzai Bank was no exception. Of course, great importance was attached to the opinion of managers, and therefore it was essential that a man make a good impression on his boss. But in the case of OLs, the situation was different. The bank did not seriously evaluate OLs' performance, and their individual talents were seldom taken into account because they were treated in a lump as "girls" (see chapter 1). The personnel management of OLs was considerably less important for the company than that of men.

At Tōzai, the ability of OLs was considered as more or less fixed. Departments had to make do with whichever OLs were allotted to them. The underlying assumption was that a truly good manager should be able to supervise OLs well even if they gave him slight trouble. And it was unheard of to fire employees. As we have seen, the company sometimes pressured older OLs indirectly into retirement, but outright dismissal was out of the question. In this way, an OL's position in a department was relatively secure and free from the influence of her boss.

Managers' limited power over OLs was reflected in an expression I heard OLs use frequently: "unless you do something *grossly* wrong" (*yohodo no koto o shinai kagiri*), assignment and compensation remain the same. The fact that their security was conditional on avoiding gross mistakes meant that an OL might lose her battle with a manager if she resorted to outright acts of resistance such as completely refusing to do his work. *Sōsukan*, however, was an entirely different means to resist. Because it was a movement supported by many OLs, even a high-ranking manager with power over personnel management could be defenseless against it. After all, to penalize an OL for "doing something grossly wrong" was one thing, but it was quite another to assert that many OLs had acted improperly. A man who made such an assertion embarrassed himself by disclosing his inability to supervise OLs.

Conclusion

To annoy and trouble a man, OLs can refuse to take the initiative to help him, they can decline to do him favors, they can refuse to work for him, they can inform the personnel department of his disagreeable behavior, and they can shut him out with *sōsukan*. In the first three forms of resistance, women adopt uncooperative attitudes toward a man and thereby affect the efficiency and effectiveness of his work. The latter two acts of resistance harm his reputation. These acts of resistance, however, do not necessarily take place independently. In fact, an unpopular man is likely to meet OLs' defiance in various forms. In particular, a man being given *sōsukan* usually cannot escape other rebellious attitudes of women.

Such resistance disturbs men, because men are usually dependent on women for clerical assistance. Division of labor between the sexes and frequent job rotation for men reinforce their unfamiliarity with how things run in a particular office. Men often have to rely on OLs to show them where certain documents are kept, how forms must be filled out, and how to operate office machines. Under such circumstances, OLs' refusal to cooperate can be considerably annoying. Likewise, the threat to damage men's reputation is effective on many occasions, because the keen competition for promotion renders men vulnerable to suspicion about their ability to supervise subordinates.

Why can't men prevent OLs' defiant behavior? James Scott argues in his research on resistance that powerless groups are rarely allowed the luxury of direct confrontation with the powerful and that they therefore resort to disguised resistance. He maintains that subordinate groups are usually subtle and that their ideological resistance is "disguised, muted, and veiled for safety's sake" (1990, 137). Similarly, researchers who have examined women's informal means of control emphasize the covert and indirect nature of women's power (Bourdieu 1977; Boddy 1989; Gullestad 1984; Rogers 1975). According to these analyses, we would expect that men are unable to take action against OLs' resistance because OLs disguise their defiance.

Indeed, some of the OLs' acts of resistance are ambiguous in nature. In not taking the initiative to assist a man, an OL does only what she is told to do. She just does not do anything beyond that even if she recognizes that she can help. Although a man sometimes becomes suspicious of her goodwill, he has no way of proving that she has intentionally looked the other way when she could have spared him trouble. Postponing work is also not easy to reproach, because assigning job priority is left to a woman's discretion. An OL usually works for a number of men, and it is awkward for a man to insist that she attend to his job first.

Yet in examining OLs' resistance to men, it is the audacity and overtness of some of their actions that surprise and impress me. Contrary to the argument that subordinate groups exercise self-control and employ indirect expression, Japanese OLs often do not hide their angry feelings from men. They write bad things about their bosses in the performance reviews conducted by the personnel department. Various men have repeatedly described how they take pains to soothe women who complain uninhibitedly about their male bosses and colleagues. An OL working for a real-estate company said that she had once told her boss that perhaps she could speak more freely than he could:

There are not many men who speak to women in a highhanded, authoritative tone. My *kachō-san* laughed when I told him that I could probably say what I want to say more than he could. It's the truth, though. Men cannot say things, because the thought of getting promoted fetters them. . . . I don't think women feel that they are oppressed. It's true that we're not entrusted with an interesting job, but our position is not that uncomfortable. You get paid reasonably for working reasonably, and if you think it's only for a short period of time until you get married, it's really not that bad.

The OL was comfortable with her current working arrangement, because she could have her say. She said that when she was busy, she did not hesitate at all to decline a man's request for help.

As suggested by the preceding quotation, OLs can take overtly uncooperative attitudes toward men because OLs hold a belittled position within Japanese organizations. Most OLs have limited authority with regard to their work, and they lack ultimate responsibility. They are seldom penalized for performing poorly. It matters little to them if something goes wrong when they neglect to take the initiative to help a man they dislike. It is generally regarded as men's task to nurture OLs' willingness to do a good job. If an OL refuses to work for a man, he is often held equally, if not more, responsible for her lack of enthusiasm. In many cases, a man cannot use his formal power to enforce compliance, because doing so declares his inability to gain women's support. Women usually do not hesitate to give *sōsukan* to even a high-ranking manager, knowing that the manager has relatively little practical power over personnel management. Because most men are saddled with the burden of proving themselves competent managers, it is to their disadvantage to call to the personnel department's attention the fact that OLs won't cooperate with them.

Most OLs are excluded from the benefits of the internal labor market that men enjoy. They have limited opportunities for promotion, and their compensation usually rises at a fixed rate and only by a small percent. Lacking incentive to care about their performance or the impression they leave on their bosses, they remain largely indifferent to organizational hierarchy. A man's high rank has far less effect on OLs' attitudes toward him than it has on other men's attitudes. Women do not need to please managers and are seldom intimidated into doing favors for them. Because most OLs do not intend to stay with the company for the rest of their lives, they need not put up with men they do not like. They record what they wish about their bosses in performance reviews. And if worse comes to worst, they can quit the company, unlike men, who must almost always continue working to support their families.

The system rarely rewards OLs who should be rewarded or punishes those who should be punished. The combination of low incentive and minimal penalty makes some OLs take unmistakably bold actions. As the woman working for a construction company said, OLs "turn their weakness into strength" when they interact with men in an almost blunt manner.

To conclude, I wish to consider the limits and implications of OLs' acts of resistance. The reason why OLs are able to assume such strong attitudes toward men is because they take advantage of the discrimination against OLs. They do not have to worry about getting work done, being promoted, or holding onto their jobs as men must do. What makes their acts of resistance possible, in other words, is the renunciation of their responsibilities as professional businesspeople.

This is not to say that all OLs lack awareness of themselves as professionals. Indeed, some OLs said they hesitate to refuse to do any work for a particular man, because they think such refusal is unprofessional. An OL who used to work for a general trading company commented, "If you remember that you're being paid, it's hard to go that far." Another OL working for a different trading company, who had a longer tenure (seventeen years) with the firm than most OLs, did not enjoy being indulged by men. She explained:

Men treat women with utmost care not to offend us. They never scold women. Even if women chit-chat endlessly and neglect their jobs, the boss says nothing. I hate that. You know why? I hate it, because it's not real kindness. It's better to be scolded when necessary. Managers raise their voices at men, but never at women. That's discrimination, don't you think? They just want women to create a cheerful atmosphere and quit in a couple of years. It's depressing. They don't expect anything more from us, and so they indulge us. If you work long enough [like me], you begin to understand. It's very, very difficult to work seriously in such an environment.

The woman told me that she had once written a report on behalf of a man and submitted it to a section manager. The manager, however, asked the man instead of her a question about the report. When the man replied that it was the woman who had written the report, the manager became angry and yelled at him, "You're an integrated-track staff member, aren't you?" The manager's remark discouraged the woman. At the end of the interview, the OL said her current problem was that she could not take ultimate responsibility for work. She commented, "Sure, it's an easy way of life because you don't have to take any responsibility. But it also means that your position is that much weaker." Though not having to take responsibility for work provided leverage for some women to resist men's power, it caused this woman distress.

Women who seek a serious career with a company do not welcome men's acquiescence to OLs' defiant attitudes. Such women are not comfortable with their fellow OLs' acts of resistance, because they see that the resistance does not help them obtain, and indeed may prevent them from obtaining, the "real" power that would enable them to share the responsibilities of their male colleagues. Being hesitant to take advantage of their position as OLs, these women seem, if anything, more vulnerable to exploitation by discriminatory company policies. Because they cannot take irresponsible attitudes toward work, they often work hard and overtime with little reward in either pay or promotion. In contrast, those who do not attempt to shoulder professional responsibilities under the present conditions have less difficulty in expressing resistance. It is a sad irony that power can sometimes be more effectively resisted when it is accepted than when it is opposed.

Although OLs' resistance has its limits, it is important to acknowledge that smiling OLs who bring tea to customers often have more leverage in an organization than is apparent at first. Takie Lebra describes as typical Japanese homes where patriarchy is interlocked with domestic matriarchy (1984). Similarly, this study shows that in the workplace, men's authority frequently exists alongside women's informal means of control. In fact, the relationship between men and women in Japanese companies demonstrates how privilege can impose its own limits just as disadvantage can provide opportunities. Being powerful means having simultaneously fewer and more constraints. Similarly, being powerless means having both less and more freedom. Men's inability to prevent women from resisting effectively against them is, in a sense, the price that men are obliged to pay in order to discriminate against women. It is not surprising, then, if some men think that perhaps they are paying too much for discriminatory company policies. Chapter 6 looks in detail at how men indeed pay dearly for such policies.

6

Men Curry Favor with Women

In chapter 3 we learned that a man's generosity to office ladies helps determine his popularity. While working in the bank, I witnessed men treat OLs to meals and other gifts many times and was often surprised by the extent of their generosity. In this chapter, I examine why men treat OLs so liberally. I analyze men's White Day gifts to women in the context of this extensive gift-giving custom in Japanese offices and discuss the possible roles that the wives of businessmen play in the gift-giving process.

Before I begin, I should remark on Japanese gift-giving practices in general. To some American readers, the Japanese in the following discussion may appear cold, calculating, and obsessed with monetary value. Moreover, their gifts may seem bribes. Although there is no space in this book for a complete discussion of Japanese gift-giving customs, I should point out that gift-giving is frequent, highly conventionalized, and symbolically rich in Japan.

People in different societies vary in terms of where they draw the line between gift and bribe. Matthews Hamabata illustrates this in his study of elite families in Tokyo (1990). He describes how he was led to reinterpret the expensive gift he received from his Japanese acquaintance as a combination of *on* and *ninjō* presentation (appreciation of gratitude and embodiment of intimate feelings), despite his initial assessment that it was an attempt to buy him and his services. For more on the complex subject of gift-giving in Japan, readers are advised to refer to Hamabata, among others.[1]

Treats

The tea room on the floor of the bank never ran out of snacks for the OLs. Men frequently received from customers sweets and cookies, which they then often presented to women to enjoy during the tea breaks that OLs took in twos and threes toward the end of the day. Groups of OLs also kept candy on one of their desks. Vice-general manager Ōtani liked candy very much and often came over to women's desks to help himself. But he remembered to contribute a generous amount of money occasionally to the "candy fund."

It was customary for a man who was to be transferred to another section of the company to present about ten thousand yen to the OLs to buy themselves pieces of cake. One day, for example, I was asked by Nakagawa-san, an OL on the floor, to help her buy forty pieces of cake with the money that a man named Nishizawa-san had left as a farewell gift. The woman explained that men usually donated ten thousand yen, but because Nishizawa-san gave fifteen thousand yen, we could buy really superior cakes. Because new appointments were all made on the same date, sometimes more than two parting presents were given simultaneously. At such a time, OLs arranged that all the money would not be spent on the same day.

The cakes we bought were placed in the tea room at about four o'clock in the afternoon. Every time an OL came into the room to have a tea break, Nakagawa-san emphasized that the present was from Nishizawa-san, who had contributed fifteen thousand yen. Nakagawa-san also delivered cakes to the male members of Department II at their desks. When she came back to the tea room, she reported to Yamada-san, her partner OL, that one man looked irritated when she told him that the cake was from Nishizawa-san. She supposed he was annoyed because he was reminded that he must also donate money when he left. Yamada-san thought he had better give generously, because the OLs had gone to a great deal of trouble to look after him. Just then, Omi-san, one of the men who belonged to Department II, came into the tea room. Yamada-san asked Omi-san to be sure to leave as much money as Nishizawa-san when he transferred. Nakagawa-san added jokingly that Omi-san should feel free to send her on a cake-buying errand at any time.

OLs not only expected men to give them farewell gifts but also to treat them for lunch and dinner. Two OLs complained that a man had promised them to take them out for lunch a long time ago but had not kept his word. Hearing them grumble, a third OL recommended that they suggest to him a date when they could lunch together. The tactic proved successful: the man treated the OLs to lunch a week later. "It was the first time he ever gave us a treat," commented one of the OLs.

OLs talked about presents, such as purses and perfumes, that men occasionally brought back to them from overseas business trips. In addition, men gave OLs gifts that their customers had given them. These included an expensive pair of tennis tournament tickets, movie tickets, and discount coupons for discotheques. (See chapter 3 for more discussion on men's generosity.)

There is a scene I remember vividly from life at Tōzai Bank, which indicates the relations between men and women in the workplace. One day during work, an OL complained that she had a headache, which she feared might be the beginning of flu. When she spotted half a dozen of bottles of a special vitamin-rich drink on a section manager's desk, she went straight up to him. Although the manager and the OL belonged to the same department, they had never worked together and were not well acquainted. Nonetheless, without even a smile, she asked the manager if she could have a bottle. The manager looked surprised but quickly said, "Please, please, take them all! Give them to the other women, too."

In his study of confrontations between the powerless and the powerful, James Scott argues that the "public performance of the subordinate will, out of prudence, fear, and the desire to curry favor, be shaped to appeal to the expectations of the powerful" (1990, 2). Scott assumes that it is the subordinate who fears and curries favor with the dominant. However, I have found the opposite to be true in Japanese offices: it is men who more often fear women; men who are afraid to offend women; and, finally, men who curry favor with women. Why is this? What makes some women bold enough to ask men for various treats? Why do men often yield to pressure from OLs and lavish gifts on them?

We have seen how Japanese companies' discriminatory policies attach low incentives and minimum penalties to OLs' performance and thereby encourage OLs in acts of resistance. Excluding women from the benefits of the internal labor market ironically strengthens their position within an organization. Because they have little to gain from being compliant, they do and say whatever they wish far more frequently than men. By denying women prospects for promotion, men have effectively relinquished their ability to influence them. In other words, discriminatory

company policies have deprived men of much of their capacity to impose, or to successfully threaten to impose, penalties for women's non-
compliance. One means left for men to influence women is to offer rewards. Many thus curry women's favor and give them lavish gifts.

A male manager working in a paper company admitted that he gave
treats to OLs from time to time. He compared the ease with which he
could gain the compliance of his male subordinates with the difficulty
of obtaining the OLs' compliance: "Male *kōhai* [junior members] are
subject to my control, but girls are not. Men are obliged to obey my
orders because their promotion depends on how I evaluate them. Girls
are not evaluated seriously, and so I have no way of influencing them."
Because the man could not influence OLs as he could his male subordinates, he had to buy them pieces of cake to ask for their cooperation. When they offer generous gifts, men attempt to compensate for
the loss of control over OLs that results from discriminatory company
policies.[2]

White Day Gifts

White Day is a quasi-holiday invented by Japanese com-
mercial interests. It developed much later than Valentine's Day and
gained popularity only toward the end of the 1980s. White Day takes
place on March fourteenth and is primarily an occasion for men to reciprocate by giving gifts to the women who gave them Valentine chocolate.[3] Though there is an overwhelming emphasis on chocolate as the
gift on Valentine's Day, there seems to be no agreement on what makes
an appropriate White Day present. Businesses such as candy manufacturers, traditional rice cracker makers, and lingerie companies have promoted their products as White Day gifts. According to my informants,
men choose to give, among other things, toffee, cookies, chocolate, tea,
handkerchiefs, towels, or underwear, or to treat women for tea, lunch,
or dinner on White Day.

OLs at the bank took interest in White Day just as they did in Valentine's Day. However, the two quasi-holidays differed in that the atmosphere of the office on White Day was much more lively and cheerful. A man, representing a section, handed out the same presents to all
the OLs in Department I at about two o'clock in the afternoon. The
woman seated next to me said in a loud, cheerful voice that could be
heard throughout the floor, "Why, thank you! I wonder what it is."

She opened her package at once. Inside was a beautiful handkerchief. She and another OL compared the design of their handkerchiefs. Then a woman working at the counter came over and said, "Oh, yours are [designed by] Kenzo. Mine is [by] Renoma." The three women got together in the middle of the floor and examined each other's presents, happily complimenting each other on the color and the design of the handkerchiefs.

Women's attitudes about receiving gifts were in stark contrast to men's. On Valentine's Day, many men looked embarrassed to receive gifts, awkwardly murmured "thank you," and swiftly put away the parcel. I did not see any man open his package, much less compare his gift with another's. On White Day, OLs, deliberately or not, made a show of receiving gifts. Because of this, it was difficult for men not to recognize that women were given presents. When I came back to my desk at about four o'clock in the afternoon on White Day, the OLs sitting near me were gasping with laughter. I asked them what was so funny, and one of the women explained that a man named Komatsu-san had just come back from somewhere and handed them a box of cookies. She was sure that because they had made so much of the handkerchiefs, Komatsu-san thought that he had better give them something as well. Komatsu-san was known among the women to be quite stingy.

Not only did women compare gifts when they were given them, they also exchanged information later on what they received on White Day. For example, two days after White Day, Kurimoto-san described to her female colleagues over lunch the gifts that she had received. She and Maeda-san, her OL partner, each received a beautiful bath set consisting of two soaps and a ceramic perfume bottle from men in Section VIII. Her colleagues exchanged an approving look. Next, Kurimoto-san told her fellow OLs that men in Section IX gave her and Maeda-san boxes of chocolate. When she noticed that her colleagues were not particularly impressed with this gift, she quickly added that the men deserved high marks because they had presented the gifts to the women early in the day. Then Kurimoto-san complained that a man working in Section VII came to her late in the afternoon to ask if she and her partner OL had received anything from men in other sections. She answered that they had, and only then did he shop for gifts.

Long after March fourteenth, women continued to talk about White Day gifts. Whether a man gave a suitable present in return on White Day was an important factor in women's appraisal of him. For example, men in Department II were denigrated, because they gave very small presents. An OL fumed that the men as a group had given her and the other OL gifts worth only about five hundred yen each on White Day the year before. Because there were only two OLs to give Valentine chocolates to as many as sixteen men, each OL had to contribute a considerable amount to purchase the chocolate. The OL thought that at the least a woman should be able to "recover the cost" of Valentine chocolates on White Day.

Valentine's Day was a touchy subject for men, a number of whom were reluctant to talk about the holiday. But women did not hesitate to discuss who gave them what on White Day. Because the number of chocolates a man received indicated his popularity among women, a man who did not receive chocolate was embarrassed. In contrast, a woman was not ashamed if a man neglected to reciprocate her gift on White Day. Apparently, a man's failure to return a gift was considered his fault and not hers, because the man was severely condemned by women for his lack of consideration. White Day gifts were yet another means to assess a man's generosity.

OLs enjoyed being able to make men reciprocate gifts on White Day, just as they delighted in soliciting other gifts from men. Therefore, how a Valentine gift is reciprocated on White Day was often regarded by OLs as of equal importance to the White Day gift itself. As the preceding conversation between Kurimoto-san and her fellow OLs indicates, a man who prepared a gift and gave it early in the day earned greater approval than one who, having forgotten to arrange a present, went out hurriedly to buy one later in the day. Dorothy Holland and Margaret Eisenhart report that the ways in which a man treats a woman on an American college campus, including whether he pays attention to her, gives her things, and shows regard for her feelings, are often considered as indicators of how much the man appreciates the woman (1990). Similarly, in Japanese White Day gift-giving, a man who prepared a gift and thus demonstrated his thoughtfulness to the OLs was regarded more highly than a man who did not. By remembering White Day, the former showed that he cared about them. In contrast, the latter's failure to remember showed that the OLs' power to make him reciprocate gifts was incomplete and that he did not care as much about them: he decided to go shopping only after learning that other men gave them presents.

The fact that most men reciprocate gifts on White Day is all the more surprising given men's embarrassment at handing out gifts to women in the open office environment. Japanese culture has traditionally emphasized roughness and reticence in men. Although such values are rapidly changing, men in general still hesitate to show kindness to women in public. Indeed, most men I interviewed said they felt awkward in presenting gifts to OLs. The following sentiments, voiced by a man working for a manufacturer of general electrical and electronic products, are typical:

I gave a gift to a woman in my department first, and then asked her to give gifts to OL so-and-so in so-and-so section and OL so-and-so in so-and-so section. Buying presents is OK, but giving them out is embarrassing. Just think about it! I go to the other floor [of the building] and ask for so-and-so-san. What if she's not there, and I have to say I'll come back? That's really embarrassing. But leaving the present on her desk is even more embarrassing.

It was a strange sight: usually serious and proud bankers in dark suits scurrying around the building, carrying shopping bags full of small presents wrapped in pretty papers and gaily ribboned. I must even say they looked somewhat ridiculous.

Some men also said that even if the gift from a woman cost her only two hundred or three hundred yen, a man's gift could not be the same price. Because "it was a matter of a man's honor," they felt it only appropriate to spend about one thousand to two thousand yen per gift. A banker observed, "Valentine's Day tickles men's hearts. We feel good when we receive chocolates, and if we receive them, we feel we must reciprocate, and if we are to reciprocate, we feel that our gifts must be at least twice as expensive as women's gifts."

In fact, I argue that although Valentine chocolate has value that transcends its material worth, this is not the case for White Day gifts. Receiving chocolate on Valentine's Day has a special meaning; even if a man does not like chocolate, he appreciates receiving *Valentine* chocolate. Moreover, OLs convey different meanings through the gifts they give. Because of the emphasis placed on impartiality and harmonious human relations in the Japanese workplace, one is supposed to be on good terms with all coworkers and give gifts of equal value to all. Overt, public displays of close friendship or antipathy that cannot be accounted for by work relations are, at least in principle, discouraged. Nonetheless, OLs can and do send gifts that suggest varying degrees of affection and aversion. This is because all Valentine presents ostensibly look the same—they are all chocolate—and yet in price, number, condition, and hour of bestowing, they allow women to attach different interpretations to supposedly interchangeable gifts (see chapter 4).

Men's gifts lack the rich symbolism of women's gifts because there is no White Day equivalent of Valentine chocolate. A man must choose from many possible gifts, and yet he hesitates to use the difference in possible gifts to express preference or dislike—as in giving lingerie to one OL and cookies to another—because making such an obvious distinction would disrupt the smooth functioning of human relations in the office.[4] He may give the same product in slightly different colors or designs, but he usually leaves it up to the OLs to choose from among the variations. Valentine gifts are pregnant with meaning, whereas White Day gifts are not. In the end, men's gifts are appreciated primarily for their material worth. Japanese Valentine and White Day gifts show, counterintuitively, that one gift (chocolate) may contain divergent meanings, whereas different gifts (lingerie, cookies, bath sets) lack individual messages. When one is not supposed to express preferences or antipathies, perhaps one can more safely voice them through a universal medium of exchange such as chocolate than through disparate instruments.

By returning gifts that may be twice as expensive as women's chocolate, are men able to discharge the debts to women they have incurred, as suggested by Peter Blau's social exchange theory (1964)? No. Men cannot wipe out their obligation to women completely, because whereas women's gifts carry (or are considered to carry) the message "I like you," men's message is simply, "Thank you for giving me a Valentine chocolate." Giving chocolate on Valentine's Day is an active behavior, implying that women have selected certain men among many to convey their feelings to. In contrast, men's behavior is essentially passive: the women who receive White Day gifts are predetermined by the women themselves.

Observing the difference between the gift given first and that given in return, Georg Simmel writes, "Once we have received something good from another person, once he has preceded us with his action . . . we no longer can make up for it completely, no matter how much our own return gift or service may objectively or legally surpass his own. The reason is that his gift, because it was first, has a *voluntary character* which no return gift can have" (Simmel 1950, 392; emphasis added). Women's Valentine chocolates are voluntary gifts, whereas men's White Day presents are not. Because White Day gifts are given primarily as a gesture of politeness, they are insufficient to discharge men's debts to women.

Japanese Valentine's Day and White Day exchanges illustrate that reciprocity does not always discharge obligation and that the *sequence* of the transactions may be crucial in determining power. Moreover, they indicate the extent to which people can be "trapped" in an exchange relationship, not because they do not have enough resources to repay, but because the meaning of the exchange precludes the possibility of paying back. No matter how much men wish to square their accounts by returning gifts on White Day, they are unable to do so completely.

The Wife's Role

When I went to a department store several days before White Day, I was surprised to see many women shopping at special sales counters for the quasi-holiday. White Day is supposed to be a day for men to give gifts to women. Why were women buying presents? I soon learned that some men ask their wives to prepare gifts for them to give to women at work. For example, an OL at Tōzai received a White Day gift from her former male colleague working in the Hiroshima branch. Although the parcel was posted in Hiroshima, it was apparent that the gift was bought in Tokyo: it was wrapped in the paper of one of the famous department stores in the area. Because the man was on *tanshinfunin* (transferred without one's family)—popular arrangement nowadays among Japanese businessmen—the OL presumed that the gift had been prepared by his wife in Tokyo and mailed by the man from Hiroshima.

A few days before White Day, I overheard a conversation between two middle-aged women walking through a subway station. Looking at the legs of a young woman walking in front of them, one woman said to the other, "I'm supposed to buy White Day presents for my husband so that he can give them out to young girls in his office. Do you think a pair of panty hose like that one would make a nice present?"

In order to investigate the role that wives play in White Day gift-giving, I conducted series of telephone interviews with wives of *sararī-man* working in large Japanese corporations. I interviewed thirty wives, asking mainly about their husbands' White Day gift-giving practices, the role they played, and their opinions concerning the quasi-holiday. (The results are summarized in appendix E.) Because of the small size and the nonrandomness of the sample (I asked my friends to introduce their acquaintances), no conclusive argument can be made. However, I think the findings are so compelling and consistent that they deserve to be mentioned here.

The first surprise was the strong interest the wives in general took in their husbands' White Day duties. Many believed that their husbands should return gifts to OLs on White Day and took an active part in the proceedings. When their husbands came home with Valentine chocolate, a number of wives advised them to reciprocate. Some, fearing that their husbands might not be well acquainted with the custom of White Day, reminded them of the date and later confirmed that they had not forgotten to return gifts. Others provided their husbands with information they gathered from newspapers and magazines and through their network of friends concerning the latest practices. A woman whose husband worked in a manufacturer of electronic instruments explained how she gave her husband advice on White Day gifts: "The word that reached my ears this year was 'investment chocolate.' Valentine's Day chocolate used to convey a love message. Then it became obligatory chocolate, and this year, it's investment chocolate. I think I read about it in a magazine. It was also talked about in the company [that I now work for]." According to the woman, the Valentine's Day gift was called investment chocolate because an OL received a gift worth about two thousand to three thousand yen in return for giving chocolate that cost her no more than five hundred. The woman therefore advised her husband that even if he received a five-hundred-yen chocolate, he must return a present worth far more. She said that she made sure her husband knew about these latest developments.

Another woman, who had returned to Japan after an eight-year absence occasioned by her husband's overseas assignment, was curious to learn how the custom had evolved while she was gone. She heard from several of her married friends that, nowadays, White Day presents were getting increasingly burdensome, because men were supposed to give gifts worth twice as much as those they received from women. Surprised, she told her husband, who worked for a general trading company, what she had learned and suggested that he take OLs out for dinner on White Day.

Still others recommended that their husbands give White Day gifts even though the men had initially decided not to. One woman, whose husband worked for an electric wiring company, persuaded him to give gifts despite the fact that he had intended to forgo the troublesome process. She explained: "When I was working in a company as an OL, girls around me always discussed whether they would be given back gifts [on White Day] after they gave [chocolate] on Valentine's Day. So I thought my husband had better return gifts, too." Another woman noted that her husband, an automobile company employee, might not have returned gifts had it not been for her advice that he do so.

In addition, many women took active part in White Day gift-giving practices by buying presents on behalf of their husbands. The wife of a man working in a food-processing company said she bought her husband's White Day presents every year because he asked her to. Because he did not specify what he wanted her to buy or how much she should spend, she decided what to purchase. In fact, this woman said that it was she rather than her husband who insisted that they prepare White Day gifts. This year, she read in newspapers and magazines that men frequently gave White Day gifts that were two to three times as expensive as the Valentine chocolate they received. She therefore thought that her husband should also return slightly more expensive presents than those he had received, and she wound up buying small ceramic vases for a little over one thousand yen each. Similarly, a woman whose husband was a computer software engineer bought White Day presents on his behalf because she believed that he should return gifts but knew that he did not have the time to shop and did not particularly enjoy shopping. She also thought that he did not know what would make nice presents for OLs.

All in all, two-thirds of the women interviewed (twenty-two, to be exact) professed that their husbands should give reciprocal gifts to OLs on White Day (see appendix E). One characteristic of these women worthy of special mention is that all except one woman either had worked as OLs or were currently employed as part-time workers and thus had close contact with young OLs. Their opinion concerning their husbands' White Day practices seemed greatly influenced by what they knew about OLs. The following view, voiced by a wife of a man working in a marine and fire insurance company, is representative. She considered Valentine's Day chocolate as a special kind of gift, because it was a present given to her husband by women at work. She cared very much whether her husband returned appropriate gifts. Although it was not necessary for him to buy particularly clever gifts, it was not good if he gave the impression that he was ungrateful or unfeeling toward OLs: "It's better if [my husband] is thought well of [by the women]. You know, in a typical Japanese company, a man is greatly helped by OLs. OLs work as his assistants. If he's not well thought of, I think he would have a hard time doing his job. I pay attention [to what my husband gives] so that [he] will be well taken care of by the women."

A woman married to a fellow worker in a computer software company also thought her husband's job would go more smoothly if he gave White Day gifts. She explained: "These things often come up in OLs' talk—what to do on Valentine's Day, and then, what they received in return on White Day. If a man doesn't give something back, he's called

a miser. Girls point out that this man and that man didn't give something back, don't they? So I think it's better if my husband gives gifts
on White Day." Her advice extended beyond White Day: she advised
her husband to treat OLs to coffee in a coffee shop when they worked
overtime.

A woman whose husband was a software engineer likewise thought
that a man would be spoken badly of if he did not give White Day gifts.
She firmly believed from her experience working as an OL that OLs expected to receive gifts on White Day. One woman without any apparent
familiarity with OLs also said she checked whether her husband, who
worked for a chemical company, had properly reciprocated on White
Day. She thought it unwise for a man not to present gifts to his female
coworkers, because he would be criticized behind his back if he did
not give them anything. When I asked her how she knew about OLs,
she replied that female friends who were OLs often told her how they
viewed men in their offices.

These women's views were in stark contrast to six wives who were
unconcerned with their husbands' White Day practices. It is interesting
to note that none of the six women had ever worked as or with OLs.
The wife of a man working in a construction company said, "I don't
know what my husband does for White Day. I've never paid particular
attention to it. It's only an exchange of obligations, so I suppose my
husband is doing whatever he thinks fit." Her husband does not talk
very much at home about what happens in the company. Because she
lacks office experience, she tries not to interfere. Similarly, a woman
married to a man working in a credit association expressed her indifference to what her husband did on White Day: "I've never taken part [in
my husband's White Day practices]. I don't have much interest in Valentine's Day and White Day. I don't have the experience of working in a
company and have never given a Valentine's Day chocolate myself."
This woman did not know that some wives prepared White Day gifts
for their husbands until a friend told her that it was a great deal of trouble to prepare them.

The remaining two informants had worked as OLs, but both of their
husbands upheld a policy of not returning gifts on White Day, and the
women respected this. According to his wife, a man working in a marine
and fire insurance company believed that Valentine's Day is a conspiracy of chocolate manufacturers. Although he was not unhappy to receive chocolates, he feared that once he started giving White Day gifts,
there would be no end to it. He hoped that if he didn't return their

gifts, women would stop giving him chocolate on Valentine's Day. The wife of the man added, however, that even though she was not involved in her husband's White Day practices, she was not indifferent to the women in his office. She tries to maintain a good relationship with them by dropping by the office once in a while and presenting cakes to them.

Although the sample size is small, the pattern that emerges from the interviews is surprisingly persistent: women who had never worked as or with OLs were unconcerned with their husbands' White Day practices, whereas the overwhelming majority of those who had worked as an OL or were in close contact with OLs thought that their husbands should give reciprocal gifts on White Day and took active part in the process. The latter group of women believed that OLs judged a man according to whether he gave White Day gifts. They knew that OLs often kept detailed records of who reciprocated gifts and criticized a man who did not as stingy. Because they feared that the failure to reciprocate would interfere with their husbands' ability to get work done smoothly, they paid attention to their husbands' White Day practices and supported them, if necessary, by doing such things as giving advice and buying presents.

As might be expected from our previous discussion, men did not differentiate their White Day gifts in the way women did their Valentine chocolates. Readers may recall that a number of women enjoyed making subtle distinctions among the gifts they gave to men. For example, a group of OLs contrived to give their boss, whom they disliked, fewer boxes of chocolate than other men in their office. Anything from product, cost, size, and number, to wrapping and hour of delivery could become the means by which OLs differentiated gifts. Through such differentiation, some women hoped to convey "secret messages" to men. In contrast, men bought, or asked their wives to buy, the same product for all the OLs. This was in spite of the fact that men had more freedom of choice than women, whose present was limited to chocolate—and in spite of the fact that there was good reason for a man to differentiate his gifts, because the chocolates he received from OLs naturally varied in cost and size. He might have received a small, two-hundred-yen chocolate bar from one OL, whereas another OL might have given him a fine box of chocolate worth one thousand yen.

Despite these facts, men seemed to ignore differences in the Valentine gifts they received, buying exactly the same product as a White Day gift for all the women. One reason given by both men and wives of such men for buying the same gifts was that it was too much of a nuisance to do otherwise. However, many wives also pointed out that men do not have the luxury of discriminating. The following view, offered by the wife of a man working in a computer software, is representative: "The reason for buying the same product is because you must be impartial. Besides, making a distinction among gifts to women sounds stingy. I mean, returning a cheap gift for cheap chocolate and an expensive gift for expensive chocolate is like estimating the value of chocolate you received, and it looks stingy." This wife thought that different gifts might be all right if the women did not know each other, but she knew that they often met in the company cafeteria and talked about White Day presents. If they found out that her husband had given some women cheaper gifts in return for cheaper chocolate, it would shame him, so she decided not to make any distinction among the presents and bought the same product for all women on behalf of her husband. She tried to select something that was slightly more costly than the most expensive gift her husband had received.

Likewise, the woman whose husband worked in a chemical company explained why White Day gifts must be identical: "Girls talk among themselves, so it would become known if [my husband] gave different things to them. Then they would compare their gifts and start saying that so-and-so received a better gift. That's not good. My husband must treat all girls equally, because they are his assistants." The woman therefore believed that if the gifts were socks, they could be in different colors but ultimately must be the same product. The playful act of making a distinction among gifts may be tolerated in "girls," but not in men. Men in responsible and respectable positions must be careful not to give the impression of being biased or impulsive. It is also interesting to note that the combination of the two factors—that all the products must be the same and that many felt that "a man's gift" must be more expensive than women's—jointly functioned to increase the amount men spent on White Day gifts.

The preceding analysis of the role some wives play in White Day gift-giving at the office suggests that wives' views may significantly influence their husbands' daily interaction with OLs in general. This seems to be particularly the case with wives who have worked as OLs in the past. Indeed, some men and women voluntarily offered information about the part wives played in determining how their husbands interacted with OLs. For example, a man working in a home electronics company described how his wife's advice helped him get along with OLs:

My wife worked as an OL in a real-estate company for four years before we got married. I tend to think it's too much trouble to buy souvenirs for OLs when I go on business trips, but my wife says it's important to do so. She also insists that I take women in my office out to dinner from time to time. She says that a man is given completely different treatment according to whether he is well thought of or not.

Similarly, a woman married to an engineer in an automobile company explained the role she played in buying presents for OLs in her husband's office—not only White Day gifts but souvenirs from their holiday trips. In the office where her husband worked, there were women called tracers who sketched technical drawings for male engineers. There were only a few of them, and orders poured in from men. The woman recalled how she and her husband decided to buy Thai silk scarves for the female tracers when they went on an overseas vacation: "I remember spending quite a lot of money on them. My husband told me that he was asked by the women to buy them souvenirs, and I thought if we were going to spend money anyway, we'd better buy something that they'd really appreciate." The wife believed that women at work frequently neglected the job of a man they did not like. In her words, "Women tend to put low priority on work for a man they don't like and refuse to do anything more for him than what is strictly required. I don't know why, but I am convinced that women work in such a way from my own experience [as an OL]. And I think how women work for a man makes a huge difference to his job." She supposed that if a man was exceptionally capable and thought nothing of women's defiance, then how he was viewed by women might make little difference. But when she heard from her husband that there were only a few women tracers and that they were always busy, she felt it was important for her husband to maintain a good relationship with them. Because she believed from her experience working as an OL that a man disliked by OLs had a difficult time, she advised her husband to buy expensive souvenirs for the women in his office.

Conclusion

We have seen that on many occasions OLs pressure men to treat them for lunch and dinner, to give them cakes and sweets, and to bring them souvenirs from overseas business trips. Women enjoy their power to make men grant such requests. Many men give in to their

pressure and lavish gifts on them, because discriminatory company policies have ironically deprived them of other effective means of controlling
women. When OLs have little to lose to begin with, inducement may be
one of few available methods for men to influence women.

White Day gifts are not much different from the ordinary gifts that
men generously give to OLs from time to time. Many men feel compelled to give reciprocal gifts on White Day, because they know that
they risk their reputation among OLs if they fail to do so. Those who do
not reciprocate can rarely escape OLs' criticism. Perhaps even more
than the men themselves, the wives of these men are conscious of their
husbands' reputation among OLs and keep an alert eye on their White
Day practices. The wives who have worked as OLs themselves are particularly aware that their husbands must maintain a good relationship
with OLs. These wives advise their husbands and buy White Day gifts
for them in the hope that this will ensure better treatment from OLs.

Conclusion

What accounts for the curiously restrained manner in which many Japanese men interact with women in the office? Men's frequent lack of confidence, their discomfort, and their feelings of constraint in the presence of women at first seem incongruous with their positions of authority. However, detailed examination of the Japanese workplace reveals the reason why men with power may not necessarily feel powerful.

Most office ladies are not entrusted with work that fully exercises their abilities, but are instead assigned simple, routine clerical jobs. They have little prospect of promotion, and their individuality is seldom respected, as evidenced by the fact that they are often referred to as "girls." And yet such complete denial of power to OLs has, ironically, empowered them. With considerably fewer benefits to protect than men, women have little to fear. They are therefore indifferent to threats—such as a boss's scornful look or a suggestion about demotion—that keep men under control.

Legitimate authority is assumed to have ultimate control over employees in modern bureaucratic organizations. However, this study shows that it is ineffective in ensuring women's cooperation because of the numerous loopholes that enable OLs to act counter to men's interests. For example, OLs seriously affect the efficiency of a man's work by refusing to take the initiative to help him or to do him favors. They frequently decide on the priority of assignments in an arbitrary manner. They can sometimes even refuse outright to cooperate. In comparing modern disciplinary forms of control with a ruler's reliance on terror,

Dennis Wrong observes: "An overseer's whip may suffice to keep galley oarsmen, cotton-pickers or ditch-diggers adequately performing their tasks, but complex skills, including the operation of machinery, are more vulnerable to 'conscientious withdrawal of efficiency,' in Veblen's phrase, and even to covert forms of sabotage" (1988, 98). He argues, therefore, that although bureaucratic organization facilitates extensive, centralized power structures, the power holder at the center becomes, ironically, more dependent on subordinates. Indeed, men in Japanese companies are dependent on women for their loyal and reliable assistance. In the final analysis, it is women's willingness to cooperate that determines how much help men will receive.

It is costly for a man to actually use his power. Relying on his authority to get what he wants from an OL is considered too abrasive and damaging to harmonious relationships in the office. A good manager is one who can obtain women's cooperation based on his personal charm (*jintoku*). A man must give the impression that women work hard of their own accord because they like him and want to help him, not because they have been ordered to do so. Therefore, although men possess the right to command, few will readily wield the power they have over OLs. This research illustrates how and why dominant groups may be reluctant to use their power (for other cases see Abu-Lughod 1986; Stacey 1991; Swartz 1982; and Upham 1987). Moreover, it shows that this reluctance is not the result of factors outside the power relations. Rather, it is integral to them.

Sometimes a man is endowed with rare personal qualities that arouse OLs' desire to please him. For example, he may be exceptionally good looking. However, for ordinary men without such endowments, one of the most effective means of influencing women is to offer inducement. Hence many men lavish gifts on OLs. Men's frequent and generous treats to women, and their (and their wives') concern over giving appropriate White Day gifts, indicate how eager men are to favorably impress their female colleagues. I argue therefore that interaction and emotion management on the micro level are not mere reflections of power relations on the macro level. They may, in fact, reverse them.

A Collective Body of Office Ladies

In examining OLs' defiance, I am struck by the diversity of ways in which they are able to cause men distress. Women can embarrass men by their constant scrutiny and gossip, they can humiliate them through their gift-giving practices, and they can annoy them while at work. Men's egos, their reputation, their business, the efficiency and effectiveness of their work, and, finally, their prospects for promotion have all been the target of women's defiance.

OLs muster forms of resistance that differ in the degree to which they disrupt office relationships. Some are on surface milder and more consensual, whereas others are openly confrontational. I hypothesize with some evidence that OLs resort to means that are less disruptive more frequently and with more ease. Many OLs admitted that they often did not take the initiative to help a man they disliked, or declined to do a favor for him. In contrast, refusing to work at all was considered an extreme measure, which some women found difficult to take.

Methods of disguise identified by James Scott (1990), such as keeping the meaning of an act ambiguous and the actor anonymous, allow women to voice defiance while avoiding direct confrontation with men. They are therefore important elements of many of OLs' acts of resistance. However, it should also be remembered that not all OLs' acts of resistance are disguised: sometimes OLs take a step that is openly offensive, such as refusing to do any work. Although OLs do not often feel the need to resort to such drastic measures and accept the consequences, it is important that they can do so if they choose.

Another feature of OLs' defiance that deserves attention is its collectivity. It might be somewhat misleading to characterize OLs' efforts as collective: this is not a study of formally organized social movements, and it is difficult for OLs to unite for the common good because they are divided by company policies and pressured to retire early. OLs' resistance should not be described as collective if this implies that they gather periodically to discuss their working conditions, or that they have their own representative body to negotiate wages and hours with the employer. However, women's resistance is collective insofar as they succeed in putting pressure on men primarily as a group.

For example, a female assistant's uncooperative attitude may annoy a man, but he is far more disturbed by hostile feelings harbored against him by many women. A man who does not get along with an OL has nothing to boast of, but that fact alone may not bring his managerial ability into question. After all, human beings do have likes and dislikes. Being unpopular among many OLs, however, is an entirely different story. A man who is disliked by many women is judged to be a poor manager: he will either not be promoted to management or, if already in management, will be denounced as unqualified. This is why a man in as high a position as vice-branch manager could not ignore OLs' *sōsu-kan* to him. *Sōsukan* is dangerous even for a high-ranking man, because it reveals that he is having difficulty managing not just one but many women.

As readers may recall, a man whose assistant OL refused to work for him was devastated not only by her uncooperative behavior but also by the antipathy of the many other OLs whom she influenced. Likewise, on Valentine's Day, a man cares less whether an individual OL gives him chocolate than about the aggregate number of gifts he receives, which measures his popularity among women. Collective opinions of OLs are a powerful weapon that can affect a man's prospects for promotion. During interviews, men spoke of their female colleagues collectively as having power, but they rarely talked about particular individuals. They referred, rather, to women, or more often "girls," as a collectivity. It is primarily as a group that women gain leverage.

Men cannot belittle a group of OLs. They also find it difficult to neglect individual women, because women appear to them to be closely connected with one another. Many men I interviewed described OLs in their office as "flocking together." They feared women's gossip, saying that it spread like wildfire, affecting the views of many. Some even held that being disliked by one OL was the same as being disliked by all.

OLs, then, do not negotiate power with men only collectively: their respective positions are further strengthened by the appearance of maintaining close coordination with one another. After all, if one woman's opinion has, or seems to have, considerable effect on her fellow OLs' opinions of a certain male coworker, a man cannot afford to take individual women lightly. Although working environments in Japanese offices undermine OL solidarity, it is noteworthy that OLs nonetheless manage to put pressure on men as a group. OLs are not formally organized, but they manage to resist men's authority collectively.

A Boss Is Not a Boss without Subordinates

It may by now be apparent to the readers that because OLs prey upon the limits of men's authority, they can effectively resist it. The curious leverage a weaker party comes to hold against the dominant has been documented by a number of researchers. James Scott argues that "any dominant ideology with hegemonic pretensions must, by definition, provide subordinate groups with political weapons that can be of use" (1990, 101). Eugene Genovese (1976) illustrates how the oppressed make use of such political weapons: he contends that slaves in America were able to turn the paternalistic dependency relationship to their own advantage.

A parallel argument is presented by Lila Abu-Lughod (1986) in her insightful analysis of how Bedouin women use poetry as a discourse of rebellion to official, male values of honor. According to Abu-Lughod, power in Bedouin society depends on demonstration of the moral virtues that win respect from others. A superior must protect his dependents' dignity by drawing as little attention as possible to their unequal relationships and by minimizing open assertion of his power over them. When he publicly mistreats a dependent, he invites rebellions that undermine his position. Abu-Lughod maintains that "figures of authority are vulnerable to their dependents because their positions rest on the respect these people are willing to give them" (1986, 103). The fact that a man needs his dependents' respect in order to hold an honored position limits the abuse of power.

In her study of superior-subordinate relations and dependency in Japanese homes (1984), Takie Lebra likewise points out that although the husband's childlike dependency on his wife is an attribute of patriarchy, it gives the wife latitude to wield power by making her services indispensable. From the wife's point of view, the husband who does everything by himself is less manipulable.[1]

Similarly, I argue that men often need OLs' support if they are to hold managerial positions in Japanese organizations. A man who is disliked by a female subordinate tends to be given a black mark for not getting along with her. A man who alienates many women is regarded as having little aptitude for managing people. One banker's story indicates how important a man's relationships with women can be in determining his later career. When a man is first hired by the bank, he is left among OLs in a branch office for about a year to learn clerical work. This form of training, according to the banker, is common in Japanese banks. If the man does not get along with women there, his branch manager judges him to have little potential. The banker observed:

On the one hand, there are men who people say are talented and are assigned promising jobs, and, on the other hand, there are those who are not. Well, it seems to me that those men who are not are often the ones who were given *sōsukan* by women in the branch office. Doing well in clerical jobs with women does not necessarily mean that you will do well, for example, in the Capital Market Department later on. But if you don't do your first assignment well, your branch manager gives you a poor evaluation. If you don't get along with women, you are often labeled as slow-witted and inflexible.

The banker heard his colleagues say that if a man did not get along with women, he would have a really hard time in the firm. It was extremely dangerous for men to alienate OLs. The fact that men needed to be on good terms with women limited the power they could exercise over them.

OLs often use the unequal relationships with men to their advantage. Although the power holder in a modern bureaucratic organization depends on subordinates to perform tasks reliably and efficiently, many OLs demonstrate that their reliability and loyalty cannot be assumed. Men in general work hard, because it is to their advantage to do so. In return for hard work, they are promoted and receive the benefits that accompany positions of authority, including higher compensation and prestige. OLs, in contrast, have little prospect of advancement. Because they are denied promotions and benefits that men receive, they insist that their duties are not comparable to men's.[2]

OLs have their own notion of men's and women's responsibilities in an organization. As we have seen, women sometimes make an extensive claim on men, demanding special attention from them. Many OLs regard work not as what they must perform in return for getting paid, but as a favor they do for men. Consequently, they expect men to thank them for what they do, and when gratitude is not forthcoming, they blame the man for being ungrateful. In addition, women often consider it men's responsibility to ensure congenial working arrangements, and a man's failure to do so becomes a legitimate excuse for their own negligence. Moreover, OLs expect men to treat them nicely and give them gifts.

Men in Japanese organizations are, in a sense, far more dependent on women than women are on men. In order to rise from the ranks, a man must take heed of what OLs think of him. Furthermore, even when he does come to power, he cannot enjoy control over women as he can over other men. Hoping to impress him favorably, male subordinates will often go to great lengths to fulfill his wishes. Women, in contrast, worry less about his opinions. No matter how highly he may regard a particular woman, it is unlikely that he will promote her, and no matter how ill he may think of an OL, he cannot dismiss her outright.

Accommodation and Resistance

It is extremely important that OLs assert certain rights within the terms available to them. They can refuse to take the initiative to improve their own work or the group performance, and they can turn down a request, because they are essentially not responsible for work. They can decline to do a man a favor, and they can inform the personnel department about disagreeable bosses, because they do not have to care about the impression they leave on the management. They can make fun of men and criticize men's struggle for promotion, because they themselves do not compete in the race. What enables OLs to take subversive actions, in short, is their accommodation to company policies that set separate career paths for men and women.

This is significant, for it implies that OLs must adapt themselves to discriminatory company policies before they can voice resistance. As Shimizu Chinami, the author of *Ojisan kaizō kōza*, appropriately points out, only OLs who do not hope to be promoted and, therefore, are certain that they themselves do not have to face the same ordeal as men can laugh at men who make pathetic efforts to please their superiors. Only women who do not care how their performance is evaluated can annoy men by acting irresponsibly. This is why the woman with an unusually long tenure with a general trading company (see chapter 5) did not welcome being indulged by men. She and the minority of OLs who seek serious careers and attempt to assume responsibilities similar to their male colleagues' do not enjoy fellow women's assertion of "female" rights.

The fact that resistance is so often voiced through accommodation leads some researchers to claim that the distinction between accommodation and resistance is unreal. For instance, Genovese claims that the slaves' response to paternalism is "a record of simultaneous accommodation and resistance" (1976, 597). He observes that "accommodation itself breathed a critical spirit and disguised subversive actions and often embraced its apparent opposite—resistance" (597). He therefore suggests that slaves' accommodation could best be understood as a way to accept what was unavoidable without falling prey to the dehumanizing and emasculating pressures of the system.[3]

However, it is not only that accommodation can enable resistance. Resistance in turn may also lead to accommodation. Paul Willis's research on English working-class "lads" (1977) shows how a cultural form created to resist domination becomes the means to ensure domination. The great irony noted by Willis is that the very resistance such "lads" use against school authority prepares them for working-class jobs. Similarly, the irony for defiant OLs is that their acts often serve to reinforce traditional gender relations. An OL's acts of resistance often involve making demands that a man pay attention to her, give her things, and cater to her and her feelings in general. She in turn will demonstrate her admiration and caring for the man, assist him in various ways, and support him. In making claims on men, OLs act out the traditional gender roles.

Dorothy Holland and Margaret Eisenhart (1990) identify the "cultural model of romance," according to which favorable treatment from men provides women prestige and status. Standards of women's attractiveness are determined by men, but the reverse does not hold. Unlike the position of men, the position of women is determined not by what women do but by how and to whom they appeal. Thus, women's sexuality is more constrained and their preoccupation with gender relations more complete than is the case for men. OLs' focus on the kind of treatment they receive from men renders them vulnerable to the same sort of gender-differentiated ranking system singled out by Holland and Eisenhart.[4]

OLs' accommodating resistance and resisting accommodation shows that the distinction between accommodation and resistance is less apparent and far trickier than it appears. Indeed, this study suggests that there may not be as large a difference as is usually assumed between women who explicitly reject discriminatory company policies and those who accept them. The latter, who subjugate themselves to men, may be no happier than the former. They may be no more docile, passive, or contented. Both groups of women, in fact, may aspire to strengthen their position against men and thereby to alleviate the one-sidedness of male dominance.

Sex Stereotype

There is another equally important implication of OLs' strategies to turn the discriminatory terms of employment to their own advantage. By stressing their difference from men, OLs promote a certain image of being female. An OL who does not take the initiative to do anything beyond what she is strictly told to do gives the impression of having little enthusiasm for work. An OL who assigns priority to jobs according to her feelings about particular men rather than according to the importance of the task to the company invariably appears unprofessional. A woman who adamantly refuses to do any work for the man she does not like looks irresponsible.

Similarly, an OL who declines to do a favor for a man of high rank seems completely ignorant of the working of power in a bureaucratic organization. One who tells tales to the personnel department may be condemned as childish. One who totally neglects a man via public *sōsu-kan* may appear insensitive to human relationships in the office or incapable of properly controlling her emotions. And those who gossip foster the view that OLs are talkative, bored, and busy killing time rather than minding serious business. Indeed, women who speak about disagreeable men often appear unreasonable and emotional to men. Even Valentine's Day gift-giving, with its emphasis on festivity and the central role OLs play in it, is viewed in contrast to men's serious world of business; it is seen as an example of women's caprice, insofar as OLs distribute Valentine chocolates in a discriminating manner, reflecting their feelings toward the male recipients.

In short, the more OLs resist, the more they promote the stereotype: that women get carried away by emotion; that they are unable to make rational decisions; and that they are not seriously committed to business.[5] By making demands on men, OLs unwittingly reinforce the very excuse for discriminating against them (see Willis 1977).

However, the present study shows that the stereotype is suspect. OLs' quickness to show anger may not be because OLs are by nature emotional. OLs' tendency to let personal feelings influence their decisions may not signify that they are inherently less rational. Nor does their refusal to work indicate that they cannot take business seriously. Showing anger, working according to personal preference, and refusing jobs are the means by which women resist men's power.

Because OLs insist on going home when it suits them while their male counterparts work until late at night, they *appear* irresponsible. Because they do not put up with a disliked boss as men do, they *seem* more emotional. However, this is not the same as being inherently more irresponsible and emotional. Indeed, some men pointed out that the contrasting attitudes men and women took toward work were not really the result of a difference between the sexes but originated in what was distinct to their respective positions in the company.

Readers may recall the man working in a life insurance company, who compared women who tended to act on impulse with men who made efforts to control their feelings (see chapter 5). The man quickly added that such contrasting attitudes should not be attributed to the difference between men and women but to that between the types of occupation. Furthermore, he admitted honestly that if he were in the women's position in the company, expected to work only for a few years, he would not try to hide his feelings. It was only because, as the family breadwinner, he had to work to be promoted that he put up with the man he did not like.

Similarly, a banker related that in his workplace, male colleagues called mechanical memorization "*onnanoko oboe*" (girls' way of remembering) in contradistinction to their own approach to understanding through reason. The man, however, felt that the contrasting ways of learning reflected the difference in what the company expected from the two sexes rather than any inherently sex-specific tendencies.

Perceptive men are thus able to distinguish between acting impetuously, illogically, and irresponsibly, and being inherently impetuous, illogical, and irresponsible. However, for the overwhelming majority of men, and perhaps even for women, who witness day after day the systematically contrasting ways in which the two sex groups work, the differences come to be considered natural. During the interviews, most men and women did not hesitate to use the expression, "Men are . . . , whereas women are . . . " Even the two men mentioned previously interpreted the differences first in sexual terms and then qualified this, quickly restating that sex was not really the determining factor.

This study does not directly refute the commonly held belief that women are inherently emotional and irrational. However, it does provide a strong basis for doubting such an argument by explaining why women may appear more emotional and irrational than men in spite of there being no innate differences between the sexes. Men usually make serious efforts to perform well in the office. They put business requirements ahead of personal preference. They will not let the impulse of the moment destroy their assured career in the company. Women, in contrast, usually care less about performance or business requirements. They readily complain and otherwise show discomfort, because they know there is little to be gained by forbearance.

Men's seriousness, their rational judgment, and their self-control may not be natural endowments that women lack. Because men and women are subject to different sociocultural constraints that condition their existence, they act differently. From this point of view, it is the wider social and cultural systems that are responsible for the contrasting attitudes men and women assume in the workplace. Moreover, the data indicate that women are no less aware than men of the terms of employment and the role they are expected to play in the company. OLs demonstrate that they are capable of sound observations and cool judgment. In this respect, they are indeed very rational.

Furthermore, the study shows how existing social relations are made comprehensible in terms of gender. For example, consider again the practice prevalent in a bank of calling rote memory *onnanoko oboe*. Because OLs are provided neither incentive nor opportunity to learn why certain business should be conducted in a particular way, they have few choices but to memorize mechanically. A more appropriate expression, therefore, would refer to the occupation and not to the sex of the person memorizing. However, because the term attributes the habit of rote memory to women, it justifies the current gender-differentiated working arrangements. Because women prefer mechanical memorization to rational understanding, the argument goes, clerical work suits them. As the banker admitted, many men in his company considered women incapable of making comprehensive judgments.

Sex and position in the workplace are so conflated in Japanese companies that what is distinctive to certain occupational roles is regarded as sexually determined. As Joan Scott has argued, dispositional generalization per sex is easy to understand: "Gender . . . provides a way to decode meaning and to understand the complex connections among various forms of human interaction. When historians look for the ways in which the concept of gender legitimizes and constructs social relationships, they develop insight into the reciprocal nature of gender and society and into the particular and contextually specific way in which politics constructs gender and gender constructs politics" (1988, 45–46). Words like *onnanoko oboe* illustrate how gender serves to naturalize social arrangements. Discriminatory company policies may require men and women to assume different attitudes toward their work, but such differences are understood and legitimized in terms of gender.

Future Changes for Office Ladies

In arguing that power dynamics on the micro level may not be a simple reflection of those on the macro level, I attempt in this book to indicate the complexity of the determination of events and actions that statistical analyses may overlook or oversimplify. In addition, by accounting for the structural nature of women's ability to resist men's authority, I represent cultural forms of local life as not only autonomous from the broader social order but also constituted by it.

Specifically, I argue that it is the rigidity of institutional sex segregation that empowers OLs. In this respect, Japanese women working as clerical assistants may have more weapons at their disposal than their American counterparts, as studied by Rosabeth Kanter (1977).[6] We have seen that it is because women have little prospect for promotion to management that they can do and say what they want. Furthermore, because gender stratification is so universal and systemic in Japan, women's low status in the company is more often ascribed to their distinct sex role rather than to individual capability: the assumption is that men and women diverge in their work patterns primarily because they assume different roles in society. This view undoubtedly prevents women from attaining status equal to men's in the workplace, but it encourages women to profess certain rights. We have seen that many employers acknowledge women's assertion to some extent and do not hold them responsible for work in the way men are held responsible.

In contrast, respect for individualism and equal opportunity in the United States may paradoxically weaken some women's position. Even if as many women in the United States hold dead-end jobs as OLs hold in Japan, American women are not by fiat excluded from career paths, as Japanese OLs are. Kanter reports that it is possible, although rare, for a secretary in America to be promoted to manager. Yet the possibility of advancement in America can cause secretaries to hesitate to make demands on their bosses. Furthermore, when exclusion of women from management is not as systematic and across the board as in Japan, one is never quite certain whether the low-level job of an individual American woman is the result of her gender or of her capability. This ambiguity may give company management leeway to discriminate against women without releasing them from responsibilities comparable to men's.

That institutional sex segregation has a potentially dual function for women's welfare has been noted by Takie Lebra, who argues that the "structural embeddedness of sex roles, on the one hand, deprives women, and, on the other, protects them" (1984, 305). This study similarly demonstrates how structural rigidity of gender stratification provides Japanese OLs with leverage that may not be available to women in societies committed to a more egalitarian policy.

Although I have emphasized the opportunity structures and constraints that women face, I do not wish to imply that Japanese society and the employment system are static. Already there are signs of change. Increasing number of firms are experimenting with new programs to better utilize women in the workplace. Some companies have established new sections in their personnel departments specifically aimed at developing women's business skills. Others have set up bureaus where women can receive counseling about problems they may face in their work. Still others have initiated regular meetings between management and female employees to promote mutual understanding (*Nihon Keizai Shinbun*, 14 January 1992).

Some firms, including a number of large general trading companies and a trust bank, are reported to have introduced performance reviews of their female clerical workers. One illustrative case is Nichimen, which has announced that its clerical workers will no longer be paid according to seniority only. Nichimen will combine seniority and merit systems so that, for instance, among thirty-seven-year-old OLs, the difference in their monthly compensation can amount to approximately sixteen thousand yen. Itōchu has also introduced a similar scheme, and Mitsubishi and Tōmen are contemplating a comparable change in their treatment of OLs. Among Japanese banks, similar attempts emphasizing payment based on merit rather than on traditional seniority have been made primarily for *sōgōshoku* employees (integrated-track staff). Sumitomo Trust Bank is said to be a rare exception that plans to do the same for female *ippanshoku* (clerical) workers as well (*Nihon Keizai Shinbun*, 26 September 1994 and 20 May 1996).

What accounts for management's recent enthusiasm to use women workers more efficiently? One explanation is the economic slump beginning in the early 1990s. Recession has forced many companies to revise their cost structure, including personnel costs of clerical workers. Another reason may be the rising number of women who work for a longer period of time. This is reflected in the gradual smoothing of the famous M curve depicting the rate of women's participation in the workforce by age. The most pronounced change is seen at ages twenty-five to twenty-nine: the number of women remaining in the workforce increased by more than 10 percent in the last ten years, from 54.1 in 1985 to 66.4 in 1995 (*Sōmuchō* 1996). As women's average length of tenure rises, increasingly fewer companies can afford to appreciate "office flowers" who have little willingness to work hard.

As discussed in chapter 1, a director of Itōchu in charge of personnel is reported to have said that until recently women's tenure was very limited, and the company did not feel the need to differentiate among them. However, as women remained in the company for longer periods, the company realized it needed to find ways to better utilize its female clerical workers (*Nihon Keizai Shinbun*, 26 September 1994).

This study has shown, however, that without drastic measures to remodel the existing employment system, it will be difficult to nurture women's willingness to work hard and thereby enhance their utilization. Women's office morale is a structural problem. If, for instance, OLs are to have real performance reviews, this change will undoubtedly affect their lives. Much of women's collective resistance, after all, is based on the assumption that they are not as seriously evaluated as men are. But it is too early to tell how profound the changes will be. For one thing, we do not yet know if the move to evaluate OLs will be limited to a number of firms in specific industries, or if other firms will adopt similar policies. There is also a question about the difference in compensation and ranks employers will and *can* make among their female clerical workers. Will OLs find this difference large enough to be motivated by it? The personnel manager at Nichimen says that as long as a woman is in a clerical position, she will never be promoted to senior management (*Nihon Keizai Shinbun*, 26 September 1994). What will promotion with such an apparent ceiling mean to OLs?

There are two other developments we need to watch carefully. One is the recent cost-cutting move on the part of companies to replace a portion of their retiring clerical workers with temporary employees, instead of hiring new graduates as regular employees (*Nihon Keizai Shinbun*, 27–31 May 1996). Because the overwhelming majority of Japanese firms continue to refrain from firing regular employees and replacing them with temporary workers, I do not foresee that this will have immediate impact on the advantages and disadvantages of OL status. However, the number of women who can enjoy the limited benefits of working as OLs may decrease in the future, when more women are employed as temporary workers for less money and with less stability.

The other development to watch is the recent increase in the number of women hired as *sōgōshoku* (integrated-track) staff (*Nihon Keizai Shinbun*, 2 December 1997). The attrition rate of *sōgōshoku* women has been high, however, so the absolute number of *sōgōshoku* women has not expanded as much as one would expect. Moreover, there is a difference between male and female *sōgōshoku*. Male *sōgōshoku* are generalists who undergo frequent job transfers as a form of managerial training, but women *sōgōshoku* are often treated as specialists in certain fields, such as sales, where the geographical location of employment is limited. We have yet to see what these limitations on *sōgōshoku* women imply for their promotion into management.

It will be intriguing to observe in the years to come how slow but steady changes in the employment system will affect and be affected by the lives of Japanese women.

Data and Methods

Participant Observation

Anthropologist Michael Jackson points out the alienating effects of visualism and argues that "perspective . . . becomes the principal Western conception of space from the early fifteenth century and has the immediate effect of privileging the way things appear from a fixed, detached point of view—that of the observer" (1989, 6). As an alternative to visualism, Jackson suggests "working through all five senses, and reflecting inwardly as well as observing outwardly" (8). Likewise, my aim in participant observation was not to "study" what it was like to be an office lady—to observe an OL as someone whose life is to be read, deciphered, and interpreted as a text. I did not intend to just watch OLs and take notes on what they were doing. I wanted instead to learn their lives by myself doing what they did. I wished to join OLs in making copies and typing documents. Rather than asking questions with notepad and pen in my hands, I preferred to carry cups and saucers on a tray and serve tea.

It was difficult, however, to gain an entry into a Japanese corporation. Both my experience with Japanese firms and the advice I received from experts told me there was little chance of obtaining official permission from top management to conduct research among their employees. Japanese companies, especially large, well-established ones, are very sensitive to publicity and avoid getting mixed up in anything unconventional.[1] In the end, I decided to sign up at several agencies for temporary workers.

Temp agencies were thriving in Japan at the time. Companies found it advantageous to replace OLs with temporary workers and thereby reduce their fixed costs. (Personnel expenses were considered fixed costs in most Japanese companies, because they customarily refrained from laying off their regular employees.) Hiring temporary workers was much cheaper than employing regular workers, and the contract did not have to be renewed if the company had no need or desire to retain a given temp. Many ex-OLs worked for the agencies in spite of the fact that their pay was reduced considerably compared to what they had received as regular workers. These women were attracted to a temp's freedom to take time off between jobs. Indeed, an advertisement for one of the agencies enticed women into becoming "an OL who did not work during the summer."

When looking for a job, I did not consider pay, business hours, and other working conditions that normally would concern an applicant. My main criterion was whether the workplace was suitable for conducting research on gender relations in large Japanese corporations. Because it was vital that I find a job in such a corporation, I turned down a number of offers from smaller firms and foreign-affiliated companies. Although it would be interesting to see how the Western business customs of a parent company influence work relations in a Japanese subsidiary office, that issue deserves a study of its own. Other workplaces were equally unsuitable, either because there were too few women in the office, or because women working there were temporary workers rather than regular employees. In addition, I preferred not to work in a small, isolated room whose occupants were not likely to interact often with other members of the company.

The job in Tōzai Bank was ideal in many respects. First and foremost, it was a large, well-known corporation in Japan, employing approximately seven thousand people. Second, the banking industry relied heavily on OLs' womanpower. In a bank, it would be possible to meet more OLs than I would in a company that employed relatively fewer women, and it was likely that gender relations would be more central and visible than in a firm where OLs had a marginal presence. Third, because the location of the office might influence how people worked, the fact that my job was in the bank's headquarters located in the central business district of Tokyo meant that my findings might also apply to the many other, similar, large companies that had offices in that same part of the city. Fourth, in the headquarters where top officials as well as rank-and-file employees worked, it was possible to see how people in different positions interacted with each other.

The office in the bank headquarters where I was to work was a desirable place for participant observation: it was a large open space without any partition, where as many as sixty-two employees worked for three departments. In addition, the employees on the floor covered a broad spectrum of hierarchical rankings, including three general managers (*buchō*), two of whom were also board members; three vice-general managers (*jichō*); ten section managers (*kachō*); thirty-five men in nonmanagerial positions; and eleven OLs.

While in the office, I worked closely with OLs but refrained from asking questions that did not fit naturally in the flow of daily conversation. In order to immerse myself in the lives of OLs, I tried to shed the signs of an outsider observer. The fact that I was a Japanese woman, relatively close in age to OLs, seemed to help. Sharing the drudgery of OL work day after day and relaxing with them during lunch and occasional tea breaks, I became close to the OLs. I came to know some of them so well that they confided their dreams and problems to me. I was obviously delighted, but, at the same time, felt a little uneasy, because I was not sharing my hopes with them. When my term with Tōzai ended, I maintained contact with the OLs through mutual visits, telephone calls, and exchange of letters. What I learned in this way about the "most recent developments in the office" proved to be important information for my research.

In hindsight, my decision to live the life of an OL was correct: it was only by doing so that I came to share something of their sorrows and triumphs. For instance, if I had not actually served tea, I do not think I would have been able to appreciate fully why OLs were more annoyed by tea serving than by other tasks that seemed equally trivial. Neither do I think I would have truly understood the frustration and miseries that OLs felt in being treated as "girls" if I had not experienced the loss of individuality in wearing the identical uniform and doing work that could be done by virtually anyone. Nor would I have realized how much gossiping enlivened OLs' spirits in the otherwise tedious daily routine if I had not shared their boredom making copies day after day. These insights and many more would have been closed to me if I had kept myself aloof from the OLs as a sociologist.

Finally, let me comment on the important ethical issue raised by the fact that no one at the temp agencies or in Tōzai knew of my real intentions. Researchers involved in participant observation often find it tricky to decide how much of their role to disclose; they must balance delicately between being accepted and not misrepresenting themselves. The compromise I reached in the present case was, first, to give exact information on my background, including my affiliation with the University of Chicago. In addition, I explained both at the agencies and in the bank that I was looking for a job in a large corporation because I had never worked in one and was interested in knowing what it was like. Partly because of the necessity to find a suitable workplace, I also said that my preference was an office where I could observe closely how businessmen and OLs typically worked. Although I did not state explicitly that I was conducting research, I later found out that I had not grossly misrepresented myself. One of the OLs I came to know well took me by surprise when she said, "If you ever write a book about your experience working here, don't hesitate to be frank." Negotiation of my role was at least somewhat successful.

Intensive Interviews

As I worked among the OLs, I accumulated many questions. These became the basis of the interviews that I conducted with thirty *sarariman* and thirty OLs employed in various large corporations in Tokyo. In addition to ascertaining that no two interviewees worked for the same firm, I tried to talk to men and women working in a variety of industries, including manufacturing, trading, transport, finance, insurance, real estate, and services. I also paid attention to male informants' age, tenure, and position and attempted to include young businessmen as well as older and higher-ranking managers. Consequently, among the male informants, there were men in their twenties who had just started their long careers in the company and managers in their fifties and sixties who expected to work for a few more years before retirement. Age and tenure were not major factors for sampling OLs, the majority of whom were in their twenties. However, I did talk to several women in their thirties in order to understand the different perspectives that a minority of older OLs held.

I felt that it was important to talk to OLs who graduated from university as well as those who graduated from junior college. As chapter 2 shows, educational background was an important factor that divided OLs in the workplace, and I made sure that I spoke to women of both groups. Education was less important in selecting male interviewees, because most white-collar businessmen in large corporations were university graduates. I did not interview any OL or businessman who had only a high school education, because many large companies in urban areas have stopped recruiting their white-collar employees directly from high school. Because marriage and retirement were crucial concerns for many OLs as well as for the company, I included five ex-OLs among my female informants in order to speak to women who had actually experienced retirement.

The resulting profiles of sixty *sarariman* and OLs are given in appendix B. The average age and tenure of male informants was 37.9 and 14.4 years respectively—only slightly older and longer than the national average of 36.5 and 12.3 for university-graduated men working in companies with one thousand or more employees. Similarly, the average age and tenure of female informants, 26.8 and 5.6, approximated the national average of 27.7 and 4.9 for university and junior college-graduated women employed by large firms (*Rōdōshō, Chingin kōzō kihon tōkei chōsa* 1991).

Apart from the preceding considerations, I did not particularly aspire to make a "representative" sample. Sixty men and women were never going to cover all the varieties of *sarariman* and OLs, and besides, the nature of the study did not necessitate random sampling. Therefore, when someone told me that one of his colleagues suffered from OLs' *sōsukan*, a form of resistance described in chapter 5, I asked whether I could talk to that colleague. If the goal of my research was to make a systematic reporting of how frequently various forms of resistance were observed, I would not have deliberately sought an interview with a man I knew to have experienced *sōsukan*, because that would have introduced bias. However, because my interest was primarily to understand why men, the supposedly more powerful of the two sexes, seemed to be afraid of offending women, I did not consider the bias critical.

I would like to stress the limitations of my data, which corresponded with the humble aim of the study. I wanted to account for the reserved attitude men frequently held toward women in the Japanese office, which was the result more often of knowing or hearing of a man who had suffered from women's defiance than of actually experiencing it. The fact that most men and women knew or heard of such a man was extremely important in determining the nature of the relationships between the two sexes. What mattered, then, was more women's readiness to challenge men than the actual act of challenge. As Dennis Wrong observes, "[Force] is more often used to establish credibility and thus to create a future power relation based on the threat of force that precludes the necessity of overt resort to it" (1988, 41). The threat of

challenge to male domination was so important in shaping the relationships between men and women in the workplace that the number of
times various forms of resistance were observed was less of an issue.

What I hope to claim in this study is that in the Japanese office, men
in general feel powerless against women. I base this claim on the data
obtained from participant observation and the opinions expressed by
men and women working in various organizations, which is further supported by logical explanations for the cause of these feelings structur-
ally common to many large companies in Japan. I do not in any way
attempt to predict the probability that a certain man will actually meet
with women's resistance.

Interviews with *sararīman* and OLs lasted anywhere between one-
and-a-half to three hours. Most female informants preferred to see
me after work in nearby coffee shops, and some suggested that we meet
on the weekend in coffee shops near where they had errands. In contrast, many men invited me into their offices during work, and some
agreed to be interviewed during lunch. This difference between men
and women reveals the degree of independence they enjoyed in their
respective offices. Men were allowed to use their own discretion, and
consequently, felt freer than women to meet with an outsider during
work.

Women refused to see me during lunch, stating that they were only
allowed to take an hour off (some said forty-five minutes). They said it
would be too hectic to try to get to a restaurant, have lunch, and talk
within an hour. I sensed that they could not be late in getting back to
work. In contrast, men whom I met during lunch did not seem to be
as concerned about time. They said an hour was probably the appropriate time off for lunch but that it was all right to run a little behind
schedule.

Following up participant observation with interviews proved extremely useful, because I was able to ask questions that I could not ask
during my work among OLs. Yet, interviews alone would have been
ineffective, because I needed to phrase my questions correctly for a
successful interview. Without prior experience working in the office, I
would have been unable to form questions in a way that made my informants feel relatively at ease in talking about everyday occurrences
in their workplace. In order to ask questions that were specific enough
to encourage informants to speak, I had to be quite familiar with the
situation of a typical Japanese office. Whenever I lost patience and tried
to get to the point hastily, by asking, for instance, why OLs did not
rebel in spite of unfair treatment, I was met by an uncomfortable si-

lence. Informants often looked confused and annoyed and muttered something like, "It's just not the Japanese way." In contrast, when I referred to the pains of serving tea, or to the curious constraint that men seemed to feel in asking for women's assistance, informants poured their hearts out.

Because I wanted to encourage informants' willingness to speak, interviews were loosely structured with only a number of questions prepared beforehand. My efforts were directed toward understanding how and why OLs could resist male authority in the workplace. I asked female interviewees to describe men in their office whom they liked and disliked, to tell me whether they worked differently depending upon their feelings about a man, and, if so, how. Since most women told me that they took uncooperative attitudes toward men they did not like, I asked them to give concrete examples of how it could be done. Interviews with men were aimed at assessing the extent to which the OLs' acts of resistance disturbed them. I asked them, among other things, whether they took special care not to offend women's feelings, and, if so, why. Furthermore, in order to understand why men could not prevent OLs from resorting to such measures, I asked them to identify things women could do but they could not.

How I Was Received by the Japanese Business Circle

I would like to discuss how my qualifications were interpreted by the temp agencies and by the people at the bank, because I believe such discussion helps us understand this study on gender relations. I initially feared that OLs might not communicate freely with me because I was slightly older than most of them and had gone to college in the United States. I also worried that my overqualification would prevent me from obtaining a job among them. To my surprise, both concerns turned out to be groundless. There were several reasons why my background did not stand in the way of getting to know OLs: in part, a number of coincidences helped to obscure my identity. But, more important, the tenacious, generally accepted notion of what was a properly female role caused people to turn blind eyes to me and, ironically, worked to my advantage.

The major reason why my graduate education at the University of Chicago did not pose a barrier was because the university was relatively little known among lay Japanese. People often had difficulty recalling the name and mislabeled it, for instance, the University of Boston, apparently remembering only the fact that the university had the name of a famous American city. If I had gone to Harvard University, one of the few institutions Japanese seem to know and which they often regard as the American *Tōdai* (the University of Tokyo, the most distinguished institution in Japan), the story would have been radically different. However, since the University of Chicago had a low profile in Japan, it attracted little attention in the process of getting a job and during my work in the bank. In fact, at the time of registration, one of the dispatching agencies advised me nonchalantly to write in my Japanese undergraduate education as my "highest year of schooling" and to put my American graduate training under the heading "technical school."

Another reason why my graduate education in the United States did not arouse interest was the increasing tendency of OLs to quit their jobs and study abroad. After working for a company for several years, these OLs, who were mostly in their mid to late twenties, sought new opportunities by studying abroad. Although some obtained degrees, most hoped to acquire language skills by studying in English-speaking countries for about a year (Taga 1991). The difference between language training and graduate education often seemed to blur in people's minds. In fact, when the student was a woman, graduate education was easily mistaken for language training: I was often complimented on my assiduousness in having gone abroad to study "English," whereas my husband, who also studied in the United States, never received such comments.

The idea of a woman studying abroad for an academic career was foreign to most Japanese, as was graphically illustrated to me during an interview with a businessman. Before I began, I gave a brief description of my research and stated explicitly that I was a doctoral student in sociology at the University of Chicago. At the end of the interview, while we chatted casually, he asked me what I intended to do in the future. I replied that I hoped to teach. He remarked, "You mean you want to teach English conversation to kids in *juku* (private lessons) or something?"

Another factor that might have impeded my getting a job among OLs was my work experience prior to entering graduate school. For four years, I worked as a business analyst for a prominent management consulting firm in Tokyo. Indeed, the manager who interviewed me for the job at the bank fixed his eyes on that part of my résumé and asked me what business analysts did. I answered that we worked as assistants to consultants gathering and analyzing data. For a moment, he looked uncertain as to what to make of that but eventually seemed to decide that an "assistant" sounded feminine enough. He did not inquire further.

When I started working at the bank, many OLs wanted to know where I had worked before. Expecting the name of one of the well-known Japanese corporations mentioned by most previous temporary workers, they were surprised to hear my reply. Yet no OL found my work experience intimidating in any way, because none of them knew of women working in such a firm. OLs seemed to have no context for understanding my experience. I later learned that a "big career" from their point of view was working as a secretary for the president of an eminent company. One of the previous temporary workers happened to be such a woman, and OLs confided to me that they had felt awkward about asking her to serve tea.

Perhaps more than anything else, the fact that I was a married woman seemed to provide an adequate explanation for my rather uncommon background. People both in temp agencies and at the bank assumed that I had followed my husband to the United States so that he could study there. OLs often spoke enviously of my experience living abroad and wished that they could also marry a man who would "take" them there. Frustrated and feeling a little reckless, I pointed out that I had also studied there, but none of the OLs showed much interest. They all assumed that I was making the most of my time in Tokyo by working temporarily during my husband's short assignment there. They seemed never to entertain the idea that my husband and I applied together for graduate study in the United States and then came to Tokyo for the benefit of both our careers.

Overall, my experience tells me that a woman need not worry that her qualifications will make too strong an impression in Japan. If my task had required me to be taken seriously, I would have encountered many difficulties. However, because my task required little except that I fade into the background, there was really no problem at all. I am certain that, had I been a man, my qualifications would have been interpreted quite differently. Indeed, if a man with my qualifications went searching for the type of job that I did, he would have been regarded with suspicion. Luckily and sadly, the fact that I was a woman justified my doing so.

Profiles of *Sararīman*
and Office Ladies Interviewed

Company by Industry	Department/ Position	Education[a]	Marital Status	Age[b]	Tenure
		Sararīman			
Foods	Director	B	M	56	33
Paper & pulp	Manager, Corporate Planning Department	B	M	43	21
Textile	Welfare Section, Personnel Department	B	M	31	9
Chemical	Factory Manager	B	M	50	27
Pharmaceutical	Chief Researcher	M	M	35	11
Electric wiring	Factory Administration	B	S	35	12
Machine tools	System Engineer	M	M	29	5
Heavy electrical equipment	Accounting Department	B	M	36	12
Heavy electrical equipment	Manager, Employment Department	B	M	44	21
General electrical & electronic products	System Engineer, Total Information System Department	B	M	31	9
Electronic communications equipment	Assistant General Manager, Semi-conductor Division	B	M	45	23

Company by Industry	Department/ Position	Education[a]	Marital Status	Age[b]	Tenure
	Sararīman				
Home electronics	Branch Chief Secretary, Labor Union	M	M	34	12
Automobile	General Manager, Production & Market Strategy Office	B	M	48	25
Precision equipment	Leader, Planning Group, Sales Head Office	B	M	40	18
General trading	Manager, Industrial Machinery & Plant Section	B	M	39	17
General trading	Heavy Equipment Department	M	M	32	7
Shipping	Assistant Branch Manager	B	M	46	22
Banking	Marketing Department	M	M	30	2[c]
Banking	Branch Salesman	B	S	28	4
Banking	Financial Market Department	M	S	33	1[c]
Banking	Capital Market Department	B	M	30	8
Banking	Branch Manager	B	M	51	28
Banking & leasing	Ex-Personnel Manager, President	B	M	65	42
Stockbrokerage	Security Analyst	B	S	24	2
Stockbrokerage	Manager, General Planning Office	B	M	41	17
Life insurance	International Planning Group, International Administration Department	M	S	31	8
Life insurance	Personnel Department	B	M	33	10
Marine & fire insurance	Assistant Manager, Recruiting Section	B	M	35	13
Real estate	Sales Manager	B	M	34	11
Services	Researcher	M	S	28	2[c]

Company by Industry	Department/ Position	Education[a]	Marital Status	Age[b]	Tenure
		OLs			
Foods	Public Relations Department	B	S	25	3
Chemical	General Affairs Department	B	M	29	6
Pharmaceutical[d]	Sales & Marketing Department	JC	M	28	8
Rubber products	Research Laboratory	JC	S	23	2
Cement	Accounting Department	JC	S	29	9
Iron & steel	Office Automation Promotion Section	B	S	25	3
General electrical & electronic products	Heavy Electric Equipment Department	JC	S	27	7
Electronic communications equipment	Systems Development Division	JC	S	27	7
Home electronics	Legal Affairs Department	JC	M	28	8
Home electronics	Export Control Office	JC	S	22	2
Home electronics	Corporate Planning Department	JC	S	23	3
Automobile[d]	Pacific Department, Export Division	B	S	25	2
Construction	Private Sector Department	B	S	31	9
General trading[d]	Foreign Exchange Section, Financial Department	B	S	26	4
General trading	Industrial Machinery Department	B	S	31	9
General trading	Business Strategy Office	JC	S	38	17
General trading[d]	Industrial Plastics Department	B	S	25	3
Electronic components trading	Device Production, System Export Department	JC	S	22	2
Shipping	Secretariat Office, General Affairs Division	JC	S	30	9

Company by Industry	Department/ Position	Education[a]	Marital Status	Age[b]	Tenure
		OLs			
Airline	Recruiting Section	JC	S	22	2
Banking	Systems Control Division	JC	S	24	3
Banking	Branch Teller	B	S	29	7
Banking	Systems Management Department	B	S	26	4
Banking	Real Estate Development Department	B	S	24	2
Credit association	Branch Teller	JC	S	24	4
Leasing	Compensation & Welfare Office	B	M	31	9
Stockbrokerage	Securities Department	B	S	23	1
Life insurance	Financial Planning Office	B	S	26	4
Marine & fire insurance[d]	Reinsurance Department	JC	M	29	9
Real estate	Total Quality Control Promotion Department	B	S	33	11

[a]Short terms used for educational background: M = holds a master's degree, B = holds a bachelor's degree, JC = finished junior college.

[b]Average age of businessmen is 37.9 years. Average age of OLs is 26.8 years.

[c]Short tenure because of job change. Average tenure of businessmen is 14.4 years. Average tenure of OLs is 5.6 years.

[d]Recently retired OLs. Marital status, age, and tenure are those at the time of retirement.

Profiles of Fifteen Office Ladies at Tōzai Bank

Name	Education[a]	Marital Family Status[b]	Age[c]	Tenure[d]	Residence (single OLs only)
Maeda	B	S	23	0.5	At parents
Kurimoto	JC	S	27	6.5	At parents
Yamada	HS	Separated w. C	44	25.5	—
Nakagawa	B	E>M>R	26	4.5	At parents[e]
Saito	HS	S>E	28	9.5	Alone
Tsuji	HS	M w/o. C	28	9.5	—
Ueda	B	M w/o. C	26	4.5	—
Matsumoto	JC	S	23	3.5	At parents
Yasukawa	JC	S	24	4.5	At parents
Aoyama	B	S	24	1.5	At parents
Hayashi	B	S>E>M>R	25	2.5	At parents[e]
Kuze	JC	S	23	2.5	At parents
Sugisawa	B	S	24	1.5	Alone
Shimazaki	JC	M>w. C	31	11.5	—
Imai	HS	S>E	27	9.5	At parents

[a]Abbreviations for educational background: B = holds a bachelor's degree, JC = finished junior college, HS = finished high school.
[b]Abbreviations for marital and family status: S = single, E = engaged, M = married, R = retired, w. or w/o. C = with or without children.
[c]At the start of the study. Average age is 26.9 years.
[d]At the start of the study. Average tenure is 6.5 years.
[e]Until marriage.

Profiles of Interviewees
on Valentine's Day Gift-Giving

Company by Industry	Department/Position	Education[a]	Marital Status	Age[b]
	Sararīman			
Pharmaceutical	Manager, Customer Relations Section	B	M	35
Automobile	Auditor's Section, Accounting Department	B	S	29
Automobile	Sales Promotion Department	B	S	27
General trading	Fine Chemical Products Department	B	S	26
Banking	Project Development Department	B	M	31
Banking	Business Development Department	B	M	28
Banking	International Inspection Department	B	M	31
Stockbrokerage	Research Section, International Business Department	B	S	26
Stockbrokerage	International Underwriting Department	B	M	31
Stockbrokerage	Underwriting Business Department	B	S	27

183

Company by Industry	Department/Position	Education[a]	Marital Status	Age[b]
		Ex-OLs		
Textile	Publicity Section, Public Information Department	B	M	26
Chemical	Pharmaceutical Business Department	B	M	28
Home electronics	Overseas Copiers Sales Department	B	M	24
Home electronics	Secretary, Director's Office	B	M	26
General trading	Rubber Department	B	S	28
Banking	Foreign Exchange, Branch Office	B	S	25
Banking	Receptionist	JC	S	24
Public financial corporation	Food Capital Section, Agricultural Department	JC	S	27
Stockbrokerage	Recruiting Section, Personnel Department	B	S	24
Mortgage	General Affairs, Branch Office	B	M	28

Informants' profiles a year before the interview when they spent Valentine's Day in Japan.

[a]Abbreviations for educational background: B = holds a bachelor's degree, JC = finished junior college.

[b]Average age of businessmen is 29.1 and of ex-OLs 26 years.

Summary of Telephone Interviews with *Sararīman* Wives Regarding White Day

Husband's Company by Industry	Husband's Age[a]	Wife's Age[b]	Wife's "OL" Experience	Wife's Concern for White Day
Foods	34	33	Yes	Concerned
Chemical	41	38	No	Concerned
Chemical	32	32	Yes	Concerned
Iron & steel	50	46	No	Unconcerned
Electric wiring	37	33	Yes	Concerned
General electrical & electronic products	33	32	Yes	Concerned
Electronic communications equipment	35	34	Yes	Concerned
Home electronics	33	31	Yes	Concerned
Electronic instruments	45	50	Yes	Concerned
Electronic instruments	40	44	Yes	Concerned
Automobile	32	31	Yes	Concerned
Printing	33	30	Yes	—[c]
Construction	43	33	No	Unconcerned
General trading	53	51	Yes	Concerned
General trading	44	42	Yes	Concerned
Retail	38	35	No	Unconcerned
Banking	50	46	Yes	Concerned
Credit association	48	43	No	Unconcerned
Stockbrokerage	42	36	Yes	Concerned

Husband's Company by Industry	Husband's Age[a]	Wife's Age[b]	Wife's "OL" Experience	Wife's Concern for White Day
Life insurance	36	33	Yes	Concerned
Marine & fire insurance	31	31	Yes	Concerned
Marine & fire insurance	29	28	Yes	—[c]
Land transportation	42	37	Yes	Concerned
Shipping	64	59	Yes	Concerned
Broadcasting	33	35	Yes	Concerned
Communications	35	31	No	Unconcerned
Publishing	37	38	Yes	Concerned
Services	45	37	No	Unconcerned
Services	39	32	Yes	Concerned
Services	32	32	Yes	Concerned

[a]Average is 39.5 years.
[b]Average is 37.1 years.
[c]The husband upheld a policy of not returning gifts on White Day.

Notes

Introduction

1. Ōsawa Machiko (1993) conducted a detailed analysis of why the gap between the wages of males and females has not decreased in Japan despite the expansion of women's activities in the labor market and improvement of their education. She has found that in large companies the discrepancy between labor productivity and wages increases as female workers accumulate tenure. She concludes that it is not women's short tenure that limits their chances for developing a career, but the seniority wage system and assignment of assistant-type jobs to women that necessitate companies to prompt their early retirement.

Ōsawa Mari (1993) argues that women play an important role in maintaining the competitiveness and flexibility of the permanent employment system that protects the "core" male employees. She describes how middle-aged women reentering the labor market after marriage and child rearing do not have any other option but to work as part-time employees with low wages and instability. She adds that employers frequently use the term *part-timer* to distinguish a worker's employment status. Many of the so-called part-time employees, the overwhelming majority of whom are women, work as many hours as permanent regular employees but lack the permanent employees' job security and benefits. The system that guarantees lifetime employment to a select few is made possible at the expense of these less fortunate workers.

Mary Brinton (1988, 1993) offers a powerful explanation of how Japanese gender stratification is supported by major social institutions, which provide and constrain individual men and women's choices. She compares Japanese and American human capital development processes and argues that both the educational and employment systems in Japan encourage sponsorship. Because critical human capital development decisions must be made in a few years in the individual's early life, someone other than the individual—usually parents and employers—plays an important role in making those decisions. Such sponsored contests and the structure of intrafamilial exchange promote "underinvestment" in women's capabilities and maintain gender stratification in Japan.

2. Glenda Roberts (1994) gives a valuable portrait of women working on the assembly line in a large lingerie factory. Dorinne Kondo (1990) writes perceptively about the construction of self of female part-time employees in a small, family-owned business in *shitamachi* (downtown) Tokyo. Anne Allison's exceptional research on corporate nightlife (1994) introduces us to a rarely studied dimension of Japanese white-collar workers' lives and discusses how the identities of female hostesses and male customers are structured in the nightclubs. Other accounts include the studies of professional women by Takie Lebra (1981) and Masako Osako (1978), office ladies by James McLendon (1983), women in politics by Susan Pharr (1981), geisha by Liza Dalby (1983), all-female Takarazuka theater actors by Jennifer Robertson (1992), urban housewives by Anne Imamura (1987) and Suzanne Vogel (1978), and rural women by Gail Bernstein (1983) and Robert Smith and Ella Wiswell (1982). See also Janet Hunter (1993); Joyce Lebra, Roy Paulson, and Elizabeth Powers (1976); and Jeannie Lo (1990).

3. According to Iwao Sumiko (1993), Japanese people differ fundamentally from Americans in that they let pragmatism rather than principles guide their behavior. The Japanese woman can therefore more readily accept becoming a loser in one game if she can be a winner in another.

4. Anne Allison writes that although "[o]n the surface, men may seem to have gotten the better of the deal," the company man must eventually retire to a home that has long been managed and controlled by his wife (1994, 204).

5. For example, Jane Collier (1974) argues that women in a Mayan community in southern Mexico use domestically available resources to suit their ends, such as seeking divorces and using their sons' loyalty and allegiance to weaken lineage solidarity. Similarly, Margery Wolf (1972) describes how women in China cultivate a power base and emotional support by defining their family as a uterine unit in opposition to its socially recognized definition as a patrilineal unit and by working to maintain close, loyal bonds among its members in their capacity as the head of the uterine family. On the basis of information gathered by listening to the conversations of female friends at their kitchen tables in a Norwegian city, Marianne Gullestad (1984) has found that women are more articulate and influential than men in setting moral rules concerning love, sex, and other aspects of personal relationships. Women are the ones who debate, maintain, and change cultural ideas and values about the rights and wrongs of sexual expression.

6. See Susan Rogers (1978) for a detailed discussion of her theoretical orientations. She has since made adjustments to her original model in her comparative study of two French communities (1985).

7. Women's informal access to power while giving the credible performance of male dominance is also illustrated by Janice Boddy (1989). In her excellent study of spirit possession in Hofriyat, northern Sudan, she describes how a woman possessed can express her grievances against her husband and other male relatives and make demands that are under normal conditions prohibitive. According to Boddy, women must exercise skill and strategic acumen to achieve

their goals. Inspired by Pierre Bourdieu (1977), she asserts that it is only in losing to men that women can win—"only in losing, and losing judiciously, that they can activate their fertility, pursue reproductive careers, and attain their social goals. Women who wield power must do so implicitly, leaving the appearance of power to men. . . . Through strategic compliance, women might negotiate their subordination" (1989, 185).

Much as I appreciate Boddy's discerning argument that men who appear to be winning are as subject to cultural constraints as women, my analysis departs from Boddy's insistence on separating power from agency. I am concerned less with forms of impersonal domination as studied by Foucault (1979; 1980), to whom Boddy refers, than with personal domination and the ways in which it is opposed by human action. For example, although modern companies are run by "scientific techniques" and bureaucratic rules, these disciplinary forms of control are mediated by agents, in the sense that they are experienced by subordinates as personal and arbitrary exercises of power. In addition, *culture*, as used by Boddy, is by definition hegemonic. There is little to gain in establishing power as a separate concept, if we ascribe the workings of power to culture.

8. On how rational, technical, and allegedly gender-neutral organizational systems hide a gendered substructure, see Joan Acker (1990) and Dorothy Smith (1988).

9. A similar argument can be found in Tsuneyoshi Ryoko's study of American and Japanese primary schools (1992), in which she compares prevalent leadership styles. She maintains that leadership in Japan typically depends on emotional agreement, whereas leadership in the United States is often based on a formal authority structure.

10. I am interested in analyzing symbolic resources and cultural repertoires that subordinate women rely on to maneuver. However, I do not intend to theorize away the obvious point that dominating men have more economic and political resources than women. Furthermore, although both groups are bound by a set of practices, men usually have more freedom to use their resources than women do.

11. I am unaware of any book-length scholarly research on Japanese female office workers. Shorter, but nonetheless useful, works include Rose Carter and Lois Dilatush's observation based on interviews with selected office ladies (OLs) (1976), Alice Cook and Hayashi Hiroko's depiction of sex-discriminatory customs observed among Japanese institutions (1980), Karen Kelsky's reassessment of OL subculture (1994), Jeannie Lo's fieldwork at an electronic company (1990), James McLendon's description of the short and superficial careers of OLs (1983), and Susan Pharr's application of a status-conflict model to OLs' refusal to pour tea for fellow male workers (1984; 1990). Journalist Jane Condon also has a chapter on OLs in her book about Japanese women (1985).

12. *Sararīman* (salaried man) is an English expression coined in Japan and is usually used to indicate a male white-collar worker.

13. Matsunaga Mari and Hioki Kōichiro (1996) and Kōnno Minako (1996) argue that we need to understand how women become marginalized in the workplace, in contradistinction to studies that emphasize how women's career patterns are determined before and outside their work experience.

14. Michele Lamont (1992), who conducted 160 interviews in her comparative study of class boundaries among the American and French upper-middle class, maintains that her blurred cultural identity as a Quebecoise allowed her to question taken-for-granted notions more freely than either a native American or French researcher. At the same time, having lived in both the U.S. and France, she was sufficiently familiar with both cultures to appreciate subtle nuances and to probe speakers fruitfully. Likewise, Rebecca Klatch (1987), who spoke to thirty conservative women in American politics, attributes part of her success in earning their trust to her identity as a graduate student, which placed her in a nonthreatening position as someone who was keen on obtaining new information. She found it beneficial to have familiarized herself with the issues so that she could ask intelligent questions. Faye Ginsburg (1989) similarly relates that although she was in many ways "culturally strange" to her informants on abortion issues in North Dakota, this fact did not pose serious communication barriers. Her questions about and interest in people's feelings about marriage, birth control, and motherhood were treated as the natural curiosity of a single woman. According to Ginsburg, speakers often framed their responses as if to counsel her about her own future conjugal happiness.

15. Tōzai is a pseudonymous name that means "east and west."

16. Some of the material in chapters 3 and 5 has appeared in Japanese in "Shokubanai no jendā kankei" (Gender relations in the Japanese workplace), *Soshiki Kagaku* 30, no. 2 (1996): 27–36 and "Kigyō ni okeru OL no teikō kōi" (Women's acts of resistance in Japanese companies), *Shakai Keizai Shisutemu* 15 (1996): 51–6. Portions of chapters 4 and 6 have appeared in "Meanings of Chocolate: Power and Gender in Valentine's Gift Giving," *International Journal of Japanese Sociology* 5 (1996): 41–66.

Chapter 1: The Japanese Labor Market and Office Ladies

1. For a complete description and analysis of women's employment patterns, see Brinton 1989, 1993; Brinton, Ngo, and Shibuya 1991; Brinton and Ngo 1993; Ōsawa Machiko 1984, 1993; Ōsawa Mari 1993; Shimada and Higuchi 1985; Takenaka and Kuba 1994; Tanaka 1987; Yashiro 1981.

2. Thomas Rohlen maintains that the crucial watershed is the rank of *kachō*, which is higher than *kakarichō*, and that little social distinction is connected with the ranks below it: "In the white-collar world, a man's achievements become worthy of general notice and respect when he is appointed to head a section or branch. The rank connotes a leader, a man of responsibility, and, particularly, a person with a group of subordinates" (1974, 26).

3. Unless otherwise indicated, all translations are mine.

4. Some of the more well-known books include *All that's OL!; Gendai OL repōto: Shuki de miru shigoto, jōshi, kekkonkan* (Report on OLs today: Their views on work, bosses, and marriage disclosed in diaries); *Imadoki OL daizu-*

kan (The encyclopedia of contemporary OLs); *It's OL show time!: Torendī OL no 24 jikan o yomu 42 kō* (It's OL show time!: Forty-two lessons on the fashionable OLs' day); *Josei ga wakaranakunatta ojisamatachi e* (For men who can no longer understand women); *Nippon no OL tachi* (Japanese office ladies); *OL jutsu* (The art of being an OL); *Saigo ni warau OL wa dareda?* (Who is the last OL to laugh?); *Shin OL zukan* (The new OLs' pictorial book); *Tonari no OL zubari 36 gyōkai* (OLs next door in thirty-six industries speak frankly); and the series *Ojisan kaizō kōza* (Lessons for transforming men). There are numerous books written as manuals for new and intending OLs, including *"Muteki" na OL ni naru hō: Furesshāzu ofisu gaido* (How to become an "invincible" OL: An office guide for newly hired women) and *OL hajimete monogatari: Shinnyū shain ga kaita kaisha seikatsu manyuaru* (First-time-being-an-OL story: A guide to life in the company written by newly hired women).

5. Although it is impossible to provide a complete list of surveys on OLs, recent examples include Arutoman Kenkyūjo, 1990, "Tōsei dokushin OL katagi: Renai kekkon hen" (Contemporary, single OL spirit: A section on love and marriage); Arutoman Kenkyūjo, 1991, "Tōsei dokushin OL katagi: Shigoto hen" (Contemporary, single OL spirit: A section on work); Chiyoda Seimei Hoken Sōgo Kaisha, 1992, "Shinguru bijinesuman, OL kinsen kankaku ishiki chōsa" (Survey on single businessmen's and OLs' monetary senses); Citzen Tokei, 1991, "OL no shūkan jikanbo chōsa" (OLs' weekly hours survey); Dōwa Kasai Kaijō Hoken Kabushiki Kaisha, 1988, "Dokushin OL ni miru 'goji kara onna' no kōdō chōsa" (Survey on single OLs' 'after-five women" behaviors); Dōwa Kasai Kaijō Hoken Kabushiki Kaisha, 1992, "Yangu bijinesuman, OL no 'risuku manejimento' ishiki" ("Risk management" consciousness of young businessmen and OLs); Heiwadō Bōeki, 1990, "Bijinesuman, OL no 'jikan' chōsa" (Survey on businessmen's and OLs' "time"); Kabushiki Kaisha Yakult, 1990, "Gendai OL no kenkō ishiki to 'haiben' ni kansuru chōsa" (Survey on contemporary OLs' health consciousness and bowel movements); Kanebō Kabushiki Kaisha, 1990, "'Kiriya zoku' ni kiku kyariyado chōsa kekka" (Survey results of career-mindedness of "kiriya" women); Kokusai Bunka Kyōiku Sentā, 1991, "'Ryūgaku' o kangaeru OL ishiki chōsa" (Survey on OLs who consider studying abroad); Nihon Keizai Shinbunsha, 1992, "Wākingu ūman 500 nin no gifuto raifu" (Gift-giving lives of five-hundred working women); Nikkei Sangyō Shōhi Kenkyūjo, 1989, "Dokushin OL no shōhi kōdō" (Single OLs' consumption behavior); Pōla Bunka Kenkyūjo, 1989, "Nijūdai shinguru futsū no OL tachi" (OLs in their twenties, single, and ordinary); Sanwa Ginkō, 1992, "Dokushin sararīman, OL no seikatsu jittai tettei chōsa" (Complete survey on the true lives of single salaried men and OLs); Sumitomo Ginkō, 1991, "Sararīman, OL no natsuyasumi sō-kessan ankēto chōsa" (Questionnaire surveys on summer holidays of salaried men and OLs).

6. I avoid giving the equivalent dollars for yen in this book. Because the purchasing power of money in the Japanese and the American economies is so different, I find such "equivalents" misleading. However, readers may wish to note that the average exchange rate was 126.65 yen to one U.S. dollar in 1992, according to International Financial Statistics.

7. The names of the OLs as well as other employees of the bank have been changed to protect their identities.

8. On the definition of *OL*, see for example *All That's OL!*; *Imadoki OL daizukan* (The encyclopedia of contemporary OLs); *Saigo ni warau OL wa dareda?* (Who is the last OL to laugh?); and *Tonari no OL zubari 36 gyōkai* (OLs next door in thirty-six industries speak frankly).

9. For excellent research on the effects of the EEO Law on the Japanese employment system, see Alice Lam (1992). She finds that although there have been improvements, the law does not fundamentally change Japanese business practices that discriminate against women. Frank Upham has also written a chapter on the passage of the EEO Law (1987). For a more technical aspect of the law, refer to Lorraine Parkinson (1989).

10. Although I feel it inappropriate to refer to adult women as "girls," I use it in translation when it is the word used by the interviewee.

11. I thank Glenda Roberts for calling my attention to this point.

12. Both at Tōzai and in the bank where the interviewee worked, if a woman in the integrated track married a colleague, the custom was that she stayed.

13. For a detailed analysis of the gap between the wages of men and women in Japan, see Kawashima Yoko (1983, 1985), Ōsawa Machiko (1984, 1993), Shinotsuka Eiko (1982), Tomita Yasunobu (1988), and Yashiro Naohiro (1980).

14. Ōsawa Machiko questions the legitimacy of such claims repeatedly made by employers to discriminate against women (1993). She maintains that it is the seniority wage system and the assignment of low-level clerical jobs to women that make women retire early, not women's tendency to retire that make companies assign them low-level jobs. For an analysis of women's rate of leaving jobs, see also Higuchi Yoshio (1991) and Tomita Yasunobu (1988).

15. The cost of evaluating OLs may not be limited to nonpecuniary matters such as damage to human relations in the office. In recent years, women's length of tenure has increased, and a number of companies have reconsidered their policy of not evaluating women. (For further discussion on this issue, see the conclusion of this book.) According to one male interviewee, the reaction of the overwhelming majority of employees in a firm where it was announced that they would start evaluating not only male but female workers was that it was such a nuisance (*mendō*). Everyone who was to assess at least one subordinate's work had to participate in three special training sessions to learn ways to assess another's work. The man felt that it was difficult to justify such training and other expenses accompanying the appraisal of OLs when their work was not taken seriously.

16. On the marriage metaphor, see *Nihon Keizai Shinbun*, 16 March 1992, "Tachiagare! Kaishazuma-tachi musume-tachi" (Stand Up! Office wives and office daughters), and *Nihon Keizai Shinbun*, 1 June 1992, "Iwaneba naoranu 'shanaizuma atsukai'" (Men will not stop treating women as "office wives" unless we speak up).

17. The OLs at Tōzai had a nickname for men with no sense of using office machines: they were called *pīchi-chan* (peach-chan). I do not know the origin of the term, but suspect that it has something to do with both words, *copy* and *peach*, sharing the same sound element, *pī*.

18. On tea pouring, see Nihon Hishokurabu Nōryoku Kōjō Kenkyūkai, ed. (1992).

Chapter 2: Why Office Ladies Do Not Organize

1. See Susan Pharr (1984, 1990) for a rare study of Japanese women's rebellion against tea pouring.

2. On a popular conception of friendship among women, see Mayuzumi Madoka (1996).

3. TV programs called *torendī dorama* (trendy drama) were popular among OLs at the time of my research. They were so well liked, in fact, that quite a few OLs watched at least one every night. *Torendī dorama* were love stories with many twists and turns involving a young heroine, often an OL, and set in a fashionable town with "trendy" restaurants and smartly decorated apartments. Because the same programs were watched by many OLs, they offered shared experiences. According to one viewer, "It's as if all of us were riding a jet coaster together everyday" (*Nihon Keizai Shinbun*, 19 February 1992).

4. A similar phenomenon is observed by Rodney Clark at a medium-sized box manufacturer (1979). When the company was new and small but growing rapidly, there weren't enough university graduates to fill the upper ranks. Therefore, a number of high-school graduates occupied important positions, including department heads and deputy heads. However, as the company became bigger and more established, there was increasingly less opportunity for high-school graduates to achieve such high ranks because it was impossible for the company to promote them ahead of university graduates.

5. Glenda Roberts makes a similar comparison between men and women working for a large lingerie manufacturer. According to her, men know precisely where they stand in the hierarchical order and where to set their goals from the time they join the firm, whereas women experience little status differentiation. She describes how difficult it is when women who have diverse backgrounds—young and old, unmarried and married, childless and with children—are "thrown together on a daily basis and expected to work harmoniously" (1994, 108).

6. Mary Brinton has found that in Japanese firms more than twice as many male workers as female workers experience job rotation in their first job. According to her, this is because employers restrict job rotation, a particularly important type of training in the Japanese workplace, to employees who can be expected to remain with the firm over a long period (1991).

7. Because of the absence of young men on the floor, the *chiyahoyasareru* treatment of younger OLs by men at Tōzai also was not as apparent as the treatment described by interviewees from other companies.

8. Kathleen Gerson (1985; 1993) and Arlie Hochschild with Anne Machung (1989), among others, have shown how work and family decisions are inseparable for men and women. Expectations held and choices made in one sphere

depend critically on the opportunities, incentives, and limits in the other. Similarly, Madeleine MacDonald (1981) and Mariam David (1978) point out that the processes of class and gender reproduction occur simultaneously in the school and the family. Some scholars further argue that the separation of work and family is an ideological construction that renders women "invisible" in political and economic arenas (Powell and Clarke 1976; Joan Scott 1988).

9. Intended retirement from a company in some cases emboldens a woman, who no longer needs to maintain a harmonious relationship with her boss and colleagues. Occasionally such a thought leads the woman to pursue radical measures and express her displeasure. This aspect of "voice en route to exit" is discussed in chapter 5.

10. My findings are consistent with analyses by both Mary Brinton and Jeannie Lo, who argue that employers encourage OLs to regard marriage instead of work as their ultimate goal. Brinton describes how employers play the role of stakeholders in women's mobility into marriage and out of the firm (1992). According to her, some employers hire as clerical workers attractive young women with the hope that they become possible future wives for their promising young male employees. Similarly, Lo describes how the personnel division of a large electric and electronic equipment manufacturer attempts to attract women who wish to work for a few years, marry, and then leave the company (1990).

11. One distribution firm considered a woman's exit upon marriage or first childbirth "convenient to the company" (*kaisha tsugō*) and increased the amount of retirement allowance she received. The premium paid was five hundred to six hundred thousand yen in the case of a twenty-eight-year-old junior-college graduate. An iron and steel manufacturer reportedly admitted that although the retirement premium was meant to be primarily a congratulatory gift, it might indirectly promote women's early withdrawal from the workplace (*Nihon Keizai Shinbun*, 15 December 1993).

12. As provided by the Labor Standards Law, a working woman may take maternity leave for up to six weeks (ten weeks in case of twins or more) before the birth of a child and must take at least six weeks and may take up to eight weeks after the birth. Although the law does not establish policies concerning payment, many firms pay salaries to women taking maternity leave. In case a firm fails to do so, health insurance provides for 60 percent of the salary, so most women are assured at least that much of their income. The more recent Childcare Leave Law, which gives parents the right to a leave from work until a child turns one year old, was enacted in 1992. One of the major problems for parents taking childcare leave, however, was economic, as no payment was usually made during the time. In order to promote childcare leave, several improvements were made in 1995. First, 25 percent of the salary is to be paid from unemployment insurance (20 percent paid during the leave and 5 percent six months after resuming work). In addition, a person may waive paying the health and welfare annuity insurance and defer paying the inhabitants' tax. Since these changes, much of the discussion concerning childcare leave has fo-

cused on various informal pressures in the workplace that prevent employees from taking it. For more on childcare leave, refer to Hayashi Hiroko (1992) and *Rōdōshō* (1995).

13. See Glenda Roberts's study at a large garment manufacturer, where she reports a similar phenomenon (1994). In addition, Roberts observes that women working in the factory found it difficult to organize in support of an issue that did not affect all women equally right away, because those who asked for improved working conditions were often accused of being self-indulgent.

Chapter 3: Gossip

1. I thank Glenda Roberts for calling my attention to this aspect.

2. Needless to say, OLs' seemingly irresponsible attitudes toward work stemmed from the fact that women were seldom seriously evaluated and that they had little prospect for promotion. OLs often had more freedom to express their feelings straightforwardly than men, many of who had to struggle in the race for promotion. Therefore, it is absolutely misdirected to conclude from OLs' attitudes that women are less serious and more emotional than men. (See chapter 5 and conclusion for more discussion.)

3. See, for example, *All That's OL!*; *Imadoki OL daizukan* (The encyclopedia of contemporary OLs); *It's OL Show Time!: Torendī OL no 29 jikan o yomu 42 kō* (It's OL show time: Forty-two lessons on the fashionable OLs' day); *Josei ga wakaranakunatta ojisamatachi e* (For men who can no longer understand women); *Nippon no OL tachi* (Japanese office ladies); the series *Ojisan kaizō kōza* (Lessons for transforming men); *OL jutsu* (The art of being an OL); *Saigo ni warau OL wa dareda?* (Who is the last OL to laugh?); *Shin OL zukan* (The new OLs' pictorial book); and *Tonari no OL zubari 36 gyōkai* (OLs next door in thirty-six industries speak frankly).

4. It may seem that Tōzai OLs' practice of calling younger male employees "those young ones" or "the young people" contradicts with the use of the term *ojisan*. The former expresses the men's objective position in the hierarchy, whereas the latter denies that position. However, in both instances, OLs choose terms that show their detachment from office hierarchy. Some OLs call men older than themselves "those young ones" because they consider themselves outside of the hierarchy. The word *ojisan* does away with rank and title altogether. In both cases, OLs declare that office hierarchy cannot bring them to their knees. They are not part of it. Moreover, OLs alternate between the two terms as it suits them. When they call young members of a company "those young ones," they emphasize their lowly position within the organization, whereas for older *ojisan*, they ignore their important titles.

5. On the relationship between gender and the power to look, see also Sandra Bartky (1982). In his study of the distorting effects of the male, colonial gaze on Algerian women, Malek Alloula (1986) analyzes picture postcards of Algerian women produced by the French during colonization. He shows how

the postcards represent not so much Algeria and Algerian women as French-men's phantasms and stereotypes of the Oriental female.

6. David Gilmore similarly asserts that just as women are forced to forgo public life, men are forced to forgo the tranquillity and comfort of the home (1990). Neither deprivation, according to Gilmore, can be said to be more re-pressive than the other.

Chapter 4: Popularity Poll

1. The analysis is based on data collected through participant observation conducted at Tōzai Bank as well as interviews with ten Japanese businessmen from large Japanese corporations attending business school at the University of Chicago and ten wives of such men who had in the past worked as OLs in Japa-nese offices. (Appendix D shows detailed profiles of the interviewees.) These Japanese men were company-sponsored students, who expected to return to their original organizations after completing the two-year curriculum.

Couples were not interviewed; that is, a wife was not interviewed if her hus-band had been selected as an interviewee, and vice versa.

2. This woman is not the wife of a student at the University of Chicago, but belongs to the primary group of sixty interviewees. Her story is included be-cause she volunteered information on Valentine's Day in her office.

3. In her study of literary reception in three different parts of the world—the United States, Great Britain, and the West Indies—Wendy Griswold (1987) argues that cultural power derives in part from a work's ability to sustain diver-gent interpretations.

4. For an excellent study of how people turn money—a homogeneous, im-personal instrument of material exchange—into a sentimental personalized gift, see Viviana Zelizer (1994).

Chapter 5: Acts of Resistance

1. It should be noted that in Japan, wives do not usually participate in cor-porate social events and entertainment.

2. Arlie Hochschild reports in her remarkable research on two-career fami-lies that a husband's irritated or glum expression can discourage a wife from asking for his help in domestic chores (Hochschild, with Machung 1989).

3. The OL seemed to find it easier to decline a request made by a vice-general manager than by another OL. When the man seated next to her asked her whether she would similarly decline a woman's request, the OL replied, "Of course, not! I wouldn't be aggressive toward another woman. Besides, I know that the woman is making a request on behalf of another man. No, I would never flatly refuse a woman's request."

4. See Judith Stacey's compelling account of fundamentalist family life in Silicon Valley (1991) for a parallel discussion of men's formal power that is sel-

dom used. She describes a wife's subordination to her husband dictated by the Bible as "patriarchy in the last instance" (133), because an occasion when she actually yields to his authority is rare. Marc Swartz also provides an example from Swahili marital relations in which husbands rarely use the power they have over their wives because the exercise of their power is made costly in a society that offers men few alternative sources of intimacy and emotional support (1982). Refer also to Tsuneyoshi Ryoko's comparison between prevalent leadership styles in United States and Japan, which she characterizes as formal and informal respectively (1992).

5. Managers were concerned with OLs' marriage plans because they had to ask the personnel department to fill vacancies when OLs married and retired.

6. A similar phenomenon is observed by Rodney Clark in his study of a medium-sized Japanese producer of boxes. He notes that on the confidential questionnaire forms distributed by the personnel department each year, "only women went so far as directly to criticize their superiors" (1979, 208).

7. As we have seen, most large Japanese companies recruit OLs only from among new graduates. As a result, new OLs join organizations only in April, after graduating from school in March.

8. Although many companies expect OLs to retire from the workplace early in their careers, it is important to note that companies do not want OLs to retire too early. Most companies hope that an OL will work for at least three years before retirement so they can recover recruiting and training expenses.

Chapter 6: Men Curry Favor with Women

1. On gift-giving in Japan, see for example Befu 1968, 1971; Bestor 1989; Hendry 1993; Itō and Kurita 1984; and Murobushi 1989.

2. In some cases, a man may use gifts in an attempt to try to date, have an affair with, or seduce an OL. Because in Japanese firms romance is thought to interfere with employees' dedication to work, people usually avoid an open display of sexual interest in a coworker. Even couples intent on getting married keep their engagement secret until the right moment comes for them to announce their plans (Rohlen 1974). Under the circumstances, a man who wishes to give gifts to a woman as a form of courtship is most likely to do so in private. I say with some confidence, therefore, that the public gift-giving I observed was primarily an act of currying favor in order to gain women's cooperation, and not a romantic gesture.

3. None of the men I interviewed gave gifts on White Day to women who had not given them chocolate on Valentine's Day, and none of the women received gifts from men to whom they had not given chocolate on Valentine's Day.

4. Lingerie is a popular White Day gift. The point here is that, when lingerie is given, it is given indiscriminately: one general manager gave lingerie as a White Day gift to all the OLs working on the Tōzai floor.

Conclusion

1. Anne Allison provides a comparable example in her discussion of Japanese businessmen who frequent nightclubs and depend on hostesses to successfully promote camaraderie among them for the benefit of business or work (1994).

2. A similar way in which the weaker party claims entitlement from the dominant is observed by Eugene Genovese in his brilliant study of American slavery (1976). According to Genovese, the masters felt an extreme need for the gratitude of their slaves; without that gratitude, they could not define themselves as moral human beings. However, the slaves considered their masters' protection and care their due. From their point of view, gratitude implied equality, whereas paternalistic dependency emphasized reciprocity. The slaves felt they earned masters' support for services they loyally rendered. Genovese thus maintains that the slaves' accommodation to paternalism enabled them to assert certain rights.

3. Similarly, Dorothy Holland and Margaret Eisenhart (1990) report that the resistance they found among female students in an American college consisted of strategic compliance. Because the high-pressure peer system propelled young women into a cultural world of romance, school authority could not be personified as a target for opposition. Resistance against gender hierarchy, therefore, tended to remain internalized and idiosyncratic. According to Kathleen Gerson (1985), women who chose to affirm traditional gender arrangements saw that they had less to gain and more to lose from the erosion of traditional female "protection." Gerson therefore argues that their compliance should not be understood as a passive acceptance of domination. It was rather an active effort to protect their own interests.

4. Dorinne Kondo (1990) likewise examines how female workers in a small, family-owned factory in Tokyo reject their structural marginality by enacting their conventional gendered identities. However, she questions the adequacy of words such as *accommodation* and *resistance*, because "apparent resistance is constantly mitigated by collusion and compromise at different levels of consciousness, just as accommodation may have unexpectedly subversive effects" (1990, 299). Even if we agree with Kondo's rejection of what she calls "easy definitions of accommodation" that indicate complete submission of the self to the dominant culture, it still seems useful to retain concepts such as *resistance* and *accommodation*. Although, as she says, accommodation may have unexpectedly subversive effects, distinction surely must be made between accommodation with such unintended outcomes and accommodation meant to be subversive. Japanese OLs' efforts to mitigate existing power relations were not subconscious or unconscious reactions to male dominance; they were attempts accompanied by explicit awareness and articulation.

5. Rosabeth Kanter reports that American secretaries' power tactics similarly reinforced stereotypes of women as gossip-prone and emotional (1977).

6. Although Kanter's study is more than twenty years old and American women's situation has certainly changed, I believe that the comparison here remains valid.

Appendix A: Data and Methods

1. Japanese organizations in general seem somewhat more open to non-Japanese students. Although it is difficult to understand why this is so, one explanation is that they tend to lower their guard against foreigners, considering (perhaps erroneously and arrogantly) that *gaijin* (foreigners) will not be able to comprehend Japanese ways of life. On this point, see Matthews Hamabata (1990, 8, 137) and Dorinne Kondo (1990, 13).

Glossary

Japanese words that appear only once in the text and are clearly defined there are excluded from the glossary.

arigatō	"thank you"
BG (*bijinesu gāru*)	"business girl," a popular expression for female office workers during the late 1950s and early 1960s
buchō	general managers, some of whom may be on the board of directors
-chan	a diminutive form of-san, used primarily after the names of (girl) children, but also after those of intimates, lovers, subordinates, and *kōhai*
chiyahoyasareru	to be puffed up by others' attentions; to be danced attendance on
dōki	those who joined an organization such as a company or school in the same year as the person concerned
enman taisha	harmonious separation from the workplace, such as when a woman quits to marry
gokurō(san)	an expression used to indicate appreciation for someone's services or efforts
ippanshoku	clerical-track workers whose primary responsibility is to assist *sōgōshoku* staff; also sometimes referred to as *jimushoku*
jichō	deputy-general managers
jintoku	personal charm; natural virtue
kachō	section managers; attaining this rank is said to be

201

	the crucial promotion watershed in the white-collar world in Japan
kakarichō	chiefs who usually enjoy nominal social distinction
katatataki	a custom in which a manager taps a subordinate on the shoulder to suggest that it is time for the person to resign
kōhai	one's junior; those who joined an organization such as a company or school after the person concerned
-kun	the masculine form of -chan
ochakumi	tea pouring
ochashitsu	kitchen where OLs prepare tea for customers
ojisan	a term originally meaning an unrelated, middle-aged man, but now sometimes used disparagingly to emphasize a man's estrangement from the youth subculture
OL (ofisu redī)	"office lady," used to indicate a female office worker engaged in simple, routine, clerical jobs usually without any expert knowledge or management responsibility
onnanoko	girls
onnanoko oboe	girls' way of remembering things
otoko no yūjō	male comradeship
sararīman	"salaried man," implying male white-collar worker
senpai	one's seniors; those who joined an organization such as a company or school before the person concerned
shomushoku	employees in the "miscellaneous job" category, who work as company chauffeurs, messengers, mailpeople, bookbinders, building receptionists, and the like
sōgōshoku	workers in the integrated track who are trained to become managers
sōsukan	to be completely shut out, ignored, or ostracized by a group of people
soto	outside
uchi	inside
yohodo no koto ga nai (o shinai) kagiri	unless there is (or one does) something grossly wrong
zaibatsu	constellation of companies extending over a range of different industries, often with cross-holdings of shares and common directorships

References

Abbeglen, James C. 1958. *The Japanese Factory: Aspects of Its Social Organization*. Glencoe, Ill.: Free Press.

Abu-Lughod, Lila. 1986. *Veiled Sentiments: Honor and Poetry in a Bedouin Society*. Berkeley: University of California Press.

Acker, Joan. 1990. "Hierarchies, Jobs, Bodies: A Theory of Gendered Organizations." *Gender and Society* 4 (2): 139–58.

Allison, Anne. 1994. *Nightwork: Sexuality, Pleasure, and Corporate Masculinity in a Tokyo Hostess Club*. Chicago: University of Chicago Press.

Alloula, Malek. 1986. *The Colonial Harem*. Trans. Myrna Godzich and Wlad Godzich. Minneapolis: University of Minnesota Press.

Asahi Shinbun. 4 April 1989. "Ryūgaku OL ga fueteiru" (More OLs are studying abroad).

Bachnik, Jane M. 1982. "Deixis and Self/Other Reference in Japanese Discourse." *Sociolinguistic Working Papers* 99. Austin, Tex.: Southwest Educational Development Laboratory.

Bachnik, Jane M., and Charles J. Quinn Jr., eds. 1994. *Situated Meaning: Inside and Outside in Japanese Self, Society, and Language*. Princeton, N.J.: Princeton University Press.

Bartky, Sandra Lee. 1982. "Narcissism, Femininity, and Alienation." *Social Theory and Practice* 8 (2): 127–43.

Befu, Harumi. 1968. "Gift-Giving in a Modernizing Japan." *Monumenta Nipponica* 23: 445–56.

———. 1971. *Japan: An Anthropological Introduction*. San Francisco: Chandler.

Berger, John. 1972. *Ways of Seeing*. London: British Broadcasting Corporation and Penguin Books.

Bernstein, Gail Lee. 1983. *Haruko's World: A Japanese Farm Woman and Her Community*. Stanford: Stanford University Press.

Bestor, Theodore. 1989. *Neighborhood Tokyo*. Tokyo: Kōdansha International.

Bic Bridal. 1996. *BB hakusho* (The BB white paper). Tokyo: Bic Bridal.

Blau, Peter M. 1964. *Exchange and Power in Social Life*. New York: Wiley.

Boddy, Janice. 1989. *Wombs and Alien Spirits: Women, Men, and the Zar Cult in Northern Sudan*. Madison: University of Wisconsin Press.

Bourdieu, Pierre. 1977. *Outline of a Theory of Practice*. Trans. Richard Nice. Cambridge: Cambridge University Press.

Brinton, Mary C. 1988. "The Social-Institutional Bases of Gender Stratification: Japan as an Illustrative Case." *American Journal of Sociology* 94 (2): 300–334.

———. 1989. "Gender Stratification in Contemporary Urban Japan." *American Sociological Review* 54: 549–64.

———. 1991. "Sex Differences in On-the-Job Training and Job Rotation in Japanese Firms." *Research in Social Stratification and Mobility* 10: 3–25.

———. 1992. "Christmas Cakes and Wedding Cakes: The Social Organization of Japanese Women's Life Course." In *Japanese Social Organization*, ed. Takie Sugiyama Lebra. Honolulu: University of Hawaii Press.

———. 1993. *Women and the Economic Miracle: Gender and Work in Postwar Japan*. Berkeley: University of California Press.

Brinton, Mary C., and Hang-Yue Ngo. 1993. "Age and Sex in the Occupational Structure: A United States-Japan Comparison." *Sociological Forum* 8 (1): 93–111.

Brinton, Mary C., Hang-Yue Ngo, and Kumiko Shibuya. 1991. "Gendered Mobility Patterns in Industrial Economies: The Case of Japan." *Social Science Quarterly* 72: 807–16.

Carter, Rose, and Lois Dilatush. 1976. "Office Ladies." In *Women in Changing Japan*, ed. Joyce Lebra, Roy Paulson, and Elizabeth Powers. Colorado: Westview Press.

Chinas, Beverly Newbold. 1973. *The Isthmus Zapotecs: A Matrifocal Culture of Mexico*. New York: Holt, Rinehart, and Winston.

Clark, Rodney. 1979. *The Japanese Company*. New Haven: Yale University Press.

Cole, Robert E. 1971. *The Japanese Blue Collar*. Berkeley: University of California Press.

———. 1979. *Work, Mobility, and Participation: A Comparative Study of American and Japanese Industry*. Berkeley: University of California Press.

Collier, Jane F. 1974. "Women in Politics." In *Women, Culture, and Society*, ed. Michelle Z. Rosaldo and Louise Lamphere. Stanford: Stanford University Press.

Condon, Jane. 1985. *A Half Step Behind: Japanese Women Today*. Rutland, Vt.: Charles E. Tuttle.

Cook, Alice H., and Hiroko Hayashi. 1980. *Working Women in Japan: Discrimination, Resistance, and Reform*. Ithaca: Cornell University Press.

Coward, Rosalind. 1985. *Female Desires: How They Are Sought, Bought, and Packaged*. New York: Grove Press.

Dalby, Liza Crihfield. 1983. *Geisha*. New York: Vintage Books.

David, Mariam E. 1978. "The Family-Education Couple: Towards an Analysis of the William Tyndale Dispute." In *Power and the State*, ed. Gary Littlejohn, et al. London: Croom Helm.

Dentsū Ōeru Pawā, ed. 1991. *Saigo ni warau OL wa dareda?* (Who is the last OL to laugh?) Tokyo: Dentsū.

Dore, Ronald. 1973. *British Factory, Japanese Factory: The Origins of Diversity in Industrial Relations.* Berkeley: University of California Press.

Dubisch, Jill, ed. 1986. *Gender and Power in Rural Greece.* Princeton, N.J.: Princeton University Press.

Foucault, Michel. 1979. *Discipline and Punish: The Birth of the Prison.* Trans. Alan Sheridan. New York: Vintage Books.

————. 1980. *Power/Knowledge: Selected Interviews and Other Writings.* Ed. Colin Gordon. Trans. Colin Gordon, Leo Marshall, John Mepham, and Kate Soper. New York: Pantheon Books.

Friedl, Ernestine. 1967. "The Position of Women: Appearance and Reality." *Anthropological Quarterly* 40: 97–108.

Fukuhara, Fumihiko. 1992. "Hanako san no raifu dezain" (The life design of Hanako-san). *LDI Monthly Report* 1: 3–23.

Genovese, Eugene D. 1976. *Roll, Jordan, Roll: The World the Slaves Made.* New York: Basic Books.

Gerson, Kathleen. 1985. *Hard Choices: How Women Decide about Work, Career, and Motherhood.* Berkeley: University of California Press.

————. 1993. *No Man's Land: Men's Changing Commitments to Family and Work.* New York: Basic Books.

Gilmore, David D. 1990. "Men and Women in Southern Spain: 'Domestic Power' Revisited." *American Anthropologist* 92: 953–70.

Ginsburg, Faye D. 1989. *Contested Lives: The Abortion Debate in an American Community.* Berkeley: University of California Press.

Goffman, Erving. 1959. *The Presentation of Self in Everyday Life.* New York: Doubleday Anchor Books.

Griswold, Wendy. 1987. "The Fabrication of Meaning: Literary Interpretation in the United States, Great Britain, and the West Indies." *American Journal of Sociology* 92: 1077–117.

Group Nagon, ed. 1990. *OL jutsu* (The art of being an OL). Tokyo: Shōbunsha.

Gullestad, Marianne. 1984. *Kitchen-Table Society.* New York: Columbia University Press.

Hamabata, Matthews M. 1990. *Crested Kimono: Power and Love in the Japanese Business Family.* Ithaca: Cornell University Press.

Hashimoto, Masanori, and John Raisian. 1983. "Employment Tenure and Earnings Profiles in Japan and the United States." *American Economic Review* 75: 721–35.

Hayashi, Hiroko. 1992. *Ikujikyūgyōhō no subete* (All about the Childcare Leave Law). Tokyo: Yūhikaku.

Hendry, Joy. 1993. *Wrapping Culture.* Oxford: Oxford University Press.

Higuchi, Yoshio. 1991. *Nihon keizai to shūgyō kōdō* (Japanese economy and employment). Tokyo: Tōyō Keizai Shinpōsha.

Hill, Anne M. 1984. "Female Labor Force Participation in Japan: An Aggregate Model." *Journal of Human Resources* 19 (2): 280–87.

Hirschman, Albert O. 1970. *Exit, Voice, and Loyalty: Responses to Decline in Firms, Organizations, and States.* Cambridge, Mass.: Harvard University Press.

Hochschild, Arlie R. 1983. *The Managed Heart: Commercialization of Human Feeling*. Berkeley: University of California Press.

Hochschild, Arlie R., with Anne Machung. 1989. *The Second Shift*. New York: Avon Books.

Holland, Dorothy C., and Margaret A. Eisenhart. 1990. *Educated in Romance: Women, Achievement, and College Culture*. Chicago: University of Chicago Press.

Hunter, Janet, ed. 1993. *Japanese Women Working*. New York: Routledge.

Imamura, Anne E. 1987. *Urban Japanese Housewives: At Home and in the Community*. Honolulu: University of Hawaii Press.

Itō, Mikiharu, and Yasuyuki Kurita, eds. 1984. *Nihonjin no zōtō* (Gift-exchange among the Japanese). Tokyo: Mineruva Shobō.

Iwabuchi, Keiko. 1990. *Josei ga wakaranakunatta ojisamatachi e* (For men who can no longer understand women). Tokyo: Dentsū.

Iwanami Shoten Henshūbu, ed. 1987. *"Muteki" na OL ni naru hō: Furesshāzu ofisu gaido* (How to become an "invincible" OL: An office guide for newly hired women). Tokyo: Iwanami Shoten.

Iwao, Sumiko. 1993. *The Japanese Woman: Traditional Image and Changing Reality*. Cambridge, Mass.: Harvard University Press.

Jackson, Michael. 1989. *Paths toward a Clearing: Radical Empiricism and Ethnographic Inquiry*. Bloomington: Indiana University Press.

Johnson, Chalmers. 1982. *MITI and the Japanese Miracle: The Growth of Industrial Policy, 1925–1975*. Stanford: Stanford University Press.

Kanter, Rosabeth Moss. 1977. *Men and Women of the Corporation*. New York: Basic Books.

Kawashima, Yoko. 1983. "Wage Differentials between Men and Women in Japan." Ph.D. diss., Stanford University.

———. 1985. *Joshi rōdō to rōdō shijō kōzō no bunseki* (An analysis of female labor and labor market structure). Tokyo: Nihon Keizai Hyōronsha.

Kelsky, Karen. 1994. "Postcards from the Edge: The Office Lady Subculture of Tokyo." *U.S.-Japan Women's Journal* (English Supplement) 6: 3–26.

Kindaichi, Kyōsuke, Umetomo Saeki, and Hatsutarō Ōishi, eds. 1984. *Kokugo jiten* (Japanese dictionary). Tokyo: Shōgakkan.

Klatch, Rebecca E. 1987. *Women of the New Right*. Philadelphia: Temple University Press.

Kondo, Dorinne K. 1990. *Crafting Selves: Power, Gender, and Discourses of Identity in a Japanese Workplace*. Chicago: University of Chicago Press.

Kōnno, Minako. 1996. "Negotiating Gender in Uncertainty: A Mechanism of Women's Marginalization in the Japanese Workplace." *International Journal of Japanese Sociology* 5: 23–40.

Kyōdō Advertising Planning Dept. LIPS. 1989. *It's OL show time!: Torendī OL no 24 jikan o yomu 42 kō* (It's OL show time!: Forty-two lessons on the fashionable OLs' day). Tokyo: PHP Kenkyūjo.

———. 1991. *All that's OL!* Tokyo: PHP Kenkyūjo.

Lam, Alice. 1992. *Women and Japanese Management: Discrimination and Reform*. London: Routledge.

Lamont, Michele. 1992. *Money, Morals, and Manners: The Culture of the French and the American Upper-Middle Class*. Chicago: University of Chicago Press.

Lamphere, Louise. 1987. *From Working Daughters to Working Mothers: Immigrant Women in a New England Industrial Community*. Ithaca: Cornell University Press.

Lebra, Joyce, Roy Paulson, and Elizabeth Powers, eds. 1976. *Women in Changing Japan*. Colorado: Westview Press.

Lebra, Takie Sugiyama. 1981. "Japanese Women in Male Dominant Careers: Cultural Barriers and Accommodations for Sex-Role Transcendence." *Ethnology* 20 (4): 291–306.

———. 1984. *Japanese Women: Constraint and Fulfillment*. Honolulu: University of Hawaii Press.

L·MIT, ed. 1991. *Imadoki OL daizukan* (Encyclopedia of contemporary OLs). Tokyo: Nihon Keizai Shinbunsha.

Lo, Jeannie. 1990. *Office Ladies, Factory Women: Life and Work at a Japanese Company*. New York: M. E. Sharpe.

MacDonald, Madeleine. 1981. *Class, Gender, and Education*. Milton Keynes: Open University Press.

Matsunaga, Mari, and Kōichiro Hioki. 1996. "'Soshiki no naka no josei' o motomete" (Seeking the model of "women in organizations" in Japanese firms). *Soshiki Kagaku* 30 (2): 4–13.

Mauss, Marcel. 1967. *The Gift*. New York: W. W. Norton.

Mayuzumi, Madoka. 1996. "Onna no teki wa yappari onna" (A woman's enemies are women after all). *Nihon Keizai Shinbun*, 19 November.

McLendon, James. 1983. "The Office: Way Station or Blind Alley?" In *Work and Lifecourse in Japan*, ed. D. W. Plath. Albany: State University of New York Press.

Mitchell, Timothy. 1988. *Colonising Egypt*. Berkeley: University of California Press.

Mukhopadhyay, Carol C. 1988. "Anthropological Studies of Women's Status Revisited: 1977–1987." *Annual Review of Anthropology* 17: 461–95.

Murobushi, Tetsurō. 1989. *Okuru riron okurareru riron* (The logic of giving and the logic of receiving). Tokyo: Chikuma Shobō.

Nagasu, Kazuji, and Yasuko Ichibangase. 1963. "'BG' ron no kōzai" (Merits and demerits of the "BG" debate). *Asahi Journal* 5: 14–21.

Nihon. 1963. "Ichiryū BG 1000-nin no fuman to yokubō" (One thousand first-class BGs' complaints and desires). Kōdansha. 6: 78–82.

Nihon Hishokurabu Nōryoku Kōjō Kekyūkai, ed. 1992. *Takaga ochakumi saredo ochakumi: Shokuba no ochakumi o kangaeru* (It is no more but no less than tea pouring: Some thoughts on serving tea in the workplace). Tokyo: Jiji Tsūshinsha.

Nihon Keizai Shinbun. 5 January 1991. "Kigyō jin e no tegami 4" (A letter to the corporate man, number 4).

———. 2 December 1991. "OL ga kaita OL no hon" (Books written by OLs about OLs).

———. 14 January 1992. "Josei katsuyō nama no koe de" (Women's utilization promoted by listening to their voice).

———. 19 February 1992. "OL wa ie de dorama-zuke" (OLs are being swamped with TV dramas at home).

———. 16 March 1992. "Tachiagare! Kaishazuma-tachi musume-tachi" (Stand up! Office wives and office daughters).

———. 1 June 1992. "Iwaneba naoranu 'shanaizuma atsukai'" (Men will not stop treating women as "office wives" unless we speak up).

———. 15 June 1992. "Kanchigai shiteimasenka OL sōjūjutsu" (Aren't you misunderstanding the way to manage OLs?).

———. 9 November 1992. "OL no kotobuki taisha: Hade na shanai seremonī" (OLs' marriage retirement: Lavish display of ceremony in the workplace).

———. 15 December 1993. "Katsute yūgūsaku, imaya yūdōsaku?: Kekkon shussan taishoku iwaikin" (A courteous treatment in the past but now a solicitous device?: Marriage and childbirth retirement gifts).

———. 17 February 1994. "Josei shokuba kurō ooki otoko-tachi" (Men with no end of trouble in the female workplace).

———. 26 September 1994. "Shōsha jimushoku ni senbatsu no nami: Nōryokushugi de shōkaku ni sa" (A wave of selection of clerical workers in trading companies: Difference in ranks by the merit system).

———. 20 May 1996. "Sumitomo Shintaku zenkōin jitsuryokushugi chingin ni" (Sumitomo Trust Bank is to change all employees' payment to a merit system).

———. 27–31 May 1996. "OL ga kieru!?" (Are OLs to disappear!?)

———. 2 December 1997. "Medatsu kinmuchi gentei-gata" (*Sōgoshoku* with limited place of employment conspicuous among women).

Nippon no OL Kenkyūkai, ed. 1995. *Nippon no OL tachi* (Japanese office ladies). Tokyo: Daiyamondosha.

Ogasawara, Yuko. 1996. "Kigyō ni okeru OL no teikō kōi" (Women's acts of resistance in Japanese companies). *Shakai Keizai Shisutemu* 15: 51–56.

———. 1996. "Meanings of Chocolate: Power and Gender in Valentine's Gift Giving." *International Journal of Japanese Sociology* 5: 41–66.

———. 1996. "Shokubanai no jendā kankei" (Gender relations in the Japanese workplace). *Soshiki Kagaku* 30 (2): 27–36.

Onēsama Company, ed. 1991. *Tonari no OL zubari 36 gyōkai* (OLs next door in thirty-six industries speak frankly). Tokyo: Futabasha.

Osako, Masako Murakami. 1978. "Dilemmas of Japanese Professional Women." *Social Problems* 26 (1): 15–25.

Ōsawa, Machiko. 1984. "Women's Skill Formation, Labor Force Participation, and Fertility in Japan." Ph.D. diss., Southern Illinois University.

———. 1993. *Keizai henka to joshi rōdō: Nichibei no hikaku kenkyū* (Economic change and female labor: A comparative study of Japan and the United States). Tokyo: Nihon Keizai Hyōronsha.

———. 1994. "Otoko to onna no keizaigaku" (Men's and women's economics). *Nihon Keizai Shinbun*, 28 October.

Ōsawa, Mari. 1993. *Kigyō chūshin shakai o koete: Gendai nihon o "jendā" de yomu* (Beyond the company-centered society: Reading contemporary Japan by gender). Tokyo: Jiji Tsūshinsha.

Parkinson, Lorraine. 1989. "Japan's Equal Employment Opportunity Law." *Columbia Law Review* 89 (3): 604–61.

Pateman, Carole. 1988. *The Sexual Contract*. Stanford: Stanford University Press.

Performance Yuki. 1987. *Gendai OL repōto: Shuki de miru shigoto, jōshi, kekkonkan* (Report on OLs today: Their views on work, bosses, and marriage disclosed in diaries). Tokyo: Nihon Nōritsu Kyōkai.

Pharr, Susan J. 1981. *Political Women in Japan: The Search for a Place in Political Life.* Berkeley: University of California Press.

———. 1984. "Status Conflict: The Rebellion of the Tea Pourers." In *Conflict in Japan,* ed. Ellis S. Krauss, Thomas P. Rohlen, and Patricia G. Steinhoff. Honolulu: University of Hawaii Press.

———. 1990. *Losing Face: Status Politics in Japan.* Berkeley: University of California Press.

Powell, Rachel, and John Clarke. 1976. "A Note on Marginality." In *Resistance through Rituals,* ed. Stuart Hall and Tony Jefferson. London: Hutchinson, in association with the CCCS Birmingham.

Riegelhaupt, Joyce F. 1967. "Saloio Women: An Analysis of Informal and Formal Political and Economic Roles of Portuguese Peasant Women." *Anthropological Quarterly* 40: 109–126.

Roberts, Glenda S. 1994. *Staying on the Line: Blue-Collar Women in Contemporary Japan.* Honolulu: University of Hawaii Press.

Robertson, Jennifer. 1992. "Doing and Undoing 'Female' and 'Male' in Japan: The Takarazuka Revue." In *Japanese Social Organization,* ed. Takie Sugiyama Lebra. Honolulu: University of Hawaii Press.

Rōdōshō (Ministry of Labor). 1994. *Joshi koyō kanri kihon chōsa 1993* (Basic survey on management of female employees, 1993). Tokyo: Ministry of Labor.

———. 1995. *Shinpan wakariyasui ikujikyūgyōhō* (The new easy-to-understand Childcare Leave Law). Tokyo: Yūhikaku.

———. Various years. *Chingin kōzō kihon tōkei chōsa* (Basic survey on wage structure). Tokyo: Ministry of Labor.

Rogers, Susan C. 1975. "Female Forms of Power and the Myth of Male Dominance: A Model of Female/Male Interaction in Peasant Society." *American Ethnologist* 2(4): 727–56.

———. 1978. "Woman's Place: A Critical Review of Anthropological Theory." *Comparative Study in Society and History* 20: 123–62.

———. 1985. "Gender in Southwestern France: The Myth of Male Dominance Revisited." *Anthropology* 9: 65–86.

Rohlen, Thomas P. 1974. *For Harmony and Strength: Japanese White-Collar Organization in Anthropological Perspective.* Berkeley: University of California Press.

Sakai, Hiromichi. 1995. "Nihon 'bokei shakai' ni icchokusen" (Japan heads straight for matrilineal society). *Nihon Keizai Shinbun,* 4 November.

Sakura Sōgō Kenkyūjo, ed. 1990. *OL hajimete monogatari: Shinnyūshain ga kaita kaisha seikatsu manyuaru* (First-time-being-an-OL story: A guide to life in the company written by newly hired women). Tokyo: Nihon Keizai Shinbunsha.

Saso, Mary. 1990. *Women in the Japanese Workplace.* London: Hilary Shipman.

Scott, James C. 1985. *Weapons of the Weak: Everyday Forms of Peasant Resistance.* New Haven: Yale University Press.

———. 1990. *Domination and the Arts of Resistance: Hidden Transcripts.* New Haven: Yale University Press.

Scott, Joan Wallach. 1988. *Gender and the Politics of History.* New York: Columbia University Press.

Sewell, William H. Jr. 1992. "A Theory of Structure: Duality, Agency, and Transformation." *American Journal of Sociology* 98: 1–29.

Shimada, Haruo, and Yoshio Higuchi. 1985. "An Analysis of Trends in Female Labor Force Participation in Japan." *Journal of Labor Economics* 3 (1): S355–74.

Shimamura, Mari, and Eri Shimamura. 1986. *Shin OL zukan* (The new OLs' pictorial book). Tokyo: Tokuma Shoten.

Shimizu, Chinami. 1991. *Ojisan kaizō kōza 3: OL 1600-nin iinkai* (Lessons for transforming men: By a committee of 1,600 OLs). Tokyo: Nesko.

———. 1995a. *Ojisan kaizō kōza 4: OL 1600-nin iinkai* (Lessons for transforming men: By a committee of 1,600 OLs). Tokyo: Bungei Shunjū.

———. 1995b. *Ojisan kaizō kōza 5: Watashi no kaisha ni asu wa nai!* (Lessons for transforming men: There is no future for my company!). Tokyo: Bungei Shunjū.

———. 1996. *Ojisan kaizō kōza 6: Kaisha osorubeshi!* (Lessons for transforming men: Formidable companies!). Tokyo: Bungei Shunjū.

Shimizu, Chinami, and Yoshi Furuya. 1986. *Ojisan kaizō kōza: OL 500-nin iinkai* (Lessons for transforming men: By a committee of five hundred OLs). Tokyo: Nesko.

———. 1989. *Ojisan kaizō kōza part 2: OL 800-nin iinkai* (Lessons for transforming men, part 2: By a committee of eight hundred OLs). Tokyo: Nesko.

Shinotsuka, Eiko. 1982. *Nihon no joshi rōdō* (Female labor in Japan). Tokyo: Tōyō Keizai Shinpōsha.

Simmel, Georg. 1950. *The Sociology of Georg Simmel.* Ed. Kurt H. Wolff. Glencoe: Free Press.

Smith, Dorothy E. 1988. *The Everyday World as Problematic.* Boston: Northeastern University Press.

Smith, Robert J. 1987. "Gender Inequality in Contemporary Japan." *Journal of Japanese Studies* 13 (1): 1–25.

Smith, Robert J., and Ella Lury Wiswell. 1982. *The Women of Suyemura.* Chicago: University of Chicago Press.

Sōmuchō (Management and Coordination Agency). Various years. *Rōdōryoku chōsa* (Survey of the labor force). Tokyo: Nihon Tōkei Kyōkai.

Stacey, Judith. 1991. *Brave New Families: Stories of Domestic Upheaval in Late-Twentieth-Century America.* New York: Basic Books.

Swartz, Marc J. 1982. "The Isolation of Men and the Happiness of Women: Sources and Use of Power in Swahili Marital Relationships." *Journal of Anthropological Research* 38: 26–44.

Taga, Mikiko. 1991. "OL ryūgaku būmu no hikari to kage" (Hope and despair of the study abroad boom among OLs). *Gekkan Asahi* (October): 130–33.

Takenaka, Emiko, and Yoshiko Kuba, eds. 1994. *Rōdōryoku no joseika* (Feminization of the workforce). Tokyo: Yūhikaku.

Tanaka, Kazuko. 1987. "Women, Work, and Family in Japan: A Life Cycle Perspective." Ph.D. diss., University of Iowa.

Tomita, Yasunobu. 1988. "Joshi no koyō kanri to danjokan chingin kakusa" (Management of women employees and the male-female wage gap). In *Sho-*

kuba no kyaria ūman (Career women in the workplace), ed. Kazuo Koike and Yasunobu Tomita. Tokyo: Tōyō Keizai Shinpōsha.

Tsuneyoshi, Ryoko. 1992. *Ningen keisei no nichibei hikaku* (Japan-U.S. comparison of human development). Tokyo: Chūō Kōronsha.

Ueno, Chizuko. 1987. "The Position of Japanese Women Reconsidered." *Current Anthropology* 28: S75-S84.

Uhl, Sarah C. 1985. "Special Friends: The Organization of Intersex Friendship in Escalona (Andalusia) Spain." *Anthropology* 9: 129–52.

Upham, Frank K. 1987. *Law and Social Change in Postwar Japan*. Cambridge, Mass.: Harvard University Press.

Vogel, Ezra F. 1963. *Japan's New Middle Class*. Berkeley: University of California Press.

———, ed. 1975. *Modern Japanese Organization and Decision-Making*. Berkeley: University of California Press.

Vogel, Suzanne H. 1978. "Professional Housewife: The Career of Urban Middle-Class Japanese Women." *Japan Interpreter* 12 (1): 16–43.

Weedon, Chris. 1987. *Feminist Practice and Poststructuralist Theory*. Oxford: Basil Blackwell.

Weiner, Annette B. 1976. *Women of Value, Men of Renown: New Perspectives in Trobriand Exchange*. Austin: University of Texas Press.

Wetzel, Patricia J. 1994. "A Movable Self: The Linguistic Indexing of Uchi and Soto." In *Situated Meaning*, ed. Jane M. Bachnik and Charles J. Quinn Jr. Princeton: Princeton University Press.

Willis, Paul. 1977. *Learning to Labor: How Working-Class Kids Get Working-Class Jobs*. New York: Columbia University Press.

Wolf, Margery. 1972. *Women and the Family in Rural Taiwan*. Stanford: Stanford University Press.

Wrong, Dennis H. 1988. *Power: Its Forms, Bases, and Uses*. Chicago: University of Chicago Press.

Yamada, Yūichi. 1960. "Biru no naka no kodoku na BG" (Lonely BGs in the building). *Nihon* 3: 70–74.

Yashiro, Naohiro. 1980. "Danjokan chingin sabetsu no yōin ni tsuite" (Factors responsible for wage discrimination between men and women). *Nihon Keizai Kenkyū* 9: 17–31.

———. 1981. "Women in the Japanese Labor Force." Ph.D. diss., University of Maryland.

———. 1983. *Joshi rōdō no keizai bunseki* (An economic analysis of female labor). Tokyo: Nihon Keizai Shinbunsha.

Yoshizawa, Norio, and Toshio Ishiwata, eds. 1979. *Gairaigo no gogen* (Etymology of words of foreign origin). Tokyo: Kadokawa.

Zelizer, Viviana A. 1994. *The Social Meaning of Money*. New York: Basic Books.

Index

Abu-Lughod, Lila, 159
Accommodation, 161–62, 198n2, 198n4. *See also* Compliance, strategic
Age: of bank employees, 36; and marriage of OLs, 58–59, 62; of OLs, 25, 26, 28, 57–59, 181, 182; and seniority, 53; and tension among OLs, 53; and women's employment patterns, 17, 19, 167. *See also* Interviewees
Algerian women, 7, 195–96n5
Allison, Anne, 5, 88, 188n4; on corporate nightlife, 188n2, 198n1
Alloula, Malek, 195–96n5
All That's OL!, 89, 190n4
Amaeru (ask for indulgence), 78
Ambiguity: as disguised resistance, 106, 157; in gifts, 107, 113
Anonymity, 106, 157
"Around-the-body care" (*mi no mawari no sewa*), 4
Arrogance, 73, 79, 94, 124
Authority: abuse of, 74; and control, 155–56. *See also* Power; Subordinates

Banking industry: discriminatory policies of, 36; employees by age and sex, 36; interviewees in, 179, 183; salaries in, 34–35; use of OLs in, 170. *See also* Financial institutions; Tōzai Bank
Bedouin women, 159
Berger, John, 95

Bernstein, Gail, 188n2
Blau, Peter, 146
Blue-collar workers, 19, 37, 188n2, 198n4
Boddy, Janice, 188–89n7
Bonuses, 31–32
Bourdieu, Pierre, 7, 189n7
"Boycotting," 123, 125
Brinton, Mary: on employers' encouragement of marriage, 194n10; on gender roles, 63, 187–88n1; on job rotation, 193n6; on women's economic roles, 4, 10–11
Buchō (general managers): at Tōzai Bank, 22, 85, 171; women as, 19–20, 21. *See also* General managers
Bureaucratic organizations: authority and control in, 155–56; dependence on subordinates in, 160; human side of, 101
Burikko (woman who acts "cute"), 81
Business cards, 34
"Business girl" (BG), 23–24
Business trips: OLs', 116–17, 118–19, 124; souvenirs from, 77, 85, 141, 153

Carter, Rose, 189n11
Charm, personal (*jintoku*), 125, 156
Childbirth: OLs' plans for, 25–26; and retirement, 61, 65, 66, 194n11
Childcare leave, 66–67, 194–95n12

Indexer: Susan Stone
Compositor: Prestige Typography
Text: 10/13 Galliard
Display: Galliard
Printer and binder: Braun-Brumfield, Inc.